# One Among Many

**Our Lady of the Prairie Retreat Center**

# One Among Many

*Sister Bernadine Pieper
and the Humilities of Iowa*

### KATHLEEN MULLEN

ISBN: 978-0-9852953-5-6

Published in association with Samizdat Creative, a division of Samizdat Publishing Group, LLC.

Cover design by Colleen Hayes. Interior design by Sonya Unrein.

Author photo by Peter Bryson nooknose.com

Photos provided by the Congregation of the Humility of Mary, Davenport, Iowa. For information, visit http://www.chmiowa.org.

*To Sister Bernadine Pieper and the Humilities of Iowa.*

*May your spirit live in all who read this book.*

# CONTENTS

## BOOK II
## THE HUMILITIES OF IOWA

# Introduction

On February 20, 2000, Sister Bernadine Pieper, just shy of her 82nd birthday, died of cancer in Davenport, Iowa. By societal norms, she was not a famous or "important" person. Her life and passing were not chronicled in the country's leading newspapers or published broadly in electronic media.

To those who knew her, however, Bernadine was a remarkable and treasured woman. And so, at the time of her death, they came in large numbers—current, former and associate members of the Congregation of the Humility of Mary (CHM), family, friends, Quakers, social activists, ministers, priests and bishops, farmers and city folk—to celebrate her life and share stories of how she touched their lives.

For these people and many others, Bernadine will live on through oral tradition, stories about her passed down from generation to generation. Her ideas, the breadth of her vision, courage, determination and love of the earth and its people will continue to guide their lives. As part of her legacy, a cadre of committed people from various walks of life will continue Bernadine's work seeking justice and peace courageously, no matter how unpopular.

So why write a book about Bernadine? Bernadine and I were friends for over forty years. For twenty-five of these years, I was a member of the CHM community and witnessed firsthand the remarkable transformation of the community under Bernadine's leadership. When I was asked to do a eulogy at her funeral, I declined. I come from a long line of Irish people who are better keeners than eulogists. I have to mourn before I can speak or write about the dead, particularly those whom I love. So I promised to write a book about her instead.

Bernadine was an uncommon woman rooted in the heartland of Iowa. As one of her friends, Sister Cathy Talarico, describes, "She was the earthiest woman I have ever known, an earth woman sprinkled with stardust."[1] Her "stardust" was her unique combination of a deep faith in God, a razor-sharp creative intelligence, an insatiable curiosity about the world and the whole cosmos, a love of and trust in people, her humor, common sense, and magnificent heart. She had an amazing ability to lift people up and give them the confidence and skills to take charge of their own lives, as well as improve the lives of others.

During her sixty-two years in the Congregation of the Humility of Mary—commonly known as the "Sisters of Humility" or the "Humilities of Iowa"—Bernadine led many distinct and disparate "lives," which this book will chronicle: fourth grade and college science teacher, college administrator, president of the Sisters of Humility, peace activist and executive secretary of the North Central

**Sister Bernadine Pieper**

Region of the American Friends Service Committee, rural pastoral minister and small farm advocate, a restorer of the prairie in southeastern Iowa, tutor and advocate for poor children and adults (including inmates in the Mississippi Madison County jail) and one of the founders of and landscaping consultant for Our Lady of the Prairie Retreat, one of the most beautiful and serene places on the earth.

But the significance of Bernadine's life cannot be fully appreciated except in relationship to the religious community to which she committed a substantial portion of her life. The centerpiece of her life was the renewal of the Sisters of Humility, which she and the sisters accomplished together during her tenure as president of the community from 1966 to 1976.

The simple design for the community's renewal was a stroke of genius grounded in midwestern common sense. The sisters decided that the strength of the community is rooted in the gifts of its individual members—their talents, faith, and pioneering spirits. The individual sisters, therefore, must be given the freedom to determine where and how they serve, consistent with the values the community holds in common. By adopting the principle of "self-determination," the community made a leap of faith and bet that the sisters would use their talents in new ways to serve those most in need all over the world. They would inspire others through their leadership to join them thus multiplying exponentially the community's effort to create a more just and peaceful world. Over the past fifty years, that bet has paid off. The Sisters of Humility have become one of the most fearless, caring and effective communities of women religious in the United States, benefiting hundreds of thousands of people all over the world.

So if Bernadine were alive today, I believe she'd say, "Don't focus on my life alone. Include the lives and works of other sisters. I am simply one among many. It is our lives taken as a whole that reflect the meaning and purpose of the Sisters of Humility." And so I have. Book I describes Bernadine's life, while Book II portraits the lives and works of individual Sisters of Humility, women who are representative of the Sisters of Humility as a whole.

Bernadine was fond of quoting Antonio Machado's admonition:

*Walker, there is no road,*

*the road is made by walking.*[2]

She believed that each person must make his or her own path in life. But Bernadine also believed that one can benefit from studying the lives of others. As she observed in *Footprints: The Early History of the Sisters of Humility,* "The more I studied the lives of those [who preceded us], the more I came to appreciate their faith, creativity and courage, their honesty and mutual love, their persevering trust in God." Even though their footprints were "sometimes uncertain, perhaps even moving in circles, often into unknown territory," for Bernadine, they at least pointed the way toward a better, if challenging future.[3]

Similarly, the lives of Bernadine and the other Sisters of Humility portrayed in this book model a faith-based community of persons. Through trust in God and mutual support of one another, they have used their individual gifts to make a difference in the lives of people in need of help and hope to survive. Their courage, service, and love have much to teach us.

# Book I
# Sister Bernadine Pieper

# From Iowa Farm Girl
# to Sister of Humility

Bernadine Pieper was neither a founding member of the community nor one of the pioneering Sisters of Humility who immigrated to America in the late nineteenth century. She was, however, one of the essential "re-founders" of the community during the period 1966-76.

In many ways, Bernadine's early life is reflective of the lives of the majority of the Sisters of Humility. They grew up in small towns or on farms in families of modest means, steeped in midwestern values of common sense and hard work, and were drawn to the Sisters of Humility out of respect for sisters who taught or cared for them. Bernadine was the first-born of five children of Frank Pieper and Mary (Mame) Nichting. Her family members were hardworking German people, some of whom had been in the United States for four generations.

Like many of Bernadine's ancestors, her parents were farmers. In 1924, they bought a 160-acre farm near Mount Hamill, Iowa, where they raised their children, Bernadine, Frances, James, Lucille, and Ruth. The farm, a whole family enterprise, was successful enough to withstand the ravages of the Great Depression to allow Bernadine and her four siblings to attend college in the 1930s and 1940s.

Frank Pieper was a man of principle, a man who opposed poll taxes and voted for the candidate of his choice rather than adhering to party affiliation. He was an avid reader and read every novel his children brought home from school. While he was a frugal man who cut and put soles on the family shoes, he also followed the stock market and was interested in the work of the Catholic Extension Society. But his first priority was his family, and the same was true for Mame. During the depression, when neighboring farmers sold all of their produce,

Frank and Mame determined that nutritious food for their children came first.[1]

Mame, excelled in mental arithmetic, loved fresh flowers, and was charming. She passed all of these traits on to Bernadine. Family lore has it that Mame was fascinated by the "doctor's book," which she consulted more than she consulted the doctor. She had a remarkable ability to diagnose illnesses she or other family members developed. According to Bernadine, she accurately diagnosed her own bowel obstruction, which caused her death when the doctor ignored her diagnosis until it was too late to treat her.[2] Medical diagnosis must be in the Pieper DNA. Bernadine demonstrated the same uncanny ability to diagnose medical conditions based solely on reported symptoms when she was thousands of miles away from the patient.

As a child, Bernadine was a dreamer. According to her sisters, Ruth Holtkamp and Frances Caslavka, she loved to sit on the edge of the livestock water tank and quietly watch the goldfish, the sky, and nature in general. But Frances also said "Bernadine shook up things everywhere she went. She had such an ability to relate to people that she was able to convince you of her position without you even knowing it."[3]

The Piepers sent their children to the Catholic school in Houghton, Iowa, three miles from their farm. As the eldest, Bernadine was responsible for ensuring that she, her brother and sisters got to school on time. Beginning in 1926 when she was in third grade, Bernadine drove her siblings to school in a horse and buggy on dirt roads for eight years. In 1934 when she was a junior in high school, she began driving them to school in a Model A Ford. However, when the roads were not passable by buggy or car, they walked. Bernadine led the group, including her siblings and children of neighbors, walking at a brisk clip. To keep the younger children from lagging behind, Bernadine entertained them with stories. When they complained that she was walking too fast, Bernadine told them, "If you don't keep up, you don't get to hear the end of the story." According to Bernadine's nephew, John Holtkamp, her brother Jim told him that he "struggled hard to keep up because Bernadine's stories were so doggone interesting he didn't want to miss even one little bit of them."

Bernadine learned the art of storytelling from her maternal grand-mother, Bernardina (Dina) Nichting. Mrs. Nichting was a gregarious, well-educated woman, who entertained family and visitors alike with jokes and stories. Her grandchildren loved to visit her as she had a Victrola they could play when phonographs were still uncommon. In these visits, Bernadine formed an especially close relationship with her.

**Sister Bernadine**

Growing up on a farm, according to Bernadine, made her appreciate and marvel at the myriad of animals, plants, rocks and sunsets. Nearly every Sunday, Bernadine's father, Frank, would take the family on rides in the car and taught them the name of every plant, bush, and tree they saw along the way. As an adult, Bernadine attributed her initial interest in botany to these Sunday afternoon drives with her father.

The Piepers had a large extended Catholic family and many Catholic friends who often would come by the farm at night just to talk. Since one of Bernadine's aunts married into the Dingman family who lived nearby in St. Paul, Iowa, one of Bernadine's childhood friends was Maurice Dingman, who became Bishop of Des Moines,

Iowa in 1968. They were kindred spirits in childhood and became supportive colleagues as adults when they civilly negotiated the disputes between the Des Moines diocesan priests and the Sisters of Humility in 1969 and the early 1970s.

Bernadine first encountered the Sisters of Humility in 1936 when she enrolled in Ottumwa Heights College in Ottumwa, Iowa. As Bernadine fully expected to return to rural Iowa to get married and have a family, she enrolled in the home economics program at Ottumwa Heights, thinking it would prepare her for the life she envisioned.

Bernadine's two years at Ottumwa Heights College, however, changed the course of her life. One of the college's legendary science teachers, Sister Joseph Marie Peters, captured Bernadine's imagination and launched her on the path to become a scientist and educator. She introduced Bernadine to the idea of God creating the universe through evolution well before the Catholic Church accepted evolution as a legitimate theory.[4] The more Bernadine learned about the evolving universe, the more her sense of mystery and joy grew. She never lost her fascination with all living things and developed as a core value the understanding that humans are not the center of the universe and our planet was not made for us to dominate. Instead, according to Bernadine, "We are part of the web of life, not the spider. We have a duty to build up and protect all living persons and things rather than destroy them."[5]

Bernadine's experience with Sister Joseph Marie and the other Sisters of Humility at the college inspired her to become one of them. At the end of her two years at Ottumwa Heights, Bernadine walked over to the section of the campus that housed the headquarters of the Sisters of Humility, rang the doorbell, and asked to talk to Mother Mary Geraldine Upham about joining the community. Mother Geraldine readily accepted Bernadine even though, according to Bernadine's sister, Frances, "she had not been particularly religious." When Bernadine told her parents her plan to join the Sisters of Humility, they supported her decision.

When Bernadine entered the novitiate of the Sisters of Humility on September 8, 1938, she joined a Roman Catholic order of women religious with approximately 235 members. The majority of the women were teachers who, in addition to staffing Ottumwa Heights College, operated twenty-one elementary and high schools in Iowa and Montana. Members of the community who held nursing licenses staffed St. Joseph's Hospital in Ottumwa. A few other sisters cared for orphans at St. Vincent's Home in Davenport Iowa and at a Torrington, Wyoming orphanage. The Sisters wore habits and lived communally in the small towns and rural areas in which they worked.

In December 1938, Bernadine's maternal grandmother, Dina, died. Bernadine just assumed she would be allowed to go to her grandmother's funeral and was devastated when she was told that she would not be allowed to do so. That decision made no sense to Bernadine and she seriously considered leaving the community. While she decided not to leave, she never forgot this incident. She felt it was a misguided policy that made discipline an end in itself when circumstances required understanding and compassion.

In 1940, when Bernadine was still in the novitiate and had not yet finished college, she was assigned to teach fourth grade at St. Mary's School in Ottumwa. As Bernadine had not taken any courses in education to prepare her for teaching, she wondered how the children would react to her. According to Bernadine, "It took me a year to get over being afraid of what the children might do. However, once I gained confidence in my ability to teach, I never lost it."[6] For the next twenty-six years, Bernadine honed her skills as a teacher and became a brilliant scientist and a skilled college science teacher who made complicated subjects easy to understand.

## The Marycrest Years: Expanding Minds and Solving Problems

In 1939, the Sisters of Humility established a four-year college for women in Davenport, Iowa in response to repeated requests followed by a demand from the bishop of the Davenport Diocese, Henry Rohlman, that "they just do it!"[1] No promise of diocesan financial support for this project accompanied the demand. And none was given. Mother Geraldine led the founding of Marycrest College. She secured the land without any collateral, built the necessary buildings, hired the initial faculty and staff, and was president of the college during its initial twenty-two years.

To make Marycrest affordable to students of modest means, Mother Geraldine held tuition, fees, room and board and other costs at below market rates. For fifty-three years, the Humilities contributed the majority of the teachers and administrators of the college from among their own ranks. As a result of the sisters' industry, thrift, and professional skills, many immigrants and other lower income persons raised both their professional and economic status by earning Marycrest degrees.

In June 1941, Bernadine and her compatriot from the novitiate, Sister Marie Ven Horst, began their careers at Marycrest. As Marycrest College needed science teachers, Mother Geraldine assigned Bernadine and Marie to take math and science courses necessary for becoming science teachers at the college.

While completing her bachelor degree in science at Marycrest, Bernadine also took some classes at St. Ambrose College from Monsignor U.A. Hauber, a nationally renowned scientist and biology teacher. Monsignor Hauber, like Bernadine, was fascinated by new discoveries in science. He reveled in the fact that he was alive when the atom was split. Even though he did not drive a car, he brought a newly minted auto to the campus so students could learn the scientific principles on which it was built.

Students and faculty considered Monsignor Hauber to be one of the wise men of the St. Ambrose campus. In classes and in sermons, he taught valuable life lessons that integrated faith and science in simple, clear ways, as in this "Spirit Day" sermon:

> A complete education should look beyond wealth to wisdom. . . . Wisdom, as distinct from knowledge, consists largely in putting everything in its proper place. . . . Out in California there are trees that were saplings in Abraham's day, still alive and growing . . . During this time of year in Davenport one sees swarms of dayflies emerging from the river; they appear one day and are dead and gone the next. One of God's creatures lives a thousand years; another only a few hours. The longest life will sometime end, only he is wise who plans for eternity, which does not end.
>
> My word to you is this: Do not be selfish in your plans. Don't think too much about yourself; you will be a failure if you do. What you do for your neighbor in the concrete is what counts. If here and there some people are happier because of our presence, our life has been a success. Whether you live like the Pacific redwoods to be a hundred years old or more like the Mississippi River dayfly in which your day ends tomorrow, is a minor matter. The report you make to your Creator on what you have done with the time and talent he gave you is all that matters.[2]

Bernadine, like Monsignor Hauber, had the same ability to clearly explain core values in simple language using images from science or nature to illustrate them.

On top of their academic and other duties, Bernadine and Marie also had to comply with the daily religious regimen set forth in the community's Constitution and Book of Customs. According to Bernadine, "Mother Geraldine expected the Marycrest sisters to exactly follow these rules as she had been instrumental in obtaining church approval of them." As these rules imposed cloister as well as other time consuming duties and restrictions on the sisters' lives, they made fulfillment of their professional responsibilities at times difficult. Mother Geraldine also asked the sisters to model their behavior on that of the Sisters of Charity of the Blessed Virgin Mary (BVMs), who, she said, were considered "ladies," while the Humilities were "too friendly."[3] Despite Mother Geraldine's fondest hopes, she was never able to transform the Humilities from being friendly, hospitable women to distant, regal ladies.

After getting their Bachelor of Science degrees from Marycrest/ St. Ambrose Colleges, Marie and Bernadine began graduate studies at Saint Louis University in September 1942. When they arrived, the graduate school dean informed them that Bernadine would be studying biochemistry and Marie, chemistry. They were quite surprised because Bernadine had completed more undergraduate chemistry courses and Marie had taken more biology courses.

Bernadine, however, was unable to enroll in the St. Louis University Biochemistry Department, as it was not accepting new students because of its involvement in the war effort to produce penicillin. Therefore, she sought admission to the biology department even though she lacked the pre-requisite courses. The dean of the graduate school waived the requirements for her admission in order to give her a chance to prove she could do the work required. Because the Humility Book of Customs prohibited them from going out after 6:00 p.m., Bernadine and Marie had to miss some required classes. Nevertheless, through hard work and good humor, both of them survived the two years and earned their Masters of Science degrees in 1944.[4]

In 1950, Marie and Bernadine enrolled at the University of Iowa to pursue doctoral degrees. Bernadine was the only woman in the PhD program in zoology and botany. When she showed up for her first class, the men in her class were joking and smoking their cigars. But when they saw her walk into the classroom in a habit, they became deadly silent. Bernadine introduced herself to the men and joined their conversation. From then on, Bernadine and her fellow students were cordial colleagues during the two years of the program. Bernadine earned her PhD degree with majors in zoology and botany and Marie secured her PhD in chemistry in 1952.

Bernadine later became a Danforth scholar and pursued post-graduate studies at Penn State University, Michigan State University, University of Michigan, and the University of Colorado. She was recognized as a leader in her fields of zoology and botany and was one of the first women listed in the American Men in Science, the premier biographical directory of the leading scientists in the United States and Canada. While Bernadine was a gifted scientist, she was at her core a dedicated teacher.

After each period of graduate and post-graduate study, Bernadine and Marie returned to Marycrest and joined the other Sisters of Humility teaching at the college. Teaching, however, was only one of their jobs. They did everything from scrub floors, paint buildings, serve as proctors in the dorms, act as their own secretaries, and serve as switchboard operators for the college in order to keep tuition low and at the same time pay down the debt incurred in establishing the college.

As the Marycrest budget did not provide for laboratory or personal care supplies for the sisters, Bernadine and Marie, using invention rather than cash, helped to provide them. Marie made deodorant and hand lotion for the sisters in her chemistry lab. In the early years, they used tin cans instead of beakers in their labs. For dissection in anatomy class, Bernadine secured free lungs and hearts from a local packinghouse. In order to get samples of antibodies for her microbiology students to study, Bernadine asked a student who had had typhoid whether she would be willing to give a sample of her blood so that the students could study the antibodies her body created to fight the typhoid virus. The student, Sister Elizabeth Anne Schneider, thought Bernadine's request, while funny, was reasonable and gave the blood sample.

In later years, Bernadine and Marie, through their grant writing abilities, secured National Science Foundation grants sufficient to help build the science building needed to accommodate the expanding nursing and medical technology programs at the college. They also attracted students interested in science to enroll at Marycrest by traveling the state to provide science workshops for high school students and promote science fairs and competitions.

During most of the twenty-five years Bernadine taught at Marycrest, she and other Sisters of Humility lived very simply. As they did not have their own bedrooms, they slept on cots rolled out of closets in their daytime classrooms. In Bernadine's case, she shared her "bedroom" with a skeleton that rattled its bones throughout the night.

Both Marie and Bernadine were creative teachers, and drew many students to their classes over the years. Bernadine had a good eye for talent in her students. One student was Luz María Orozco, from México City, whose grandfather, mother, and sister had been trained as doctors, so she enrolled in science as her major area of study. After Bernadine taught Luz María several science courses, she called her in and told her, "You are a bright young woman, but you don't belong in science. You would be more at home in the humanities." Based upon this advice, Luz María switched majors and became a nationally recognized scholar and teacher of literature of the Middle Ages and the eighteenth century.

Sister Bernadine and Sister Luz María Orozco

Luz María became a Sister of Humility in 1958 and, for the next fifty years, used her unique gifts of humor, satire, and drama, as well as her encyclopedic knowledge of the literature of the Middle Ages and of the eighteenth century, to regale and educate undergraduate students at Marycrest College and Marycrest International University. In 1993, she was inducted into the World's Who's Who of Women for her contributions to the fields of English and Spanish literature. For Luz María, teaching allowed her "to unfold her students' talents." The key to good teaching, she says, is "listening to the students to understand their interests and strengths and then tailoring the curriculum to challenge them individually while helping them expand their knowledge and attitudes towards literature and the world."

According to Luz María, Bernadine remained her "friend, sister, guide, confidante, confessor, mentor, and role model" for nearly sixty years. At the time of Bernadine's death, Luz María summarized the life lessons she learned from Bernadine in an article, "Vintage Bernadine," published in the Marycrest newspaper, *The Crest*:

- By giving it all, you receive it all. Or maybe not. But then it hardly matters.
- Place people first, second, third. The rest will take care of itself.
- Make your weakness your strength. Acknowledge it.
- The process to achieve a goal is sometimes more valuable than the goal itself.
- A sign of success in a job is that when you are done, people don't even notice it.
- You can endure more than your body tells you.
- In time, trophies tarnish and scars heal. Don't fret overmuch.
- People are no less precious simply because they don't share your sense of humor.
- "Off with their heads!" should be used sparingly and never as your first course of action.[5]

Bernadine also befriended students who lacked confidence or who found science and math difficult to understand. She was able to give them the confidence necessary to succeed. One student, Sister Mary Martin Lane, was a very talented student of literature, but lacked the confidence to compete with her peers. She approached Bernadine with a request that she withdraw from the field of literature and transfer to social studies. Bernadine heard her out, then quietly said, "But that would be a great loss." According to Mary Martin, "That was a unique moment of being known and valued as I had never before experienced." Mary Martin continued her studies and became an accomplished poet and teacher.

Another student, Sister Lisa Marie Staebel (now Lisa Mullins), who was accomplished in her chosen field of literature, just could not grasp math concepts. According to Lisa, when she and another sister approached Bernadine for help:

> This brilliant Ph.D. biology teacher worked patiently with us, using corn and other objects to help us "get" math for the first time ever. We both had "eureka" experiences, moving from the shame we had previously felt to a sense of empowerment through her down-to-earth, practical approach.[6]

Bernadine firmly believed that it is not difficult to teach and for a student to learn if each of the elements of the subject is simplified. According to Sister Jude Fitzpatrick, "She was an unbelievable teacher, brilliant but able to translate complex matters into simple terms. For example, she could use a single piece of paper to describe the entire circulatory system."

Sister Penelope Wink, who majored in biology at Marycrest in the early 1960s, often would stop by Bernadine's office at night to talk. She would find Bernadine sitting at her desk with her bandeau pushed up on her head to give her forehead breathing space, her shoes off, and her feet up on her desk. Usually, Bernadine was reading theology texts, poetry, current affairs magazines, history books, or novels in addition to science journals and texts. Penelope was amazed at the breadth of Bernadine's interests and her global vision. According to Penelope,

> Bernadine was a woman who approached life with her arms wide open. She was unlike many people, who see life through the picture frame of their own preconceptions of what life really is or their personal vision of the future. Instead, Bernadine was open to life experiences without the strictures of such preconceptions and experienced life from others' perspective as well as her own. In turn, she was able to synthesize the life experiences of many people and share them in a coherent way with others thereby broadening their perspectives as well. Her broad vision helped the community move into the future with a zest to discover and contribute to building the future in cooperation with others.

Another student, Roberta Kealey, describes herself as "an immature, disconnected college student who never would have made it through

Marycrest without Bernadine's support and encouragement." During the three years that Roberta worked as an assistant in Bernadine's science lab, they developed a friendship lasting forty years, which included Roberta's husband, children, and grandchildren.

To Roberta, Bernadine was a very accomplished and successful person, who was never interested in climbing the proverbial ladder of success. Bernadine, she says, "never reached upward; she reached outward."[7]

With children, Bernadine had a special touch. They were drawn to her because she, like them, was curious and loved a good time. When children were around, they became the focus of her attention. As her nephew, John Holtkamp, who as a child overcame a severe speech impediment with Bernadine's help, described her: "She had the ability to focus on just you and never gave the impression that she wanted to be somewhere else with someone other than you. You were important when you were with Bernadine."[8]

Bernadine was a strong supporter of young sisters in the CHM community. From 1960 to 1966, she served as the appointed superior for Sisters of Humility who returned to Marycrest each summer to complete bachelor degrees. Rather than treating these sisters as persons to be supervised, Bernadine treated them as friends. Bernadine spent a lot of time listening to these sisters' hopes and frustrations. From these conversations, Bernadine concluded that it was time to reform the outmoded customs and rules of the community. She also determined that, if given the opportunity, she would make it possible for these and other sisters to refocus the mission of the community and use their talents individually and jointly to respond to the changing needs of the world, particularly the needs of poor and disadvantaged persons.

In 1963, the Humilities established a house of studies in Davenport and began sending larger numbers of sisters to Marycrest to complete their degrees before sending them out on the "missions." I was one of the newly professed sisters sent to Davenport in June 1963. As was the tradition in the community, members of my novitiate class went to Marycrest early to help prepare the college for the new academic year. When we arrived at Marycrest, we had no idea what we would be studying.

During my second year in the novitiate, I had asked the novice mistress to allow me to take philosophy and literature courses that were being taught to newly professed sisters. She told me that individual sisters like me were not allowed to decide the course of studies they would pursue, the timing of such studies, the type of work that they would be assigned, or the location of such work. These decisions, she said, were made by the Mother General of the community.

The novice mistress also suggested that my goal of being a teacher of literature and philosophy might not be consistent with the community's needs or commitments, and that she would recommend I be among the sisters sent out to teach in elementary school after two years of college. Such an assignment, she said, would test my willingness to serve community needs rather than pursuing my individual goals.

The novice mistress' words made me think long and hard about whether I would trust the community's centralized decision-making process to somehow match my skills and interests with the community's needs or commitments. Ultimately, I decided to stay in the community because I could not conceive that it would not use the talents and interests of its members to carry out its mission.

I also stayed because of the women I had come to know in the novitiate. I felt a kinship with these women whose camaraderie and humor allowed all of us to survive the "boot camp" of the novitiate and gave me the confidence to take the risk that the choice I had made in joining the Sisters of Humility would work out.

When our group arrived at Marycrest, I, by the luck of the draw, was assigned to work with Bernadine. As the Assistant Academic Dean, Bernadine was responsible for determining the class schedules for all Marycrest students based upon their declared majors and interests. I was assigned to help Bernadine with these schedules. I had never met her before. When I arrived at her biology lab, I encountered a woman with brilliant blue eyes, a rumpled habit, and welcoming smile. She clearly explained to me the process for determining the schedules and left me to make them.

A couple of days later, Bernadine came in to check on my work. She scanned the schedules I had made and then asked me what I wanted to study. Although I was surprised to be asked, I immediately replied, "philosophy and literature." She said with a smile, "Make yourself a schedule." She then told me to find out what the other sisters in my group wanted to study. The next day, I reported what each sister wanted to study. In response, she said, "Make them schedules as well."

To Bernadine, it was only common sense to allow each sister to determine her course of study consistent with her interest and talents. By these decisions, Bernadine changed a longstanding community policy that generally did not allow individual sisters to determine their own professional training and thus the nature of the work they would do. This small, quiet reform was just the beginning of a comprehensive reform and renewal of the Sisters of Humility under Bernadine's leadership.

# Changing Course by Reclaiming the Community's Roots

On October 11, 1962, Pope John XXIII convened the Second Vatican Council. He called upon the church to modernize itself through dialogue with the world, including other Christian traditions, other faiths, the culture, and the political and technical milieu. The pope knew there would be substantial opposition to his plans for the church. In his opening address to the council, Pope John urged the bishops and cardinals not to listen to the "prophets of doom" and to tackle present-day problems joyously and without fear." His call for a joyful renewal through dialogue both within and outside the Catholic Church represented a sea change for the church. According to Cardinal Franz Konig, "It was a bolt out of the blue even for those of us who realized that reform was necessary."[1]

While John XXIII is the pope with whom Vatican II will always be associated, he died in June 1963 after only one session of the council. On his deathbed, John XXIII said: "It is not that the gospel has changed: it is that we have begun to understand it better. Those who have lived as long as I have. . .know that the moment has come to discern the signs of the times, to seize the opportunity and to look far ahead."[2]

His successor, Pope Paul VI, had to guide the council through the substantial, contentious issues that were unresolved. Paul VI both reaffirmed the mission of Vatican II as envisioned by John XXIII and led the council in enacting the *Pastoral Constitution on the Church in the Modern World* and other important decrees aimed at modernizing the Catholic Church.

Toward the end of Vatican II, Paul VI in October 1965 issued *Perfectae Caritatis,* the decree that specifically called upon religious communities of men and women to renew themselves and adapt to the modern world. The primary guideline set forth in *Perfectae Caritatis* is that religious communities "must return to the sources of all Christian life, the gospels, and to the original spirit of their institutes as adapted to the changing conditions of our time."[3]

On August 6, 1966 Paul VI issued an apostolic letter, *Ecclesiae Sanctae,* which allocated the most important role in the adaptation and renewal of religious life to the religious communities themselves, working through their legislative bodies, which at the time were called "general chapters of affairs.[4] *Ecclesiae Sanctae* specifically authorized general chapters to allow experimentation in customs and practices, modify their constitutions, issue new norms, and adapt their mission to the needs of the modern world. It also urged religious communities to consult with their members and educate them regarding the social conditions of the times in which they live so that they might be able to serve more effectively. The gospel mandate to serve the poor and the *Pastoral Constitution on the Church in the Modern World's* call for enlarging the church's mission to serve people of all places and faiths were to be the primary guides for the renewal of religious communities.

Within these general guidelines, religious communities throughout the world and, particularly in the United States, began the process of reform and renewal. The interpretation of the gospel mandate to serve the poor adopted by the bishops of Latin America during conferences in 1968 at Medellin, Columbia and in 1979 at Puebla, Mexico also profoundly influenced this process.

The Sisters of Humility did not wait for the Vatican II Council to conclude its deliberations in 1965 before responding to its call for renewal and revitalization of religious communities.[5] In early 1964, sisters at Ottumwa Heights College began a study of the community's existing constitution with an eye toward updating the document in light of the changing needs of the world. In November 1964, Mother Mary Nicholas Sheetz and her council called for a congregation-wide vote on a revision of the delegate selection process to be used for the CHM's 1966 General Chapter of Affairs. Through this vote, the community adopted a participatory democratic process, which resulted in the election of new chapter delegates, thereby broadening the perspective of the 1966 chapter.

In November 1964, the community also commenced an eighteen-month study of the founding principles, structure and the spirit of its members during the first hundred years of the community's existence. This study profoundly influenced the community's renewal in the late 1960s. Specifically, the sisters learned that four women, Antoinette Potier, Julie Claudel, Marie Tabouret, and Marie Gaillot, joined together in 1854 in Dommartin, a small French village, to provide basic education for orphans and children of poverty-stricken rural families. As neither the state nor the church provided education to such children, these women established a free school and a workshop in the Potier ancestral home. The free school provided instruction in religion, reading, writing, and simple arithmetic. In the workshop, the young girls learned marketable skills. To support themselves and their students, the women spun wool, made clothing and shoes for themselves and the children, bound books, tended vineyards, grain fields and their own gardens, as well as raised a pig or two and a few chickens for food.

These women, known as the Daughters of Dommartin, lived and worked together as a classless society for nearly four years without vows, prescribed rules, or recognition as a religious order by the church. In 1858, they submitted founding documents called "the rule" to Bishop Alexis Basile Menjaud in Nancy, France for review and approval.[6]

Their proposed rule mirrored the structure and ethos of the Beguine communities that emerged in Belgium in the twelfth century. These small autonomous groups of Christian women combined a life of prayer and direct service to the poor. Marked by an ethos of freedom and simplicity, members of the Beguine communities retained possession of their homes and property, but lived simply. They made promises of celibacy but were free to leave the community and marry. They alleviated poverty through a variety of works, including teaching, manual labor, care of the sick, and any other works their members were capable of performing.[7]

The Daughters of Dommartin's proposed rule specifically established an egalitarian and democratic way of life. It also explicitly provided that the members would not make a vow to observe cloister, and they would earn their own living rather than depend on church or civic support.[8]

As a community founded to serve poor people in rural communities, the rule emphasized that the spirit of poverty and simplicity would guide members both in their work and in their daily lives. Each house supported itself, but also shared any surplus with others who had less. Members of the community provided their services without regard to the recipient's ability to pay.[9]

Although the founding members were teachers, the rule did not limit the work of the community to teaching. It encouraged each member to develop her talents and make her unique contribution to the joint effort. It also charged the community as a whole to pursue "all possible works of charity that [the members] may find practicable." But the rule also encouraged the members to turn over the existing work to qualified persons as they emerge and seek other ways of serving poor persons.[10]

On August 25, 1858, Bishop Menjaud approved the proposed rule. With this approval, the Daughters of Dommartin became the Sisters of the Holy Humility of Mary, a religious order recognized by the Catholic Church.

From 1858 to 1864, the community established schools and workshops in eight rural villages, nursed cholera patients in their homes, and increased its membership to twelve members.[11] Due to their association with Father John Begel, a parish priest who often challenged both civic and church leaders, the sisters began to experience difficulty in obtaining and/or renewing their teaching certificates. In early 1864, they began transferring their schools and workshops to lay women who, in turn, planned to turn them over to religious congregations who had the credentials to operate them under French law.[12]

When civil authorities revoked the Sisters of the Holy Humility of Mary's teaching certificates in retaliation for Father Begel's refusal to ring the church bells in honor of a military victory by Napoleon, the community joined the exodus of many other religious communities from Europe to the United States.[13] Before they could leave for America, the founder of the community, Antoinette Potier, became sick and died. The remaining eleven sisters, along with four orphans and Father Begel, embarked on the uncertain journey to the United States.

The sisters arrived in New York in 1864, and went immediately by train to stay temporarily in Louisville, Ohio. The Bishop of Cleveland, Amadeus Rappe, sold the sisters a farm near New Bedford, Pennsylvania, which turned out to be mostly swampland, with wooded areas and buildings in disrepair. Its land had not been cultivated for years since two prior religious orders abandoned the property because it was too remote and unsustainable. But the sisters adapted to their circumstances, learned English, and gradually began to teach, care for orphans, and provide nursing care in homes and hospitals.[14]

From 1864 to 1870, the sisters taught children in parochial schools in rural areas of Pennsylvania and Ohio, and cared for children made orphans by the Civil War. They also nursed children in their convents and adults in their own homes during the smallpox epidemic. After the epidemic, they established a hospital to care for patients disabled by small pox.[15]

In 1870, the community responded to a request from Bishop John Joseph Hogan of Missouri to establish schools for Irish and German immigrant children in the frontier Diocese of St. Joseph. Four sisters moved to Missouri, while the rest remained in Pennsylvania and Ohio. For seven years, these sisters and several new members from the area taught in rural public and parish schools in Nordway, Easton, Chillicothe, Liberty, and Carrollton, Missouri. In 1874, this western group of Humilities separated from the Humility foundation in the Cleveland diocese and formed an independent congregation.[16] In 1944, they changed their formal name to the Congregation of the Humility of Mary.

In the frontier parishes of Missouri, the Sisters of Humility of Mary lived and worked with the people with very few resources for themselves or their schools. An egalitarian, courageous, free-spirited group of women known for their hospitality, they shared a house with twenty other boarders in Carrollton. To support themselves and pay down the debt they incurred in establishing and operating their schools, two sisters traveled the railroad lines and solicited funds from construction workers.[17]

In 1877, this small band of sisters moved to Ottumwa, Iowa and established the Sacred Heart School for Boys, as they were one of the few religious communities of women willing to teach boys. In Ottumwa, they lived among the people, responded to the changing needs of the community, and used their individual talents to do whatever was necessary to meet those needs.[18]

The Humilities, during their first sixty years in Iowa, established and staffed a hospital, two colleges, two orphanages, and a series of elementary and high schools, many of which were located in rural areas throughout Iowa, Illinois, and Montana. As the Humilities' colleges and hospital expanded and the free standing elementary and high schools grew in number, the membership of the community also increased. By 1960, the community had grown to four hundred members.

However, during the period between the early 1930s and 1966, the founding mission of the community, to serve poor people, lost its primacy. Although individual sisters continued to serve poor persons, the community at large focused its efforts on maintaining its system of schools, orphanages, and St. Joseph Hospital. These institutions, established to educate poor immigrants or to care for sick people without access to health care, gradually began to serve descendants of immigrants who were no longer poor or those for whom there were other alternative services in the community. Nevertheless, the Humilities continued to subsidize these institutions with their own labor instead of focusing this considerable resource on direct service to poor people and other changing needs of the world.

The decision of Mother Geraldine, the superior general of the community, to seek certification in 1938 of the community as a papal institute in order to facilitate the community's work throughout the world exacerbated the community's loss of focus on its founding purpose. To become a certified papal institute, the Humilities had to conform their Constitution and Book of Customs to the requirements of 1918 Code of Canon Law. This code, rather than recognizing the differing natures of religious communities, imposed cloister, uniform regimens that restricted the sisters' daily lives, ministries, prayer forms, and even clothing styles. These restrictions were unsuitable for apostolic communities like the Humilities, whose work required them to serve people in the community.

The community's 1948 Constitution, based upon the 1918 Code of Canon Law, emphasized "sanctification of its members" and narrowed the community's original purposes to "the instruction of children and youth and the care of sick in the hospitals." These purposes, according to the community's 1948 Constitution, "could not be changed or added to without authorization from the Holy See." As a result, the sisters' ability to respond to the changing needs of the people and communities in which they worked was severely constrained.

While the community's revised Constitution and Book of Customs were not uniformly enforced, the majority of the members were required to abide by their restrictions on the sisters' daily lives and mission. Over time, these restrictions became totally out of sync with contemporary life. But it was the sisters' pent up desire to address changing social, economic, and civil injustices that became the seed for the reform of the community beginning in the mid-1960s. The community's original 1858 rule became the blueprint for making revolutionary changes in the life and mission of the community.

In February 1965, the community embarked on a regional consultative process in which four regional committees open to any sister in the community studied the issues of liturgy, common life and discipline, poverty, obedience, mission/works, and formation of new members. From this study, the sisters concluded that their restrictive daily regimen and outmoded customs were not the essence of religious life, but were impediments to living out their gospel based responsibilities. The members also gained a renewed appreciation for the founders' vision of the community and its prior history of faith, pioneering spirit, and commitment to the poor, which gave them the confidence and determination to renew themselves.

Individuals or groups of sisters submitted 545 proposals for consideration by the CHM 1966 Chapter of Affairs. As Bernadine said at the time, "These recommendations included practically every facet of the sisters' lives and customs."

The Chapter of Affairs convened in June 1966. Bernadine was one of the newly elected delegates to the chapter. The delegates voted to open the chapter proceedings to all members of the community, with each community residence to receive tapes of the proceedings and the chapter decrees for review by the members.

The first agenda item was the election of the new leader of the community. As in any democratic process, there was politicking both before and during the chapter. Lists of sisters who were deemed by some to be "unsafe" to be elected the leader of the community circulated among the delegates. Supporters of specific candidates began their organizing efforts. A number of younger sisters who did not want Bernadine's sometimes rumpled habit to get in the way of her being elected to lead the community made certain that she had a newly pressed habit each day.

Initially, three contenders for the leadership position in the community each had support among some chapter delegates. The delegates debated at length which of the three would best lead the Sisters of Humility during this time of renewal. At the end of the debate, chapter delegates elected Bernadine Pieper as the Mother Superior of the Congregation of the Humility of Mary. Immediately after her election, Bernadine announced to the delegates that she would not assume the title of "mother," but preferred to be called "sister" as she considered herself "simply one among many." With the consent of the chapter, she took the title president instead of mother superior and indicated that she would involve all sisters in the vital decisions concerning the renewal of the community.

The chapter delegates set forth principles and processes for renewal and did not adopt specific legislation to determine substantive issues.

As they too were committed to involving all members in decisions regarding major issues affecting their lives, they adopted the principle of "subsidiarity," the delegation of authority throughout the community to ensure participation in decision-making by all sisters. Collegiality, joint decision-making, and transparency became the norms for Bernadine's administration of the community during her tenure as president.

The chapter did recommend broadening the community's mission, with particular emphasis on Latin American missions, supported long term planning, and set up various commissions to work with the community at large in determining other reforms necessary to renew and revitalize the community.

The chapter also voted to set aside the existing Book of Customs with its disciplinary requirements, and substituted flexibility, simplicity, and planning by the members of each house as the norms for determining local communities' daily activities. When the chapter ended, the renewal efforts by the community at large began in earnest.

# Honest Brokering of the Renewal Process

Bernadine immediately challenged the members at large to take responsibility for the renewal of the community saying, "The responsibility for the success or failure of adaptation and renewal rests with you. The general chapter and the council can only open doors, but the ultimate test is the quality of your response as free and responsible religious women."[1]

In her July 29, 1966 letter to the community, Bernadine reported that many fundamental aspects of the community's operations, including its mission, as well as the meaning and implications of the sisters' vows in the contemporary world, would be further explored and determined by the community at large. To begin the process, she announced a series of regional meetings.

Bernadine committed to write to the community frequently and visit each local community annually in order to learn directly from the sisters their views on these and other issues. During her ten years in office, Bernadine was faithful to this commitment. A voracious reader, her letters were often a synthesis of contemporary thought on a variety of issues ranging from the essentials of religious life to emerging economic, scientific, social, and political issues facing the world and thus the community. At times, they also included the "sense of the community" on issues, which she learned during local and regional meetings and in individual conversations with the members.

Bernadine early in her administration stated that she hoped her change of residency and title would not change the friendship she and the members shared. For her, personal relationships among the members were critical to the strength of the community. As she wrote to the community in November 1966:

> We need to know one another as persons rather than as role-

players. We also need the psychic support of one another to continue or at least begin to live enthusiastically the life of the Lord. Belonging to a society such as the Sisters of Humility should also mean belonging to a community in the sense that community means living with persons who really care what becomes of us, who will allow us to lean when we cannot stand, who will reinforce our courage when we do move to decision-making, and who are really concerned about our works as well as about us as people. Community does not just happen. It must be built, reinforced, and repaired in common worship, service and sacrifice.[2]

Bernadine engaged the members in basic policy decisions that had a direct impact on the sisters' daily lives. For example, on July 1, 1966, she solicited nominations of sisters to serve as elementary school principals or local house superiors for the coming year. When a newly appointed local superior, Roberta Brich, reported to Bernadine that their house had a great spirit, Bernadine told her that she had assigned to her local community sisters who had recommended her appointment as a superior, as she knew they would support her. In fact, whenever possible, she used the same process when determining the local superiors and composition of other community residences.[3]

At the same time, she requested that each sister send her copies of their resumes and educational transcripts, teaching, nursing or any other licenses, and a statement of their interests and experience so that mission assignments for the coming year would be based more closely on the qualifications and preferences of the sisters.[4] After receiving the requested information, Bernadine spent considerable time in July 1966 making the annual assignments based upon both the interests and qualifications of each sister, as well as personal characteristics that impact the quality of local community living.

Traditionally, these assignments were sent to each sister in writing with a message that such assignment represented the will of God. As Bernadine did not believe that her administrative decisions had the force of the "will of God," she did not assert that they did. Instead, she described in a meeting open to all members of the community the process and basis for decisions she and her counsel used to make the appointments. Bernadine explained that they began by attempting to match each sister's educational qualifications, experience, and interests with the requirements of open positions. Then they also took into account the human dynamics that would make or break any local community. With her usual candor, she explained: "Some of us are more difficult to live with than others. Therefore, we tried to assign such persons to communities able to accommodate them while equitably distributing such persons among various local communities."

Bernadine further stated that she thought in the future each sister would have a much more central role in determining her own work. However, before that could happen, she would have to renegotiate the commitments previously made to the various schools in which sisters were currently teaching.

Bernadine also urged the habit commission to quickly solicit suggestions from the members and promptly develop recommendations for revision of the habit. She also asked each local community to resolve as quickly as possible its own daily regimen because "so long as one is chafing about [these] relatively minor issues, one does not have the time and energy to probe the deeper questions of the meaning and value of religious life."

In September 1966, Bernadine consulted with bishops in the dioceses and pastors of parishes in which the sisters were currently working. She hoped that these consultations would foster collegial relationships with them as the community worked through its renewal and revitalization process. In the first consultation, Bernadine met with Bishop George Biskup of the Des Moines Diocese, who immediately raised the issue of habit revision. He said he "would not have a sister without a veil in his diocese." Bernadine responded by saying that many other dioceses were requesting and would welcome Sisters of Humility if he did not want them. She further pointed out that the Humilities had outstanding invitations to serve from Alaska, Hawaii, California, Georgia, Louisiana, Missouri, Nevada, New York, Ohio, Tennessee,

Texas, Japan, Butuan, and the Philippines, as well as from cities and towns in which the sisters had or were currently serving.[5] Bishop Biskup changed the subject and did not raise the issue of habits again.

However, the priests in the Des Moines Diocese did. They asserted that the sisters' experimentation with habits was subject to the agreement by the pastors. Bernadine told them politely but firmly that only the sisters would make habit-related decisions. After a few more skirmishes, the Des Moines pastors also gave up on this issue.

In the Davenport Diocese, there were no major disputes between Bernadine and Bishop Gerald O'Keefe. As soon as Gerald O'Keefe was appointed Bishop in 1966, Bernadine invited him to Ottumwa for a private meeting. They got to know each other and developed a firm bond. On the issue of the habit revision, Bishop O'Keefe said he would "never presume to tell a woman what to wear." More importantly, Bishop O'Keefe supported the Humilities on a wide variety of issues both during and after Bernadine's presidency. He once said that he did not always understand everything the Sisters of Humility were doing, but he both trusted and "sure liked them." He also admired Bernadine, whom he called the "iron woman of the diocese" because when she made a decision or agreement, she stood by it.

The issue of habit revision, however, was initially more polarizing within the community than expected. For some sisters, the habit was a symbol of their dedication to God. For others, the change from habits to modern dress signaled adaptation of religious women to modern life. And for many who had worn the habit for decades, they could not imagine not wearing it. The community's Commission on Habit Experimentation weighed all of these concerns and in March 1967 recommended a period of experimentation with more modern dress within certain guidelines, but with the alternative for any sister to continue wearing the habit either as traditionally worn or as modified. Bernadine quickly approved this recommendation.[6]

After a year of experimentation, the commission recommended and Bernadine approved on May 6, 1968 the simple guideline that the sisters dress as women of their particular professions, or alternatively continue to wear the traditional or modified habit.[7] For the past fifty years, the Humilities have followed this guideline with the support of its members and with little opposition from the people with whom they have worked.

Although the Humilities' transition from habits to modern dress was peaceful, the Immaculate Heart of Mary Sisters (IHMs) encountered stiff opposition from James Cardinal McIntyre of Los Angeles. Cardinal McIntyre ordered the IHM sisters to adopt and wear a common recognizable habit or risk being expelled from the Archdiocese's schools.[8] When the IHMs pointed out that Pope Paul VI's August 6, 1966 apostolic letter governing modernization of religious communities, *Ecclesiae Sanctae,* specifically authorized religious communities to make the decisions regarding their adaptation and renewal, the cardinal used his connections and power with the Vatican to control the lives and educational mission of the IHMs.

After attempts to resolve the dispute with Cardinal McIntyre failed, the dispute moved to the Sacred Congregation for Religious, whose members sided with the cardinal.[9] In a further attempt to resolve the conflict, Sister Anita Caspary, the leader of the IHM community, asked Bernadine and ten other leaders of religious communities active in the Conference of Major Superiors of Women to accompany her to Rome to try to resolve the conflict with the pope.[10] Although they all agreed to do so, the trip was cancelled after a cardinal in Rome advised Anita that the trip would only make the conflict worse.

When the Conference of Major Superiors of Women scheduled a vote on a resolution supporting the IHM Chapter decrees, the Vatican Sacred Congregation for Religious dispatched a representative to the meeting, Father Ed Heston, who told the major superiors they should not pass the resolution but instead should end all debate concerning the conflict between Cardinal McIntyre and the IHMs. The resolution in support of the IHMs, which required an affirmative vote of two-thirds majority for passage, lost by a very small margin. According to Bernadine, some major superiors feared that supporting the IHMs might put their own communities at risk. Bernadine was willing to take that risk, as she believed that the IHM decrees were within the authority of religious communities under Vatican II decrees and were

responsive to Pope Pius XII's 1950s call for both male and women's religious communities to eliminate "outdated customs and clothing that
estranged them from those they served."

Ultimately, the Sacred Congregation for Religious forced 455 IHMs,
who voted to affirm their 1967 Chapter of Renewal decrees, to relinquish their canonical status. These women, after relinquishing such
status, established a lay ecumenical community whose members have
continued to live in accordance with the principles and values set forth
in these decrees during the past forty-five years.[11]

In 2000, the Archbishop of Los Angeles, Cardinal Roger Mahony, in
his Lenten address, apologized for "the unfortunate dispute" between
his predecessor and the IHMs.[12]

# Reaching Accord on Basic Principles

The discussions and collaboration necessary for the Sisters of Humility to reach agreement regarding their spirit and goals as well as the community's primary mission began in the fall of 1966. As resolution of these issues involved a major culture change in the community, the process took considerable determination, courage, creativity, and a willingness to trust one another to make responsible decisions.

Bernadine led a bottom up process in which each sister had the opportunity to express her own views, hear the views of others, and work together to reach agreement on these essential issues. To provide a factual underpinning for these discussions, Bernadine in 1967 enrolled the community in the national survey of religious women sponsored by the Conference of Major Superiors of Women Religious and directed by Sister Marie Augusta Neal, a Harvard trained professor of sociology at Emmanuel College in Boston. The survey focused on women religious' understanding of and attitudes about the meaning of religious life, the renewal process in their own community and in the church, their religious vows, and broader social issues, including poverty and social justice. Eighty percent of the women religious in the United States participated in the survey. Participants received the results of the survey for their own community as well as the composite results for all participants for comparison purposes.

Initially, the Humilities' survey results as well as their discussions among themselves reflected more differences than agreement on fundamental issues facing the community. For example, sisters personally committed to teaching asserted that education provides an essential service to the church and communities in which the sisters work. Thus teaching should remain the primary mission of the community. They worried that allowing sisters to individually determine their work would undermine the resources necessary to continue the system of elementary, secondary, and higher education the community had built over the previous hundred years.

Others argued that the founders of the community and Vatican II called for them to focus specifically on the needs of poor people. According to these sisters, while the parochial school system initially focused on poor immigrants, it now served primarily middle class families, many of whom could secure comparable educational services elsewhere. Some of these sisters had other talents they were eager to use, but felt they were unable to do so due to the community's existing commitments to parochial schools or the staffing needs of the community's own institutions.

The financial cost of such change also became an issue. Some argued that the Sisters of Humility, never a wealthy community, did not have the resources necessary to serve poor people in the U.S. and establish new missions in the third world while meeting its current obligations to care for retired sisters, pay down the debt on the institutions, and continue to educate current and future members. A few sisters asserted that Bernadine would bankrupt the community and destroy its future.

Intertwined with these and other fundamental issues were the members' varied understandings of the meaning of religious life in general, the vows the sisters had taken and the underlying purpose for being a member of the Sisters of Humility in particular. Some were content to continue living their lives according to the established norms while others were eager for a wholesale reformation of the community.

Bernadine understood that these differences were real and that harmony could not be imposed. She provided all members the opportunity to voice their fears as well as their hopes. The members themselves, she knew, had to work out their differences if the community was to achieve a unified understanding of the unique identity of the Sisters of Humility and a committed position on its spirit and goals and primary mission. And so she began by confronting the differences head on. Quoting Yevgeny Yevtushenko, she said,

We are people
We argue,
  grumbling and snapping,
  at times we jealously trample on one another,
  but our separateness—
  as you know—is false, in general,
  We the people
  don't exist separately.[1]

The Sisters of Humility, Bernadine pointed out, "are a service community first, not for ourselves but for others. . . . We do not exist merely to exist or because we have existed in the past." For the community to move forward together, "each sister must ponder and pray to discern how and where she can serve. The congregation—each house, each region, the works committee, the senate—must all ponder and pray to discern the corporate direction."[2]

Regarding differences which divide the members of the community, she said: "It would be a stark world if there were no differences of opinion; however, we create a chaotic world when we do not trust one another."[3] And so, she repeatedly urged the sisters to trust one another and confront their differences directly and civilly.

For Bernadine, harmony, among people as well as in music, does not mean only one note. She believed that the diversity of its members was one of the community's assets. In fact, she often said she wished the community had more diversity to help solve the complex issues facing it.

What is needed, she emphasized again and again, is real collaboration among the members. To achieve such collaboration, Bernadine nudged and encouraged reluctant members of the community to actively participate in the renewal discussions and restrained others whose instinct and style was to take over the process in order to accomplish renewal more quickly. When a majority of sisters arrived at a particular position on an issue, Bernadine protected the minority to ensure that their concerns about the issue were heard and accommodated to the maximum extent possible. She also urged those "who have lived longer to recognize that the young sisters have the greatest stake in the renewal of the community; according to the laws of probability, they will live longer to harvest the fruits of all of our labors."[4]

In her letters and in conversations with individual sisters and groups of sisters, Bernadine urged them to study carefully the history of the community, including the principles upon which the founders established the community. These principles and the pioneering spirit of the sisters who immigrated to the United States from France in the late 1860s, she said, must be the starting point for the renewal and adaptation of the community to the modern world.

For over two years, members of the community vigorously debated virtually every element of religious life. These issues included the place of prayer and contemplation in the life of the individual sister, the bonds necessary for the community to continue to exist, the meaning of the religious vows, the particular spirit and identity of the Sisters of Humility, the mission and purpose of the community, and the interface between the overall mission and the right of each sister to determine how she might best use her talents to carry out such mission.

Bernadine was the key to a peaceful resolution of these issues. As Sister Marie Ven Horst observed, "Bernadine was a real innovator. She had good sense. Nothing daunted her; she was fearless. Deep down in her heart, she knew she was capable of solving the problems facing the community." According to Sister Ann Therese Collins, who served as vice president of the community during six years of Bernadine's tenure as president and succeeded Bernadine as president:

> Bernadine was one of the great women in the order. She was an honest woman who acted out of conviction. She understood that the upheaval in the church and society were for the good and was not afraid to say that life changes. She was also confident enough to allow the community to experiment, even if mistakes were made in the process. She was a joyful person, even in adversity. Never autocratic, she trusted the sisters and supported their decisions even though, in some instances, she would have made different choices.

In 1968, the community adopted a consensus statement called "Spirit and Goals," which the chapter formally approved on August 8, 1969. In this document, the members declared:

We Sisters of Humility of Mary are a group of women in the Catholic Church who have banded together to dedicate ourselves through a special common effort to the pursuit of life's essential meaning and to a radical response to the Christian gospel of universal love . . . This includes raising the prophetic voice in society in which we live.

They further decided that life in celibate community and simplicity of life with respect to material possessions is their distinguishing mark. Central to such life is their belief that "people joined together in a common cause can accomplish what one alone cannot do in creating a future in which every [person] can become fully human." In 1990, after further reflection and debate, the Sisters of Humility adopted the following mission statement:

We, the members of the Congregation of the Humility of Mary call one another to live the gospel with simplicity and joy following the example of Mary. Like our founders, we strive to be attentive to the call of the Spirit in the signs of our times, especially the needs of the poor and the powerless. We commit ourselves as individuals, and as a congregation, to work for justice within the human family and care of the earth itself.

To carry out these fundamental principles, they adopted and implemented a policy of "self-determination." Under this policy, each sister decides for herself the ministry she will pursue based upon her qualifications, training, or experience within the context of the community's agreed upon mission, spirit and goals.

# Greasing the Wheels of Renewal

While the community debated these policies, Bernadine anticipated practical implementation problems, which she quietly and efficiently solved before they became insurmountable obstacles. In early September 1966, three years before the policy of self-determination was first implemented, Bernadine gave notice to schools that, within two to three years, the community would no longer guarantee sisters to fill specific positions within the parochial school system. The individual sisters would make their own decisions regarding what work they would undertake. Bernadine assured the school administrators that this change would not result in the community's immediate abandonment of the schools, as she believed the majority of the sisters would choose to continue to teach in the parochial school system.

To test out this belief before the chapter formally adopted the self determination policy in 1969, Bernadine in 1968 implemented an open application process in which each sister determined the job she would like to have and submitted an application to her for either her existing job or another job that was open. Bernadine saw this process as a way of defusing the fears of those committed to teaching in the community's institutions or the parochial school system that their choice would be undermined by large numbers of sisters opting out of teaching and jeopardizing the community's colleges or the parochial school system. In fact, as Bernadine foresaw, the vast majority of the sisters remained teachers by choice and there was no immediate mass abandonment of either the community institutions or the parochial school system.

Bernadine was also the quiet "fixer" of a number of other issues confronting the community during her term in office. To cover costs related to the community's existing obligations as well as future expenses related to the new missions both within and outside the United States, Bernadine, in conjunction with the finance committee, developed a financial plan designed to generate the necessary resources to meet these needs. As Bernadine believed in transparency in community affairs, she prepared and distributed to the entire community a budget so that the sisters were informed about the community's necessary expenditures. Contrary to the fears of a few, most of the sisters voluntarily contributed to the general fund when they understood the community's internal expenses and the estimated cost of new programs to serve people with no or low-income and other disadvantaged people.

One part of her financial plan was to negotiate an increase in compensation for sisters who taught in parochial schools. In 1965, salaries for Humilities teaching in parochial schools ranged from $50 to $100 a month. In Des Moines, all of the parishes paid sisters $50 per month, or $600 for the nine month school term. During these negotiations, some pastors in Des Moines asserted that increases in sisters' compensation would be unnecessary if the sisters maintained their habits, as they could get along on $50 per month. Ignoring these insults, Bernadine pressed for more reasonable compensation for the sisters.

After many months of negotiations, Bernadine achieved agreements for graduated increases in these salaries. By 1975, in Iowa where most of the sisters taught, their compensation increased to an annual salary of $3300 plus $500 for retirement, an average of $423 per month per sister for the nine-month school term. This rate, while still substantially below the market rate for teachers, was sufficient to allow sisters to meet their own personal expenses and contribute funds to meet general community obligations.

Bernadine reported to the community in 1976 that she no longer worried about parochial schools losing sisters because the parishes lacked the money to provide the modest salaries sought by the community. She had learned through salary negotiations that most parishes had the money and were willing to pay for everything but sisters' salaries because the sisters had always been willing to do the work without any substantial payment. Bernadine believed the sisters should not be a cheap labor force for middle class schools. Rather, she said, the community should concentrate its donated services on those who are in fact impoverished, not provide services "just because we have always done so" in parishes which are no longer poor.[1]

In the summer of 1966, Bernadine established a health insurance plan. To free active sisters from increasing costs associated with supporting retired sisters, she enrolled the community in the Social Security program in 1972 when it became available for sisters, with the community paying the employer's portion of the Social Security taxes. Using unclaimed interest in patrimony funds, the community set up the CHM Retirement Trust Fund in 1976.

Although Bernadine operated the community on a tight budget, she always made room for special project funds to assist poor or other disadvantaged persons or to support projects that advanced peace and justice. One fund established early in her administration was the People's Investment Fund (PIF), which both the community's general fund and the sisters' individual contributions created and sustained. The PIF provided grants and no-interest loans to many individuals, families, and groups in emergency situations when they had no other financial resources. It paid rent, medical bills, transportation expenses, funeral costs, food, repair or modification of poor peoples' homes, as well as funded education and training to qualify poor persons for jobs. The fund also supported peace and justice organizations, migrant advocacy groups, senior citizens groups, and family crisis centers.

Early on in her administration, Bernadine had an idea for what she called a Blue Sky Conference in which experts in diverse fields like geography, demography, science, religion, politics, history, world affairs, and ethics would come together with interested sisters to explore future developments in the world and the cosmos that would radically change human life. She thought such a conference would expand the sisters' thinking about themselves and their relationship to the world, and help spur creative ideas for new ministries to carry out the mission of the community.

As Bernadine's Blue Sky Conference idea was not widely embraced by the community, she scaled the conference back and tried a different approach. After consulting with the ministry committee, Bernadine proposed to establish a seed grant fund for the members to encourage innovative ideas in education, health care, and the creation of new or expanded ministries. The community readily approved this fund and seed grants have helped many sisters, including some whose ministries are described in this book, implement innovations in their existing work or develop new ministries.

In the early 1970s, Bernadine began to review each of the community's institutions to determine whether they should be turned over to others capable of continuing their work in order to focus the community's resources on service to poor people or other unmet needs of society. Marycrest College, Ottumwa Heights College, and St. Joseph's Hospital were already separately incorporated. However, they were still considered by both the CHMs and broader community to be owned by the Sisters of Humility and would be sustained by the donated labor of the sisters. In effect, the sisters were the "endowment" for each of these institutions.

Bernadine, as the chairperson of each of these three institutions, began in 1968 to add laypersons to the board of directors of each institution. In the same year, a group of laymen and women associated with Ottumwa Heights College established a foundation to increase financial support for the college. The board also hired a layman as the development officer for the college. By 1970, majority lay boards for each institution had begun to assume responsibility for operating these institutions and by 1976 laypersons chaired the boards of each institution. As Bernadine reported to the community in 1976, these steps "are examples of daughters growing up enough to be independent of their mother institute and so are signs of progress and development."[2]

In subsequent years, Bernadine negotiated or otherwise facilitated the merger/sale of Ottumwa Heights and St. Joseph's Hospital to others with the capacity and commitment to carry out their essential missions. Marycrest College and its successor, Marycrest International

University, continued its operations until 2002 when the campus was sold and transformed into a residential community for senior citizens known as the Marycrest Senior Campus, with market rate and below market rate residences for seniors. In the aftermath of Hurricane Katrina, the Marycrest Senior Campus offered permanent housing for hurricane victims through the efforts of Sisters Cathleen Real and Judith Cararra, who traveled to Mississippi to deliver supplies and provide emergency assistance to those whose homes were lost or damaged by the hurricane.

The merger and sale of these institutions ultimately freed up substantial numbers of highly educated sisters, many of whom directed their skills to projects serving poor persons all over the world, other justice and peace work or caring for the earth programs.

# Founding the Latin American Missions

In January 1967, six months after her election as president of the community, Bernadine announced that the Sisters of Humility would establish within a year's time missions in Latin America. As Bernadine believed that mission work in third world countries required a particular set of skills, temperament, and commitment, she announced that the missions would be staffed only with volunteers found to be appropriate candidates after screening through a battery of tests and interviews. A sufficient number of sisters volunteered and the screening process began.

In June 1967, Bernadine and Sister Ana María Orozco set out to explore potential sites for the missions recommended by Father Louis Colonnese, Director of the Latin American Bureau of the United States Catholic Bishops' Conference. Bernadine chose Ana María to accompany her since she was fluent in Spanish and had already volunteered to serve in the community's Latin American mission(s). Bernadine's description of this trip, as recorded in her June 29, 1967 letter to the CHM community, describes not only what she saw, but also her thinking that led her to recommend to the community missions in San Andrés Larrainzar, México and Ambato, Ecuador:

> Very early Saturday morning we left México City for Tuxtla
> Gutiérrez by plane. A Cursillo leader took us up an innumerable number of curves to San Cristóbal de las Casas (San Cristóbal), which is almost two miles higher than Tuxtla. Everyday extremes seem more incongruous here—plowing oxen next to bulldozers; modern plastic capes over typical regional dress; trucks and cars on the same road with burros and women carrying wares to and from market; native alcohol in Pepsi bottles. We spent Sunday visiting this diocese of about

half a million people; and each place we stopped took us back another century. This is the rainy, warm (60° – 70° F.) season of a mountainous area.

We began at the Cathedral, which, like all colonial churches, has many gold-leaf altars covered with oil paintings, contrasted with a simple table for Mass, peeling stucco walls and a few rough benches. Over a thousand (I do not exaggerate) fresh lilies decorated the church.

Brother Antonio took us to the Marist school where four Méxican brothers teach the young married Indian men, who leave their home for a four-month period of woodworking, sewing, hygiene, and simple theology. We also visited the school for Indian girls, who stay three years with four Méxican Sisters to prepare for going back to their tribes as catechists. One handsome Indian couple brought their daughter while we were there . . .

Sunday morning we went up and down the mountains in a jeep with Father Álvarez as he offered Mass and visited catechists in various villages. At one place he brought communion to an old woman who got up and dressed for the occasion. Her clay-floored house contained two altars, a hundred (perhaps I exaggerate a bit) religious pictures, a dozen pictures of relatives, flowers, a bed, a box and a transistor radio . . .

In another village we went to the home of the richest man. It also had an altar and pictures in the main room, which had a rough wood floor. Another room had an open fire for cooking. Like the people, I smelled of wood smoke. The roofs of the houses are made of thatched grass or tiles and the walls, a combination of clay and wood . . .

At mass, the participation in song (led by several seminarians who went along with us and was taught earlier by the catechists) was really good. Even the men, who knelt or sat on the clay floor covered with fresh grass on the side opposite to the women, were attentive. It seems that the early Spaniards baptized everybody and now the people, who continue to be baptized, believe their souls are made of many parts, which become one at baptism . . .

The final place we stopped, the chief village of the ninety thousand Chamula Indians, was the most incredible mixture of all. Nearby, crosses can be seen on the tops of the mountains; however, these are not Christian symbols, but the goddesses of water. In the front one-fourth of the old church, Father Hernandez, who has lived there a year and-a-half, was offering Mass with several dozen people . . .

The rest of the church was a pagan temple. One group of statues had a least one hand removed and lacked the cloth dresses most of the statutes here wear. Even the priest may not touch these, for the people consider them gods in disfavor. Other statutes, originally taken from the churches in the area, were dressed in layers of cloth and worshipped. Families were kneeling before them with the men chanting and lighting candles. The chant is incredibly sad and beautiful . . .

It was in this church that the alcohol was placed in Pepsi bottles and the adults drank and drank during the daylong prayers. Two catechists are helping Father, who is respected by the Indians but not allowed to own anything. They teach hygiene, nutrition, agriculture, and religion. If they succeed, the people won't have to depend on alcohol to achieve relief from a sub-human existence . . .

The government has been trying to help the people, but they trust only those whose motives are selfless and respect the Indians for themselves, and as the religious here say, things are being accomplished, but *poco a poco* . . .

Sunday night Bishop Samuel Ruiz García showed us statistics about the diocese. Even though the country of México is relatively affluent, his diocese is one of the lowest in literacy in Latin America, lowest in number of priests, and highest in infant mortality . . .

The priests and religious here demonstrate that the spirit of Francis of Assisi and Charles de Foucauld lives on. For example, Father Locket, a priest from New Orleans whom the bishop hopes the Sisters of Humility will help serve the health, nutrition, and religious needs (which are unbelievably great) of ten thousand Tzotziles, lives in a room containing a mattress-less bed, table, chair, book and medicine cases, and a kerosene lamp. The outdoor latrine turned Sister Ana María green, and the water was drawn by a pulley and rope from an open well . . .

Monday Father Locket took us up and down and around the mountains of his parish, San Andrés, Larrainzar. Here life is quickly stripped to the barest essentials. Sisters who begin here would have to do without the benefits of electricity, plumbing, or heating, and variety in companionship, food, and amusement. They would need to be able to endure, or better, enjoy, gray days because during part of the year it rains a part of every day; continue in spite of pain, nausea, weariness; really love one another; possess ingenuity in solving practical problems of a most primitive kind; and be able to pray and think during times of traveling and waiting. They would be assured of knowing that they are serving God in the poorest of the poor. They would also be working with dedicated and *muy simpatico* priests, bishop, religious, and people helping people achieve a human existence; teaching basic ideas about God and his mysterious relation to man; living in a mountainous area of magnificent grandeur and beauty. The people have no shoes, but they have flowers and music. Travel will be by burro, jeep and plane.

Tuesday the bishop rented a plane and took his mother and us to the Jesuit mission of Bachajón, where the priests and sisters have been working for nine years, and Ocosingo, where a Dominican priest has been four years and the Presentation Sisters, one year. It would take six days to reach these places by horseback. The objective of this trip was to see what has been accomplished by committed religious. When the priest and sisters came to Ocosingo, there were only a grass-and-clay hut and an abandoned colonial church; now the place is clean and attractive. These missions already have several hundred native catechists and the means for sharing some of the things we take for granted – health, nutrition, sanitation, and tools for earning a living suited to free men . . .

When Bernadine and Ana María prepared to leave México for Quezaltenango, Guatemala, their trip was interrupted by a student revolution resulting in planes being grounded, telephone lines cut, and buses stopped for possible kidnapping of U.S. citizens. So Bernadine and Ana María returned to México City to arrange for an alternative itinerary. But as they were leaving the diocese of San Cristóbal, Bernadine thought that they should go no further. As she explained to the community in the same letter:

> To forget these people would be to follow the example of the priest and the Levite on their way to Jericho. We had seen a place of almost infinite need, a bishop with vision and purpose, and a possible structure in which the Sisters of Humility could work directly to share the vision and healing of Christ. We had experienced the cost in time and money to the bishop for us to visit his mountainous diocese. It did not seem fair to accept such hospitality from the other places since we could not promise to send sisters to most of them, particularly to those whose needs did not seem quite so great.

Rather than continue their travels to the remaining sites, Bernadine and Ana María sent telegrams and explanatory letters to those who were expecting them explaining that plans had changed. They also sent money from the community's Latin American fund to the places not visited to help support their work.

Although Bernadine had not fully committed to San Andrés being one of the community's Latin American mission sites when they returned to Ottumwa, Ana María in her heart had. While in San Andrés with Bernadine, she climbed the church tower, looked out over the highlands and said to herself, "This feels like home."

Prior to making a final decision, Bernadine did further study, consulted sisters who had volunteered for the missions, and met with Bishop Bernardino Echeverría Ruiz, OFM, who traveled to Ottumwa to encourage the community to establish a mission in Ambato, Ecuador. Bishop Ruiz described how Ecuador's clergy, few and unevenly distributed across the county, live in poverty close to the people they serve. He explained that the Andes Mountains have kept many Ecuadorian people in comparative isolation for centuries. In 1967, about forty percent of the people were illiterate; the per capita income was about $220 a year. Bernadine was already aware of the extreme poverty in Ecuador and knew that it did not have many U.S. religious communities working with its poor people.

Bishop Echeverría suggested a cooperative program with the Society of the Divine Word, the Peoria Franciscan Sisters, and the Sisters of Humility to develop a leadership formation center, operate a medical clinic and participate in a diocesan adult education program.

In August 1967, the Humilities' General Council and the Coordinating Commission of the Apostolate, after reviewing the results of Bernadine's study, approved the Dioceses of San Cristóbal de las Casas (Diocese of San Cristóbal), in Chiapas, México and the Diocese of Ambato, Ecuador as sites for the Sisters of Humility's Latin American apostolate.

In announcing this decision to the community, Bernadine explained that initially seven sisters would be chosen to work in these Latin American missions, four in Chiapas and three in Ambato. Before making the announcement of which sisters would go to the missions in the fall of 1968, Bernadine met with each sister who volunteered, but had not been chosen. One sister, Judith Cararra, said of Bernadine, "She was a real person, who was in touch with the realities of life, and honest when it took a lot of courage to be honest. I felt valued by her even when she was counseling me out of going to Latin American."

Bernadine called upon the entire community to support these new missions saying:

> A call to work in primitive missionary territory is a particular
> vocation, but missionary consciousness is an integral part of

every religious vocation. Only a few of us have received the vocation to communicate to Latin American people not our riches, but their own. As members of the Sisters of Humility of Mary, though, we share in one another's apostolate. We will also provide the sisters' daily food, clothing and travel.

Some of us can promote social, economic, linguistic, and scientific research to find adequate solutions to roots of problems. Many can work to develop a social conscience in those we teach. All of us, through faith and the courageous optimism it confers, can pray and sacrifice that the Sisters of Humility of Mary in both North and South America free men to be truly human, compassionate and capable of helping one another.[1]

In September 1968, the Sisters of Humility began their missions in México and Ecuador. Over the past forty-three years, nine Sisters of Humility worked in these missions. Some served there for only a few years; others devoted long periods of their lives to these missions. Other Humilities have also worked in Columbia, Ghana, Tunisia, Taiwan, Croatia, Haiti, New Guinea, and Brazil. While the people who were served in these missions came from different cultures, they had many of the same basic needs. These missions not only significantly contributed to the lives of the remarkable people with whom the sisters worked, but they also provided to the community a "window on the world" and broadened the global vision of its members.

# Widening the Tent /
# Extending the Community's Reach

Early on in the renewal process, Bernadine understood that changes in society would significantly impact the numbers of vowed members in religious communities and therefore new forms of membership should be considered. In the 1950s, the numbers of young women entering religious orders escalated due to the large number of children in Catholic families, the growth in the number of Catholic schools, and the relative lack of career opportunities for young women in society. Many young Catholic women had two options when they finished high school: marry and begin a family or join the convent.

By the mid-1960s, both the Catholic culture and the role of women in society had substantially changed. Catholic families were smaller and parochial schools were no longer the primary choice for Catholic families. Young women had expanded opportunities for higher education and careers. As a result, the growth in women's religious communities across the nation substantially slowed.

Other societal norms changed as well in the 1960s. Permanent commitments were less the norm in society. Just as divorce became a more acceptable option for women in mid life, so too did the decision to leave religious orders. There was no longer a social stigma attached to "leaving the convent."

Six years before Bernadine was elected president, the Sisters of Humility had their largest novitiate class. In 1960, thirty-two young women entered the community. Six years later, new members shrank to two. During the first six months of 1966, prior to Bernadine's election, ten sisters left the community. Over time, others followed.

The reasons sisters left the community varied. Some left because they disagreed with the direction of the community. Others so disagreed with Vatican policies and practices that they felt they could no longer represent themselves as vowed members of a Vatican certified religious institute. A significant number desired to get married. Others, whose work took them far away from the community, found it difficult to remain active in the community and thus could no longer justify continued membership.

Many of those who resigned as vowed members, however, remained committed to the mission of the community. They had strong ties with the sisters and a desire to continue to be part of the community. Others maintained their friendship with Bernadine and other sisters in the community and continued to live their lives consistent with the values of the community.

For Bernadine, each sister who left the community was a personal loss. Despite her sense of personal loss, Bernadine lived the words of Anne Morrow Lindberg: "[Those] that I love, I wish to be free—even from me."[1] She respected the decisions of these members and did what she could to help smooth their transition to a new life. One sister who left to marry, Lisa Mullins, dreaded telling Bernadine she would be leaving the community. But, according to Lisa, "Bernadine was kind and matter-of-fact as always, telling me that 'I already knew you wanted to do this.' The community held a farewell party for me during which Bernadine shared in the laughter and reminiscences."[2]

Bernadine told the remaining members that these departures were not an affront to the community. Rather, she said, the values developed by these women while in the community as well as the respect and support given to them that allowed them to make their decision to choose a new life validates the worth of the community.

Rather than mourning, Bernadine sought to widen the tent of the community. In 1971, in consultation with the community, Bernadine took action to add new vitality and diversity by establishing the associate membership. Through this membership, the community welcomes women and men, young and old, married or single, who carry the Humilities' spirit in their personal and professional lives, to join them.

Since 1971, over 175 people have become associate members. Currently there are over one hundred associates, twenty percent of whom are former vowed members. Associate members also include professional colleagues, relatives of sisters, former students, or other persons who are seeking a community of committed people with whom they can share their lives.

The associate membership is rooted in bonds of friendship, service, prayer, and mutual support. Associates define their individual relationship with the community through a written agreement, renewable each year. They participate actively in the life of the community by serving on committees, becoming involved in service projects initiated by them and/or sponsored by the community. They join with the community in prayer and other community gatherings. Over the past forty years, associate members have allowed the community to extend its global reach, made important contributions to the mission of the Humilities, and enriched their own lives as well as the lives of other members of the community.

Mary Martin Lane is a good example of the value of this program. After fourteen years as a Sister of Humility, Mary Martin resigned her vowed membership in 1972 due to personal conflicts with certain dogma and policies of the Church. She did so with reluctance because of

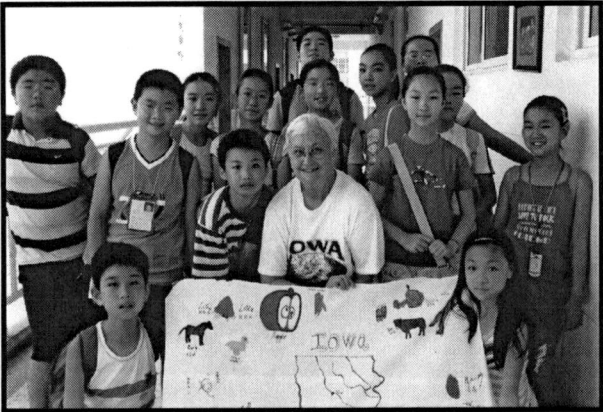

**Mary Martin Lane and students in China**

her strong bond with Bernadine and many of the other sisters, her commitment to both the spirit and mission of the Sisters of Humility, and her firm belief that committed women like the Humilities can accomplish much more together than she could alone.

According to Mary Martin,

> Bernadine's support of me when I was a student and a young
> sister and at other junctures of my life helped me understand
> and actualize my own values and talents. She always ap-
> proached me with a smile, an open heart and open mind.

So when Bernadine announced the establishment of the Associate
Program, Mary Martin immediately applied, was accepted, and has
been actively engaged with the community as an associate member
for the past thirty-eight years. She considers herself a fifty-three-year
member of the Sisters of Humility as her commitment to the values
and purposes of the community has remained unchanged since she
first entered the Sisters of Humility in 1958.

Mary Martin is a gifted teacher, who has specialized in teaching
English and U.S. culture to speakers of other languages both within
the United States and abroad. In her work with various cultures around
the world, she has taken with her the teaching skills honed in Humility
schools and the belief instilled in her by Bernadine and the community
at large that "all people have value if given a chance to demonstrate it."

From 1978 to 1980, Mary Martin served as a Fulbright "good will"
ambassador, taught English to students at Pedagoski Fakultet, developed a language curriculum and conducted in-service seminars for
teachers of English in the Republics of Yugoslavia. As a volunteer under the auspices of the U.N. High Commissioner of Refugees, she returned to Croatia in 1996 to teach survival English to refugees at the
Gasinci Refugee Center near Djakovo, Croatia.

One of Mary Martin's students in the Gasinici camp was Anesa
Kajtazovic, who was seven years old. Anesa, her parents and sister
had fled the horrors of civil war in Bosnia. According to Mary Martin,
Anesa stood out in a cold and dreary refugee camp for her "warmth,
joy, and curiosity." Her parents invited Mary Martin to their cabin and
shared their food with her. They became friends.

When approximately four thousand Bosnians, including the
Kajtazovic family, immigrated to Waterloo, Iowa in 1997, Mary Martin
created and implemented a specialized educational system for Bosnian
students to ensure their successful integration into the school system

and into the Waterloo community. She also served as a volunteer tutor for Balkan adults, especially elderly refugees, who spoke only the Croatian-Bosnian language and were heartbroken by being forced to leave their native country.

When Mary Martin learned that the Kajtazovic family was in Waterloo, she immediately adopted them and helped them get settled in their new homeland. Anesa, a middle school student, quickly become fluent in English, excelled in school and graduated from Waterloo High School in 2004. Shortly before her eighteenth birthday, she became a naturalized citizen. Working a full time job while also volunteering for the Democratic Party, Anesa completed two bachelor degrees in Business and Public Administration at Northern Iowa University in three years and upon graduation took at job in Des Moines at GMAC.

In January 2010 Anesa returned to Waterloo to campaign for election as the state representative for House District 21. In November 2010, at age twenty-one, she defeated the former mayor of Waterloo and now is the youngest person to serve as a state representative in the Iowa legislature. During her election campaign, Anesa was driven by a core value instilled in her by her family, "to work hard and give back." According to Mary Martin, these values are not only part of the Bosnian culture, but the cultures of many immigrants with whom she has worked. They are dedicated to their extended families and instilled with a culture of sharing. The aspirations of their hearts are basically uniform even if their cultures are very different.

In 1991, she lived among and taught Apple computer skills to German and English speaking Hutterite students in Manitoba, Canada. Although Hutterites did not in 1991 generally associate with persons outside their community. Mary Martin became a friend and remains a welcomed visitor in the Hutterite community.

She has also taught English and culture to international students at Concordia College in Minnesota, middle school Chinese students in Beijing and Yangzho, teachers and students from the Ukraine, elementary and middle school students in Hungary and Poland, and young Saudi men and women. In each of these societies, she found most students not only eager to learn the language and culture of the United States, but also to share their own cultures.

In turn, Mary Martin has shared the experiences and values she has gained from these cultures with the Humilities. While considering the next phase of her life, Mary Martin, at age seventy-one, is keeping in touch via Skype and other forms of communications with the people she has taught or met on her journeys, as well as continues to serve as a an active volunteer in both the CHM and Waterloo communities.

# Integrating Prayer, Simplicity of Life, Work and Community

Bernadine, throughout her life, modeled the integral relationship between simplicity of life, justice and peace work, contemplation, and community. As she understood that mandating common times and forms for prayer often led only to meaningless ritual, she instead fostered an environment that allowed each sister the freedom to find her own spiritual expression.

For Bernadine, apostolic activity and prayer are "two sides of the same coin—love."[1] She believed that religious commitment in community, which arises out of the gospel mandate to love God and your neighbor, is not possible without contemplation. Continual recollection of the presence of God in the sisters' lives is necessary, she suggested, "to ensure unity between prayer and the gift of ourselves to others; between our love for God and the love we bear our brothers and sisters." It is contemplation, she said, "which allows us to understand the teachings of the beatitudes, and so make them the practice of our daily lives."[2]

Bernadine, like Rabbi Abraham Joshua Heschel, believed deep in her bones that "prayer is an act that constitutes the very essence of being human. The dignity of man consists . . . in being endowed with the gift of addressing God."[3] For Bernadine as well as for Rabbi Heschel, "To pray is to take notice of the wonder, to regain a sense of the mystery that animates all things, the divine margin in all attainments."[4]

Thus, Bernadine gently and consistently encouraged sisters to take time for prayer and contemplation as she believed that only insofar as prayer and related reading follow the tempo of our lives as a whole will they become integral parts of our existence instead of something veneered to the rest of our activities. According to Bernadine, such prayer, if only for short periods each day, is a human necessity rather than a divine command. Quoting Gladys Taber, she said:

> A time of quietude
> brings things into proportion
> and gives us strength.
> We all need to take time
> from the busyness of living,
> even if it be only ten minutes,
> and watch the sun go down
> or the city lights
> blossom against the cannoned sky.
> We need time to dream,
> time to remember,
> and time to reach toward the infinite.
> Time to be.[5]

Although it took time for some sisters to find the balance between contemplation, prayer, and work, such balance is clearly evident in the lives of the Sisters of Humility today. Prayer and contemplation are the foundation of the sisters' efforts to promote peace and social justice, serve impoverished people, and care for the earth.

According to Bernadine, living in community is an equally important aspect of religious life, as well as a basic human need. When Bernadine became president of the community, she moved from one institutional setting at Marycrest to another at Ottumwa Heights. Initially she lived in the president's bedroom, which was close to the community's administrative offices. While the bedroom was comfortable, she felt isolated, particularly later in the evening when most of the retired sisters who lived near her had gone to bed. After a few years, Bernadine moved to the former novitiate quarters where many of the sisters teaching at Ottumwa Heights lived, and enjoyed the camaraderie of being with the sisters after she finished her work for the day. They often would come together later in the evening in a common area with a refrigerator, microwave, and television. They shared some food, had some drinks, caught up on the day's events and watched a bit of television, including *M*A*S*H* and the *Dick Cavett* show.

In 1970, Sisters Mary Boland, Vicky Reeves and I, who were teaching at Ottumwa Heights, decided we would like to live in a house rather than an institution. We found a small, inexpensive rental house on Van Buren Street, a short distance from the Heights. We told Bernadine about our plans, and she said, "I would like to join you." We were delighted to have Bernadine join us, but a few sisters initially opposed the plan. For some, it was simply expected that the leader of the community would reside at the Heights, as it was the tradition. For one of the sisters, "Bernadine's moving was like a divorce." Bernadine listened to the concerns of the sisters opposing her move and assured them she was not divorcing anyone nor was she going far way. She would be at the Heights every day when she was not traveling to visit members of the community or at other meetings. Bernadine followed through with her plan to move to Van Buren Street and the controversy faded away.

The house, while small for four people, had a yard large enough for Bernadine to have a garden. Tinkering in her garden allowed Bernadine time to relax and think, which produced as many ideas as flowers and vegetables.

We had a great two years together with many laughs and other adventures. Bernadine's bedroom was just a few feet off the living room and had a pocket door that opened wide. She liked to lie on her bed in the evening with her door open as she read stacks of books, magazines, and newspapers while talking with us in the living room. She is the only person I have known who could simultaneously read and carry on an intelligent, coherent conversation. Bernadine was always interested first in what we were doing and thinking. Then she would tell us about her work as well and what she had been reading and thinking. She was a voracious reader and kept us abreast of developments in science, politics, history, literature, the arts, and religion, as well as local affairs. In many ways, Bernadine was a true Renaissance person. Above all, she was never dull.

Bernadine, true to her reputation, was not much of a housekeeper but she was an efficient cook. She could whip up a simple, but nutritious meal in short order. She was also a good sport. One time the three of us took her shopping for clothes as her wardrobe, always small, needed serious refreshing. It was, to say the least, not her favorite thing to do. She said at the time, "I'd rather watch a movie or read a book." However, our persistence won out and we took her to a department store, put her in a changing room and brought to her a variety of dresses. Some worked, some didn't. We laughed a lot at those that didn't. She put only a few aside as possible buys. In the end, she bought only a couple of dresses, consistent with her belief that "a few dresses are all you need."

In May 1972, Mary Boland moved to Iowa City to pursue a master's degree in social work and teach part-time at the School of Religion at the University of Iowa. Vicky and I headed to Washington, D.C. where I entered law school and Vicky initially worked for an environmental organization. Later, after being commissioned to do the artwork for the 1973 Campaign for Human Development of the United States Conference of Bishops, Vicky opened an art studio. Through her artwork, Vicky gave voice to the concerns of a wide variety of social justice groups promoting the preservation of the environment as well as social and economic justice for all, but with an emphasis on poor and other disenfranchised persons.

The morning the three of us packed up to move, Bernadine worked in her garden. She was sad, but did her best not to show it. However, in her letter to the community later that month, she wrote about the value of friends and community:

> It is probably just as well that the final days of May are busy ones; otherwise, the ache of impending separation might be too much for our frail psyches. Yet, I think it imperative for each of us to take time, even perhaps more so when we do not think we have it, to reflect on the meaning of existence and the value of friends and community. I think 'it is not good that man (or woman) be alone' applies to all of us . . . and am sure that working with a community of friends is well worth their absence...It is vital, though, to remember

63

that we belong to a "human family" with members all over the world.[6]

Bernadine loved the small house on Van Buren Street, and so she lived there with other Humilities for the remainder of her term as president of the community. Like us, some of the sisters moved on when their work took them to other places. Others continued to work in Ottumwa and lived with Bernadine on Van Buren until the end of her term.

Bernadine taught all of us who lived with her the value of simple living. She lived a spare, but full life. She did not care about material goods, particularly clothes and other personal possessions, but she also believed that simplicity of life is fundamental to the life of a Sister of Humility. For her, it is the essence of the vow of poverty that each sister takes. Bernadine, who loved to read books and appreciated beautiful things, never kept them for herself. If you gave Bernadine a gift, you knew that before sundown she would likely give it to someone who needed it more. When Bernadine was first elected president of the community, she specifically asked the sisters not to give her the Christmas gifts that were traditionally given to the leader of the community. Instead, she suggested that the sisters use the money to help poor people or invest in projects that advanced justice and peace. Conserving natural resources and sharing with others whatever financial resources or other possessions she had was an instinctive response for Bernadine. Through example, she demonstrated the value and freedom of such living to all of us.

Bernadine also believed the operation of the community should reflect the same simplicity and spirit of poverty as is evident in the lives of the individual sisters. During her ten years as president of the Sisters of Humility, she built no brick and mortar institutions. As she said in her 1975 State of the Union report to the community, "It can be said of me what Sister Sacred Heart is supposed to have said to Mother Geraldine when she left office in 1939, 'Maudie, you haven't so much as built a chicken coop.'"[7] Instead, Bernadine focused on building human communities that look beyond themselves to serve others in need and instilled in members of the community the confidence and passion to do their own community building wherever they live and work.

# Risk Takers, Not Nesters

Ann Therese Collins captured one of Bernadine's important contributions to the community when she said, "She encouraged the sisters to
be risk takers rather than 'nesters.'" As Bernadine herself said, "God
gave us backbones rather than shells. We should use them."

The call to be risk takers was unsettling to some sisters.
Nevertheless, Bernadine urged all sisters to actualize their pledge
"to raise the prophetic voice in the communities in which they live."
Invoking Albert Camus' 1948 call to Christians, Bernadine asked the
sisters to be willing "to stand up and to pay up personally."[1] To do so,
she said, quoting Daniel Berrigan's letter to his fellow Jesuits:

> We must begin again where we live. The real question of the
> times is not the conversion of cardinals or presidents, but the
> conversion of each of us.
>
> There are few . . . who, if their speech is to be trusted, are un-
> accepting of change. Most of us are obsessed with its inevita-
> bility. We talk persuasively of it, we grasp at new forms and
> styles. And yet the suspicion remains; very few of us have the
> courage to measure our passion for moral change against the
> sacrifice of our comfort, our security, and our professional
> status.
>
> And yet, until such things are placed in jeopardy, nothing
> changes. The gospel says it; so do the times. Unless the cries
> of the war victims, the disenfranchised, the prisoners, the
> homeless poor, the resisters of conscience, the Blacks and
> Chicanos—unless the cry of the world reaches our ears,
> and we measure our lives and death against others, nothing
> changes, least of all ourselves.[2]

In her report to the CHM 1972 Assembly, Bernadine offered the following suggestions for how individual members and the community as a whole might keep alive the corporate commitment to peace, justice, and freedom, and strengthen the community's resolve to struggle against oppression, dehumanization and poverty:

- Move toward simpler, more sparing patterns of life in order to express solidarity with those who have little control over their own lives and a scant share in the earth's resources.
- Become more sensitive to the needs of others who lack the basics of life, and support their efforts to develop and overcome misery in their own lives.
- Act responsibly to conserve resources for future generations.
- Make a full-scale review of the active priorities of the community with the view of making action for justice as the top priority.
- Evaluate each institution staffed by the community according to its efforts to implement justice, and evaluate the contributions of graduates according to their sensitivity and commitment to justice. If any community institution does not demonstrate a commitment to justice, modify the work of the institution or withdraw from working in the institution.
- Cooperate actively with other religious communities and persons of other churches so as to organize effective power for social and political change.
- Promote among the members programs to develop social awareness, especially of global interrelationships of mankind and the impact of the U.S. on developing nations.
- Speak out on issues of peace and justice, and work with others to organize an effective voice for such issues.
- Work to achieve participation by women religious in the national leadership of the church, taking as a special focus, the reordering of the national priorities of the church, and
- Speak publicly in the church for justice in the area of women's rights, including women's right to direct their own lives and the lives of their communities, and work for full participation

for women in decision-making in the church and in the ministerial priesthood.

Bernadine intended these suggestions to be just the starting point for the sisters' decision-making. She firmly believed that each member and the community as a whole must determine what it really means to seek justice, serve the poor and powerless, and care for the earth.

As Bernadine once noted, the Humilities have never had one famous member who captured national attention by speaking out on issues of justice and peace. Instead the Humilities' power, she stressed, lies in their union of efforts among many quite ordinary, but committed persons living out the values of the community.

Over the past fifty years, the Sisters of Humility's backbones have remained strong as they have lived the values affirmed in the community's Spirit and Goals and mission statements. They have and continue to stand up and personally pay up on a variety of issues. However, they have done this quietly, day-by-day, in the communities in which they live and work.

In 1968, after the death of Martin Luther King, Humility sisters from both Minneapolis and the Quad Cities in Iowa and Illinois traveled to Milwaukee to march in solidarity with and in remembrance of him. In response to this action, the pastor of St. Austin's parish, without talking to the sisters who participated in the march, drove nearly three hundred miles from Minneapolis to Ottumwa to notify Bernadine he no longer wanted the sisters who marched in Milwaukee in his school.

Bernadine heard him out, and then called Sister Joanne O'Brien, the principal of the school, to report the pastor's demand. After consulting with the sisters who marched, Joanne replied, "We believe that our participation in the march is consistent with the values of the community. If the pastor wants to fire us, that's his choice." Bernadine reported to the pastor that the sisters stood by their decision to participate in the Milwaukee civil rights march, and that she supported their action. She then offered him lunch and saw him off as he began his trip back to Minneapolis.

The Milwaukee demonstration was just the first of many peace and justice marches, demonstrations, educational forums, and other advocacy efforts in which Humility sisters have participated over the years. In May 1970, the Senate of the Sisters of Humility, in response to the expansion of the Vietnam War into Cambodia and the government's crackdown on student protests on college campuses, enacted a resolution, which they publicized through an advertisement in the *Des Moines Register* that was paid for by individual sisters in the Senate and distributed through other media outlets. The ad read:

> As Christian women and professional educators,
> We deplore the violence rendering American society and the expansion of the war in Southeast Asia;
> We recognize the frustration and despair of our youth in their attempts to be heard;
> We affirm the right and duty of responsible dissent and the necessity of effective participation in the political process.
> Therefore, we are urging the Sisters of Humility to actively support peace candidates. We are also strongly recommending that the administrators and faculties of our schools and colleges incorporate into the educational program a period of intense involvement in the November elections.

This ad sparked many discussions both within the CHM community and the larger communities in which the sisters lived and worked regarding the Vietnam War, violence in our society, and the responsibility of schools to encourage students to effectively participate in the democratic process. In schools staffed by the Humilities, the resolution stimulated a renewed study of war and peace issues and increased the schools' focus on the importance of citizen participation in the electoral process. Individual sisters, some for the first time, became active participants in electoral campaigns. Sister Eleanor Anstey ran for election as a State Senator from Muscatine, Iowa, with Mary Boland as her campaign manager. Other sisters lobbied their elected representatives to stop the war in Vietnam. When the lobbying efforts proved unproductive, they joined local and national demonstrations against the war.

Over the past fifty years, the Sisters of Humility have used their collective voice and joined with others to advocate on peace and justice issues through the media, in the halls of Congress, and in state legislatures and agencies throughout the country. They have also been active in political organizations and non-profit organizations that seek to advance peace and justice for all people.

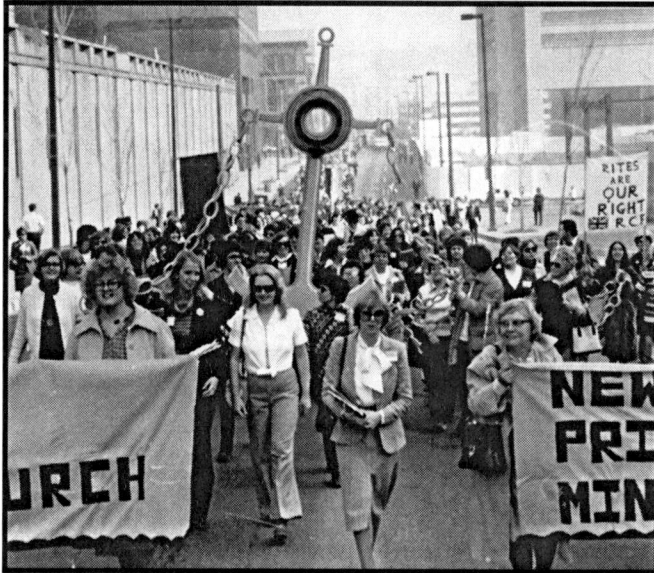

**Sister Bernadine, (far right, carrying banner)
at the Women's Ordination Conference in 1978**

# Changing Mission while Preserving Commitments

Bernadine always focused on the future. Toward the end of her term as president, she began preparing the community for the uncertain future of religious life as the members had known it. On November 11, 1975, Bernadine wrote to the community: "Religious life, as an institution codified by the Roman Catholic Church, is becoming extinct, going the way of the dodo." She further stated:

> Some communities will resist its passing because of its past value. But religious communities like other institutions will die if they fail to provide a creative response to current cultural challenges. The community must focus on the future and ask itself what part of the past do we preserve and what creative responses are necessary to meet the future.

Bernadine believed that the new form or forms of religious life were yet to be defined, and perhaps would be defined only after they are lived. She thought they might include lay ecumenical communities, networks, Latin American base communities, movement-related communities, or small communities similar to those of the early church, all with greater diversity and an emphasis on service and sharing.

Bernadine was certain that "flexibility, creativity, and faith are called for." In choosing the new leaders of the community, she suggested, "High value should be placed on flexibility, creativity, and faith —along with personal concern, courage, and an ability to listen and to delegate."[1] In the end it is the sisters, she believed, who must continue to create their own future by participating in shaping the culture in which they live. Structure is not as important as the corporate spirit and dynamism of a shared vision.

After giving her final report to the community at the annual assembly in June 1976, Bernadine moved from Ottumwa to Iowa City to allow the incoming president, Ann Therese Collins, the freedom to assume the leadership of the community without Bernadine "looking over her shoulder." Bernadine planned to spend her sabbatical year taking courses at the University of Iowa, writing the history of the Sisters of Humility, and thinking about what she would do next.

When Bernadine moved to Iowa City in the fall of 1976, she and Mary Boland again lived together. They had been friends since Mary was a student at Marycrest in 1961-65 and shared many mutual interests. They read, shared and discussed poetry, contemporary theology, politics, history, biographies, economic and political analyses, and books exploring technological and scientific advances. They were kindred spirits in their ability to synthesize what they read and spin out new ideas of their own. They also liked to debate these ideas while imagining what the future might hold for the community, the church, the country, and the world.

But they also talked about each of their own futures. Just as Bernadine was at a transition point in her life, so was Mary. After eight years of being a temporary professed Sister of Humility, Mary was contemplating giving up her formal membership in the community and forging a new course in her life. Mary told Bernadine of her pending decision and they talked it through together. Just as Bernadine had drawn Mary to the Humilities in the first place, she also gave Mary the freedom in these discussions to change the course of her life. She knew that no matter what path Mary chose, she would continue to live out the values of the Sisters of Humility with passion and grace.

During their year together, Mary and Bernadine opened their home to friends, as well as other persons in need of shelter or support. Humility sisters and other friends traveling through Iowa City often stopped to see them. Jim and Mary McCue, Iowa City residents, associate members of the community, and long-time friends of both Mary and Bernadine, would drop by to talk with them about the church, the world and their children.

As Iowa City had no shelter for abused women, Mary and Bernadine sheltered such women on an emergency basis. Most stayed only a few days, during which time Mary and Bernadine helped them obtain safe housing, counseling, and legal or financial assistance, as needed. One young woman with a small child lived with them for several months. Once she gained a level of stability and confidence, they arranged for her to rent a small apartment in a house owned by Jim and Mary McCue, knowing that Jim and Mary would provide continuing care and support for this small family.

Two other visitors that year were Jerry Solloway, president of Ottumwa Heights College and Sister Joann Kuebrich, academic dean and dean of students at the college. They reported that Ottumwa Heights College, despite an aggressive five-year plan to stabilize the enrollment of the college, could no longer compete with Indian Hills Community College and other mid-western public and private colleges. Dr. Solloway and Joann asked Bernadine if she would be willing to become the president of Ottumwa Heights, with an eye toward negotiating a merger or sale of the college. According to Joann, Dr. Solloway told Bernadine, "If the college must be sold, I can't do it. It must be done by a Sister of Humility."

Bernadine understood that many members of the community were intensely loyal to the people of Ottumwa and would oppose any merger or sale of Ottumwa Heights. But she also believed that Ottumwa Heights, as an independent organization with its own board of directors, must decide itself whether a merger or sale of the college was necessary. So she agreed to be a candidate for the presidency of Ottumwa Heights only if the Board of Trustees went through the usual search process. At the conclusion of that process, the Board hired Bernadine. She began her term in July 1977.

When Bernadine's selection was announced, one of the students complained that "hiring a nun as the president of Ottumwa Heights College would take the school back to the Stone Age."[2] That student did not know Bernadine. When informed of the student's remark, Bernadine just laughed and went to work.

One of Bernadine's first tasks was to stabilize the finances of the college, which had operated in the red for the previous two years. She balanced the budget, but the result was an austere operational budget. To increase the college's enrollment, Bernadine pursued a number of new program options, including the establishment of a cooperative program with a four-year college to offer degrees in accounting, business, and liberal arts. She negotiated a transfer program with the University of Iowa that allowed students with an Ottumwa Heights liberal arts degree to automatically transfer to the University without further requirements.

Shortly after Bernadine arrived, Dr. Lyle H. Hellyer, the president of Indian Hills Community College, came to Ottumwa Heights to welcome her back. He brought her baked goods produced by the Indian Hills bakery program. When Joann Kuebrich noted the gifts, Bernadine laughingly said: "Beware of Greeks bringing gifts." When Lyle heard about Bernadine's remark, he had a good laugh and said, "It was quickly apparent to me that Bernadine was a no-nonsense, extremely bright, forthright person and we hit it off immediately."

After assessing the future of Ottumwa Heights College over a number of months, including the pros and cons of merger of the two colleges, Bernadine packed up her research on a cold winter day and met with Lyle. As she later described to Joann, "We both put our cards on the table and had an open and honest discussion regarding the merger of the two colleges." They then developed a plan for merger of the two colleges, which they presented to their respective boards for approval. In September 1978, Indian Hills moved its entire nursing program as well as other students and faculty to Ottumwa Heights, which in practical effect began the integration of the liberal arts and technical programs of both colleges. Ottumwa Heights accepted one more freshman class. Within two years, the colleges had completely merged.

Bernadine, reflecting on her role in the merger of the two colleges, said she was ideal for the job of negotiating the merger of the Heights with Indian Hills "because I had no academic future to lose." She said she spent much of her time "helping the sisters and the people of Ottumwa to see the merger as the best option in the long run because Ottumwa could not support two colleges." In her address at the joint commencement of the two colleges in 1978, Bernadine summarized her position:

> The words of T.S. Eliot, "To make an end is to make a be-
> ginning," applies to Ottumwa Heights, Indian Hills Colleges
> and to the people of Area XV. Future increased interplay be-
> tween the liberal arts, which should provide a better under-
> standing and ability to deal with an ever more complex soci-
> ety, and vocational-technical training, which should provide
> a means for earning a living, can help students face life as a
> whole rather than in separate compartments. Further, those
> who emphasize only the liberal arts can easily become too
> academic, elitist, and unrealistic. Those who know nothing
> but work tend to become narrow-minded and boring, even
> to themselves.

> Next year, Indian Hills will administer the liberal arts pro-
> gram at the Heights campus. Interaction between programs
> of the two colleges will be mutually beneficial. For example,
> the Nursing program of Indian Hills and the Medical Records
> and Radiological Technology programs of the Heights can be
> unified to avoid duplication and make possible the exchange of
> ideas and sharing of facilities and personnel. Monetary savings
> will also be achieved through having only one set of adminis-
> trators. Continuation of the Heights' cultural programs in mu-
> sic, theater, and the visual arts is assured because of their affili-
> ation with a viable post-secondary institution.

> There is a place in U.S. society for competition; there is also
> a place for cooperation. In the face of fewer and fewer high
> school graduates in this area from which both colleges draw
> most of their students, one strong college is preferable to the
> strong likelihood of two weak ones within the next several
> years as both students and available funding decline.

> I am a graduate of Ottumwa Heights College. I was a mem-
> ber of the Board of Trustees for eleven years. I am now the
> chief administrative officer. So it is not without sadness that I
> take part in the planning of a new merged institution. I believe,

though, that this is the right direction and what we call an end is a beginning. So you and I share the experience of Eliot:

> *What we call the beginning is often the end*
> *And to make an end is to make a beginning.*
> *The end is where we start from.*[3]

In the course of the merger process, Bernadine and Lyle became good friends, which led to Lyle becoming an associate member of the Sisters of Humility. Both Lyle and his family so loved Ottumwa Heights that they asked Bernadine whether they could be buried in the Humilities' cemetery located on the campus. Before Bernadine left Ottumwa Heights, she secured the approval from Ann Therese Collins, the current president of the community, for the Hellyer family request.

After the merger, negotiations commenced for the purchase of the entire Ottumwa Heights campus. Although Ann Therese, as president of the Community, took the lead in the negotiations, Bernadine was an essential participant in the process. According to Joann Kuebrich, "Bernadine laid the foundation for the sale of the property. It was her relationship with Lyle and her business acumen that led to the sale of Ottumwa Heights for a fair price, while maintaining the community's commitments to the people of Ottumwa."

Given the history and tradition of Ottumwa Heights, there were divisions within the Sisters of Humility regarding whether the campus should be sold at all, and if so, to whom and at what price. Many in the community believed strongly that the community had made a commitment to the people of Ottumwa and should not abandon them. Bernadine shared that view.

First, Bernadine secured an agreement from Lyle that Indian Hills would continue the academic programs of Ottumwa Heights College, including its emphasis on art and music. As a result of this agreement, Sister St. John Ven Horst, the revered teacher of string instruments and the director of the Ottumwa Heights string orchestra, continued teaching at Indian Hills for an additional eight years. Sister St. John helped the arts program substantially expand with the additional financial resources that became available from the publicly financed community college system.

In addition, Bernadine, as well as other administrative staff of Ottumwa Heights, developed a plan to continue the religious mission of the college. Bernadine, as a member of the Davenport Diocesan Pastoral Council, was aware of the need expressed by adults, particularly in rural areas and small towns, for religious education. She and Joann felt that meeting this need would be an important continuation of Ottumwa Heights programs, as well as consistent with the mission of the CHM founders, who focused their work in rural areas neglected by others. To carry out this work, they created New Horizons of Faith, a 501(c) (3) organization dedicated to the provision of religious and educational programs for adults. Bernadine agreed to serve as the chairperson of the board, which she did for the next twenty years.

This resolution of the sisters' concern about continuing to serve the people of Ottumwa paved the way for the community to move forward with the negotiations to sell the Ottumwa Heights property. A number of possible purchasers, including an operator of penal institutions and an itinerant preacher, inquired about purchasing the campus. When Lyle told Bernadine about the possible bid to use Ottumwa Heights as a prison, Bernadine was horrified and said, "Don't worry, that won't happen." Bernadine and Ann Therese agreed that the primary criteria employed in evaluating bids was whether the bidder's proposed use of the Ottumwa Heights campus advanced the Sisters of Humility's values and mission. Ultimately, the community sold the Ottumwa Heights campus to Indian Hills College.

At the completion of the sale, the Humilities allocated a portion of the proceeds to fund programs offered through New Horizons of Faith to enrich the faith and prayer life of adults in Ottumwa and surrounding areas. They planned to cover operating expenses of New Horizons of Faith for the first five years to allow the new corporation sufficient time to become self sufficient.

The community also set aside an additional portion of the sale proceeds to establish the Seeds of Hope, a program to support volunteers who worked with the Humilities on projects directly serving poor people or other justice and peace or care of the earth projects. Initially, this program matched high school and college students with projects sponsored by the Humilities. The commitments of such volunteers varied from a few weeks to years. Some groups made Seeds of Hope a tradition, sending new volunteers each year. Seeds of Hope broadened over time to include seed grants to Humilities or other persons seeking funding to support justice and peace or care of the earth projects and funded such projects at twenty-three different sites, including sites in Iowa, Colorado, Kentucky, New Mexico, Mississippi, Montana, Illinois, West Virginia, and México. At each of these projects, the volunteers not only worked with the sisters, but also often lived with them. During the life of the program, about 250 people participated. One participant said, "I feel it is the greatest thing the community has going . . . it touches the poor and the powerless and lets them touch us."

Some Seeds of Hope volunteers have become active associate members of the community. Nancy Roberson was a Seeds of Hope participant who lived with the sisters while volunteering at the Café on Vine and the Humility of Mary Shelter for homeless people in Davenport. Currently, an associate member of the community, Nancy and another associate member, Evalee Mickey, now represent the Humilities on the Inter Congregational Justice and Peace Task force that is composed of representatives from five congregations of women religious who have made immigration reform one of their priority issues. Equally important, the Seeds of Hope program for many volunteers has fostered a life long commitment to serving poor people in their local communities.

# Fostering Peace and Justice the Quaker Way

In 1978, when it was clear that Ottumwa Heights would merge with Indian Hills College, Bernadine began to look for a new challenge. She applied only for jobs promoting peace, justice, and human rights. Rather than continue as the full time president of Ottumwa Heights, Bernadine decided she would seek a job within traveling distance from Ottumwa so she could return to Ottumwa on weekends to complete her work at the Heights.

A number of jobs with Catholic institutions that piqued Bernadine's interest required that she be male, a cleric, or possess a theology degree. Some agencies rejected her job applications on the assumption that the position would "take more energy and ability to travel than you have." Before making this judgment, the hiring authorities did not interview Bernadine in person. Had they bothered to interview her or check her references, they would have found that she had more energy than a person half her age.

One organization that did interview her was the American Friends Service Committee (AFSC), a Quaker organization committed to social justice, peace, and humanitarian service. As indicated in its mission statement, the work of the AFSC is based on a belief in the worth of every person and faith in the power of love to overcome violence and injustice.

In 1947, the AFSC and the British Friends Service Council (BFSC) jointly received the Nobel Peace Prize for their three hundred years of work healing rifts and opposing war. In accepting the peace prize, Henry Cadbury, then chair of the AFSC board, said the award means that "common folk—not statesmen, nor generals nor great men of affairs—just simple plain men and women like the few thousand Quakers and their friends, if they devote themselves to resolute insistence on goodwill in place of force, can do something to build a better, peaceful world."[1]

As Bernadine lived her life according to these same values, she was very much at home with the Quakers and interested in the opportunity to work with the AFSC program. The Quakers were equally interested in her. In 1979, the AFSC hired Bernadine to serve as the executive secretary of its mid-west regional office, responsible for administration of programs in the eight states of Iowa, Missouri, Minnesota, North Dakota, South Dakota, Nebraska, Kansas, and Colorado.

Bernadine worked with local, regional, and national AFSC committees to set the goals and priorities for the mid-west region and secured the financial and administrative supports necessary for staff to carry out the priority programs. Given the multiplicity of committees within the AFSC program, Bernadine made certain the oversight function of the committees facilitated rather impeded the work done by staff.

Issues of concern to the AFSC nationally and regionally during Bernadine's tenure included peace, the Cold War, nuclear weapons, the Middle East conflict between Israel and the Palestinians, Central America, racial and sexual discrimination, hunger, human rights, and Native American issues. These issues have bedeviled people of good-will for generations.

Each of the eight state offices had their own approach to these priority issues. On the issue of nuclear weapons, the AFSC Denver Office initiated the Rocky Flats Campaign focused on the local hazards of the Rocky Flats nuclear weapons plant, fifteen miles north of Denver, as a way to educate the local community about the costs of the Cold War and the arms race.

The founders of the campaign, Pam Solo and Judy Danielson, built the initiative from the ground up. They went to the neighborhoods around the plant knocking on doors, taking soil samples, and educating people about the dangers of nuclear weapons production in their neighborhoods. Once they assembled clear evidence of the real and present dangers the plant posed to the local community, they linked those dangers to the global threat of nuclear arms in a broadly circulated publication entitled *Local Hazard, Global Threat*. This publication galvanized scientists, environmentalists, Rocky Flats workers concerned about their own health and job security, neighbors concerned about risks to their health and property values, social justice advocates concerned that the arms race steals resources from the whole community, and those who opposed nuclear weapons on moral grounds. They became the core of the movement to close Rocky Flats and to stop the nuclear arms race. These citizens in turn helped organize others.

Members of the movement testified at state and Congressional hearings, organized hearings locally and nationally, and executed a sophisticated media campaign aimed at engaging ordinary people as well as experts and leaders in arms control at the local, regional, and national levels. Once the campaign developed a large citizen base, the organizers combined large rallies at the plant calling for the plant's closure with focused civil disobedience events to keep the necessary public pressure on both governmental authorities and the plant owners. Because of the campaign's focus on the hazards at Rocky Flats, government agencies kept a closer eye on the plant. In 1989, a FBI raid on Rocky Flats found systemic hazardous conditions resulting in the ultimate closure of the facility.

The Rocky Flats Campaign was also one of the founders of the Freeze Movement, an international campaign seeking to freeze the production and deployment of nuclear weapons and delivery systems. Colorado and other state offices in the AFSC mid-west region supported the Freeze Movement. The Freeze Movement garnered sufficient public support to force a popular president, Ronald Reagan, to engage in arms control negotiations with the Soviet Union in 1984. The Rocky Flats Campaign and the Freeze Movement forever changed the nature of the debate regarding the production and use of nuclear weapons.

To Pam Solo, Bernadine was a great boss to have in such campaigns. She firmly believed in both the Rocky Flats Campaign and the Freeze Movement, was open to new and innovative ideas, supported staff efforts, helped maintain the necessary organizational support for these campaigns at both the regional and national levels of the AFSC, and had a good sense of humor about both the committee process and the ups and downs of the campaigns. According to Pam, "Bernadine knew how to get things done. She quickly gained the respect of both the regional and national committees and made certain that the committee process served the campaigns rather than impeded their progress."

While the Rocky Flats campaign and the Freeze Movement were successful projects, Bernadine faced difficulties in other programs. Shortly after she was hired, shortfalls in funding led the mid-west regional committee to recommend the termination of the Indian rights program at the Pine Ridge Reservation in South Dakota. Before agreeing to the termination, Bernadine went out to the reservation to talk to the Lakota Sioux leaders and evaluate the need for the program.

Bernadine found the tribe still reeling from the aftermath of the 1973 Siege at Wounded Knee. The siege arose out of a hundred years of "broken treaties" between the federal government and the Lakota Sioux Nation. One of the broken treaties was the 1868 Treaty of Fort Laramie, which had awarded most of South Dakota west of the Missouri River, including the sacred Black Hills, to the Sioux Nation "for its absolute and undisturbed use and occupancy." But when gold was discovered in 1877, Congress abrogated the treaty and simply reasserted the government's ownership of the Black Hills after negotiations with the Sioux to buy back the land broke down.

After years of trying to reclaim the Black Hills through negotiations with the government, traditional elders of the Lakota Sioux asked leaders of the American Indian Movement (AIM) to take over the community of Wounded Knee, South Dakota and reclaim it in the name of the Lakota Sioux Nation. AIM and the traditional Sioux people then demanded that the federal government honor the Fort Laramie Treaty by returning the Black Hills to the Sioux Nation. They also demanded an investigation into the Bureau of Indian Affairs (BIA) and the Department of Interior's handling of the affairs of the Sioux tribe, including their misuse of tribal funds.

The government's response was to send FBI agents to remove the Native American occupiers of Wounded Knee resulting in a siege that lasted for seventy days. Two Native Americans were killed, two wounded, and 1200 arrested. Although a negotiated settlement ended the siege, the government once again reneged on its promises. During the next three years, the conflict between the government and the Sioux raged, with more deaths, wounded persons and arrests. In 1979 when Bernadine joined the AFSC, the dispute was still unresolved.

On her trip to South Dakota, Bernadine found that the Sioux people on the Pine Ridge reservation were living in abject poverty. Based upon these intolerable living conditions and the long history of broken promises made to the Sioux people by the United States government, Bernadine recommended to the AFSC regional committee alternative measures to make up the funding shortfall and urged continuation of the Indian rights program. She proposed two focuses for the continued program: (1) continued advocacy to redress the illegal confiscation of the Black Hills, and (2) cooperative projects with the Women of All Red Nations (WARM) to improve conditions on the Pine Ridge reservation, including stopping contamination of water on the Pine Ridge reservation caused by uranium mining and the establishment of a health clinic for the reservation. The regional committee adopted Bernadine's proposals.

In 1975, the Indian Claims Commission determined that Congress's 1877 action abrogating the 1868 Treaty was unconstitutional and amounted to the illegal seizure of Indian lands. In 1980, the U.S. Supreme Court in *United States v. Sioux Nations of Indians* affirmed the Commission's ruling and ordered the government to pay remuneration to the Sioux equal to the initial offering price for the Black Hills in 1877 of $17.5 million plus interest, or approximately $106 million. The Sioux Nation declined to accept the payment and renewed its demand that the government return the Black Hills to the Sioux Nation.

Further attempts in the 1980s to restore the Black Hills to the Sioux people failed. However, the Sioux have continued to refuse to take the federal funds, which have now increased to over $570 million, as acceptance of such payment would violate deeply held cultural and religious values of the Sioux Nation. Specifically, they believe that they are the stewards of the Black Hills, which belong to God.

The other goals of the AFSC Indian Rights program were only partially fulfilled. A health clinic was established, but the services it provides are limited due to the lack of adequate funding for the clinic.

Uranium mining continues in the Black Hills of South Dakota, and the Lakota Sioux continue to fight the pollution of water on the Pine Ridge Reservation from such mining.

Although continuing the AFSC Indian Rights project did not resolve these long-standing problems, Bernadine believed that the decision to continue the project was right and consistent with her own and Quaker belief in the importance of ordinary people standing together to challenge injustice even if the issues at stake remain unresolved for generations. During her many trips to the reservation, Bernadine earned the respect of the Indian people on the Pine Ridge Reservation and forged strong relationships with men and women leaders of the tribe. These relationships allowed her to mediate many internal disputes of the tribe both while serving as the AFSC Mid-west Region Executive Secretary and later as a consultant to the AFSC.

Bernadine's other major focus at AFSC was to facilitate the more traditional work of day-to-day education and advocacy on such issues as the Middle East conflict, the civil wars in Central America resulting in large refugee populations, racial and sexual discrimination, hunger and food policy, human rights, and peace.

Between 1980 and 1981, approximately one million Central Americans fleeing civil wars in Guatemala and El Salvador and mass murder of civilians by military forces sought asylum in the U.S. Although Congress at the time prohibited foreign aid to countries that were committing human rights abuses, the U.S. continued to provide funds, training, and arms to the Salvadoran and Guatemalan military forces. To avoid admitting its direct violation of congressional policy, the Reagan administration argued that Central Americans who sought asylum were "economic migrants" fleeing poverty rather than victims of governmental repression. As a result, the U.S. granted only a small number of Central American immigrants asylum.

In response to these policies, the AFSC became part of the Sanctuary Movement, which provided economic and legal assistance, as well as safety in churches for such immigrants. The AFSC staff campaigned to stop the U.S. support for military forces in Guatemala and El Salvador and for mercenary forces in Nicaragua during the Contra War. The public disclosure of this unlawful military support embarrassed the Reagan administration and forced the government to withdraw such support.

The eight state AFSC offices also carried out their on-going effort to educate citizens and build support for alternatives to war. In Des Moines, where she lived, Bernadine was able to take a more direct role in peace and justice education activities in Iowa while carrying out her regional responsibilities. For example, she helped the Iowa Peace Network and the Consortium on International Peace and Reconciliation establish a Peace Resource Center to coordinate peace education efforts in the Des Moines region. She worked with Catholic Peace Ministry to create a Peace Park at Nollen Plaza as a continual reminder to Des Moines' residents of the need to foster peace and reconciliation in the community. Bernadine helped the Des Moines diocesan priests' justice and peace council write their five-year plan and was also a frequent and popular speaker throughout the region on the relationship between land/food policy and the technologies of war. Finally, she was an active participant in local, national, and international demonstrations against war and in support of peace, justice, and human rights. According to Sister Ramona Kaalberg, Bernadine is still well known in Des Moines for her justice and peace work.

Bernadine, who by nature made decisions quickly, learned to appreciate and became a master at the consensus decision-making process utilized by the Quakers. As Bernadine said, "It is messy and slow but makes for committed people." In local and regional meetings, Bernadine patiently listened to debates that lasted for hours, concisely summarized the arguments, and then moved the committees toward consensus decisions.

She also used her gentle laid-back management style to support AFSC staff both personally and in their work. According to a number of staff in the Des Moines office, "She was someone you could go to without hesitation to talk about work or personal problems, and she always had time for you." At times, Bernadine anticipated the needs of staff without being asked. Mikel Johnson, a single parent and AFSC regional staff member in Des Moines, described the night Bernadine showed up shortly after Mikel had purchased and moved into a house that needed a lot of clean up and repair. That night, Mikel was tired, but working to get the house cleaned up and in shape for her children. Bernadine walked in and asked, "What can I do to help?" and started to clean cupboards. Mikel said to herself, "What kind of boss is this that senses needs not expressed and does anything she can to help?"

But it was also Bernadine's spiritual grounding that made her a respected leader within the AFSC organization. As Kathleen McQuillen, the current AFSC Iowa Program Coordinator, described her in February 2000:

> Bernadine was a skilled leader . . . one of the finest. The strength of her leadership lay in deep spiritual grounding, an unwavering respect for the value of all people, and a keen mind. As a leader, she was as 'at home' in the board room as she was on the barren plateaus of the Pine Ridge Reservation. She understood the importance of the connections between the boardroom and the everyday lives of people. Bernadine believed that everyone could make a difference, and that each of us has a role to play in creating a just society. Bernadine was an inspiration and an embodiment of the servant leader at work—living out her faith in practice as she worked to build a peaceful and just society on a daily basis.

# Building Community in the Iowa Heartland

In 1987, Bernadine decided to return to her own roots in rural Iowa. Her goal was to live and work among people in a poor rural area. After talking with Father John Zeitler, pastor of two Catholic Churches in Ringgold County, Bernadine joined the South Central Catholic Community pastoral team that served seven Iowa parishes near the Missouri border. Her decision delighted John, and he invited her to live in the rectory in Maloy. As Bernadine had worked with John in Des Moines on peace and justice issues, she felt they would be a compatible team.

When Bernadine, the first Catholic sister to live and work in Ringgold County on a full time basis, took up residence in the Maloy rectory, some of the parishioners and the town newspaper assumed that she was the priest's housekeeper. After first being incensed and then amused by this assumption, Bernadine set out to meet the people.

On the day she arrived in Maloy, one of the parishioners, Regina Lynch, invited Bernadine to have lunch and stay overnight at her family's farm. She quickly learned that Bernadine never wanted anyone "to go to any fuss or bother for her." According to Regina, Bernadine "was my kind of people."

Betsy and Brian Terrell had moved to Malloy to start a Catholic Worker community. When Bernadine learned about them, she went over to introduce herself. Betsy and Brian had two small children, Clara and Elijah, who were then two and four years old, respectively. Bernadine immediately connected with them. Soon they became an extended family, praying together almost every morning, working on a variety of projects together, and sharing weekend breakfasts cooked by Bernadine for the Terrell family and others who might be visiting the rectory. According to Brian, "Bernadine was a rare and valuable resource" to the people of the Catholic Worker "back to the land" movement. She was, he said, "a farm girl, more solidly grounded and with deeper roots in the earth than us city kids with more romantic notions than real experience with rural life."[1]

Bernadine worked with members of the Catholic Worker community on a variety of issues, including pressing a large commercial hog confinement to clean up the land and water it had polluted, and challenging the unjust treatment of Hispanic workers at a Lennox egg-processing factory. Together they sponsored public education programs on international peace issues, including a program that examined the United States' alliance with the military-controlled Salvadorian government's death squads, which targeted protestors who challenged the human rights violations perpetrated by the military. They also presented a program on the draft resistance movement in Israel as a way of exploring from a different perspective the longstanding conflict between Israel and the Palestinian people. According to Brian Terrell, Bernadine's involvement in these programs gave them credibility in the minds of Ringgold County citizens.


During her first two years in Maloy, Bernadine assisted seven Catholic parishes develop religious education programs and train parishioners to implement them. She led parishioners in each parish step by step through the process of developing the curriculum, recruiting teachers, ordering the books and materials, setting up, and teaching the classes. When the programs succeeded, Bernadine gave the parishioners the credit. As soon as the newly minted religious educators developed sufficient skills and confidence to conduct the programs, Bernadine moved on to other issues.

As Ringgold County in the 1980s was one of the five poorest counties in Iowa and Catholics constituted only a small minority of people in the entire region, Bernadine, after consulting with other South Central Catholic Pastoral team members, elected to focus her efforts primarily on the needs of the farmers and small communities of Ringgold County. Bernadine became an active participant in the

Ringgold County Ministerial Alliance, whose mission was to promote ecumenical worship and understanding, as well as address a broad array of economic and social issues affecting farmers and other rural people living in the county.

For a number of years, Bernadine took her turn leading interfaith services, participating in pulpit exchanges sponsored by the Alliance, and presiding at services for residents of long-term care facilities, a drug and alcohol recovery center and a low-income housing project in the county. While president of the Alliance, Bernadine, using a Seeds of Hope grant from the Sisters of Humility, organized an inter-denominational vacation school to which she brought minority inner-city children from Holy Trinity parish in Davenport to study with and get to know rural children and their families in Ringgold County. Her involvement in the Alliance helped to reduce the lingering anti-Catholic sentiment in both Ringgold and other counties in the region.

But Bernadine's primary work was listening to and responding to the expressed needs of people in Ringgold County. During the late 1980s and early 1990s, Ringgold County suffered a series of farm crises due to falling commodity prices and total crop failures caused by both drought and floods. Going house-to-house and farm-to-farm, Bernadine listened to the concerns and hopes of the people and did whatever was necessary to empower them to solve the problems they faced. When farmers expressed fear that they would lose their farms, Bernadine arranged for and accompanied them to meetings with insurance agents and banks to ensure their claims were fairly handled. She also helped secure financial restructuring of debt necessary to maintain the families' farms. For people who expressed a desire to start their own businesses, Bernadine got them help to develop business plans and secured other necessary supports to implement such plans.

With other Ministerial Alliance members, Bernadine delivered leaflets to farms and homes in the county that described sources of financial aid and mental health services to help people deal with the loss of income and stress caused by the farm crises. During a period of drought in the late 1980s, Bernadine was instrumental in getting water to farms and homes in the county. After the floods in the early 1990s, she wrote grant applications to get financial assistance for those whose properties or crops were damaged or destroyed by the floodwaters.

When people in the community complained that the Mount Ayr Board of Education was not responsive to their requests for a new school or their complaints about pesticides in the school, Bernadine went with them to the school board meetings and advocated on their behalf. Since Bernadine had served on school boards, she knew how to present the issues in a way that the board members could hear the concerns without becoming defensive. As Bernadine had already become a friend of the superintendent of schools prior to the meetings, the school board listened to her, resolved the pesticide issue immediately, and eventually authorized a new school.

Through Bernadine's efforts, the Vista program sent volunteers to Ringgold County. They renovated a building owned by the Immaculate Conception Church in Maloy into a cooperative store that sold local crafts and antiques, as well as bulk food items like honey, fruits, nuts, and spices. Under Bernadine's direction, the Vista volunteers also developed a business directory for the county, assisted the people to develop a farmers' market, and worked on a campaign to attract more tourists to the area.

Bernadine was also active in stewardship of the land programs. One local program, Project Harvest, provided small grants to allow Ringgold County residents to learn about successful sustainable projects in agriculture, energy, shelter, and waste management that might help revitalize their County. Bernadine, as chairwoman of the project screening committee, sent Ringgold County residents to the Adopt 100 Conference that was focused on ideas for diversifying Iowa agriculture, and to the Mid-western Rural Women's Conference. In addition, Bernadine helped John Zeitler coordinate a series of meetings between area farmers and farmers from outside the region who had successfully developed sustainable agricultural methods and projects.

Bernadine also worked regionally and nationally on land trust issues with Renewing Rural Iowa—Congregational Revitalization Community Mission project, which focused on solving the systemic problems afflicting rural Iowans. Mindful of the relationship of local issues to national and regional policy, Bernadine brought back what she learned from these activities to the people of Ringgold County in order to broaden their sense of their place in the world and the importance of being active in the global community.

One of Bernadine's personal stewardship of the land and economic development projects was the railroad prairie project. She and John convinced the Northwestern Railroad Company to donate a plot of land to be used as a demonstration plot of native prairie grass and wildflowers. They believed that restoring the prairie would serve important educational and ecological purposes. Bernadine enticed Tom Rosenberg, a doctoral student at Iowa State University in Ames, to identify the seeds of prairie grass indigenous to the area a hundred years before and grow starter plants from such seeds. On May 16, 1989, Bernadine and volunteers planted the prairie with five species of native grass and fifteen kinds of wildflowers. Two years later, they planted ten more species of wild flowers. In addition, at least another twelve species emerged from seeds that had been dormant in the land for many years. Bernadine also planted a grove of walnut, butternut, hickory, oak, and hazelnut trees, as well as basket willow and raspberry bushes, as these had also been common in the area a century before.

From 1989 until she left Maloy in 1994, Bernadine maintained the prairie and grove. At times, she had to defend the prairie against people in the county who called the prairie a "field of weeds" and wanted to return it to closely cropped blue grass. In a series of articles for the *Mount Ayr Record-News* in 1993, Bernadine described the monthly changes in the prairie over the year to educate the community about the prairie, as well as to encourage tourists to visit the prairie to see the growth of the tall grass and the wide variety of native wildflowers that bloom throughout the summer. Bernadine, the science teacher, also hosted field trips for school children at the prairie.

Over twenty years later, the tall prairie grass, wildflowers, and grove continue to provide texture and color to the landscape of

Maloy. When the Catholic Church sold Immaculate Conception Church in 1999, supporters of the prairie convinced the diocese to sell the prairie to Don Ray, a Maloy resident, who for years has cared for it on a volunteer basis and believes in its value. Mr. Ray has continued Bernadine's educational program by chronicling the beauty of the annual life cycles of the prairie on his own web site, FOXTOWNMEDIA.COM/PRAIRIE.

Bernadine's clear commitment to stewardship of the land won the deep respect of the farmers. Her gentleness, simplicity of life, and willingness to be part of the community by baking pies for the Annual Hunters' Dinner, helping out at the parish's county fair stand, and taking care of children so that their parents could attend meetings endeared her to the women of Ringgold County.

Father Dave Polich replaced John Zeitler in 1989 when the region was in the midst of a drought. Bernadine, he said, "taught me ingenious ways to conserve water." In addition, every year Bernadine planted a big garden, used only what she needed, and shared the remainder of her produce with people in the community. According to Dave, Bernadine was a "wizard both in the kitchen and with the checkbook. They ate the rabbits and squirrels in the freezer that John had hunted and produce from her garden and did not spend one hundred dollars per month for groceries."[2]

When the Des Moines Diocese reassigned him in 1990 without providing a replacement priest for Ringgold County, the Maloy parishioners, according to Dave, "were ready to secede. If Bernadine would have said so and if they had had title to the buildings, they would have ordained her and gone on ahead on their own. She had their complete and total confidence." While not ordained, Bernadine did serve as the *de facto* pastor of Immaculate Conception Church after Dave was reassigned, until she left Maloy in 1994.

Her Ministerial Alliance colleagues so appreciated Bernadine's work that they nominated her for the Lumen Christi Award given annually by the Catholic Extension Society. In support of her nomination in 1992, Carmen J. Lampe, Pastor of the First Baptist Church wrote:

Bernadine's commitment to the people of rural Ringgold

County reaches back to her own roots in rural Iowa, and reaches out to include all who work anywhere to sustain a way of life deeply connected to the land. She has an amazing capacity to offer ministry on a number of levels—local, diocesan, national, personal, communal, and systemic. From the work that Bernadine has done toward responsible land stewardship on a national level to the personal stewardship of the land as seen in her fine garden, the stretch of prairie she tends and promotes, the trees that she is forever planting and maintaining, all is seen as having an impact upon this rural place and its people . . . As she has lived and worked alongside the people in Ringgold County, she has come to be loved and respected by people not only in the Catholic parishes, but also throughout the churches in the county. Her insight and view and astonishing energy are sought out for many ecumenical endeavors . . . .Bernadine has brought to each of these involvements the breadth and depth of her personal experience, her attitude of partnership, her faithfulness to the gospel. She is an invaluable minister among us.[3]

# Promoting Literacy and Bridging the Racial Divide

After eight years in southeastern Iowa, Bernadine moved to Canton, Mississippi, a small town which serves as the county seat of Madison County. When Bernadine arrived in 1994, Canton had approximately eleven thousand residents. Approximately eighty percent of the residents were African Americans. Twenty-five percent of the households, according to the 1990 census, had annual incomes under ten thousand dollars. Nearly half of the residents lacked high school educations. In addition, more than seventy percent of Mississippi prisoners in 1994 were considered functionally illiterate.[1]

The Sisters of Humility's connection to Madison County began in the 1950s. For ten years between 1950 and 1959, approximately twenty Humilities, along with students from Ottumwa Heights College, taught summer school classes at the Sacred Heart School, founded by the Missionary Sisters of the Most Holy Trinity. The students were primarily African American children whose ancestors had occupied land once known as the slave quarters that were owned by Irish plantation owners.

The Humilities, during their first summer in Mississippi in 1950, taught in a temporary building located in a woody area of Ofahoma outside of Camden because the Ku Klux Klan had burned down Sacred Heart School in Camden. They held summer school classes in the rebuilt Sacred Heart School in both 1951 and 1952. But in 1953, a white supremacist group again burned the school to the ground. The Camden community rallied to build a new brick school, which was completed in 1955. During the period of construction, summer school classes continued in temporary housing. Between 1955 and 1959, the Humilities taught in the rebuilt Sacred Heart School, which still exists today and currently serves as a family center.

Prior to 1964, children in both Catholic and public schools in Mississippi attended segregated schools, as required by state law. In response to the Civil Rights Act of 1964, Mississippi local and state officials adopted the "freedom of choice" method of desegregation that allowed the state to maintain largely segregated schools. In 1968, the Supreme Court in *Green vs. County School Board* ruled that "freedom of choice" had proven to be an ineffective method of desegregating schools."[2] A year later, the Supreme Court, in *Alexander vs. Holmes,* issued a more pointed ruling directed specifically at thirty school districts in Mississippi, which required termination of their dual school systems and the establishment of "unitary school systems within which no person is to be effectively excluded from any school because of race or color."[3]

In response to these rulings, the majority of Mississippi's Caucasian citizens, especially those who lived in majority black school districts, abandoned the public schools in droves in favor of all white private academies. Most public school districts, however, continued to have school boards controlled by Caucasians. As their children did not generally attend the public schools, there was little incentive for such school boards to invest in schools populated largely by African American students.

Canton public schools in 1994 were and are today overwhelmingly segregated, with African American students comprising 97.97% of the student population, and Asian and Hispanic students representing two percent. Caucasian students represent less than one percent of students in public schools. Even today, public schools in Canton are not properly funded and student achievement is below national standards. The Canton School District's 2009-2010 Children First Annual Report rated one of Canton's four public schools as being on academic watch, two at risk of failing, and one as failing. The dropout rate in 2010 was thirty-one percent.

Sister Helen Strohman, one of the Ottumwa Heights college students who taught summer school in Camden in 1950s, returned to Madison County in 1988. For six years, Helen observed the substandard public education afforded African Americans in Madison County. Outraged by the lack of opportunities available to African American students and adults to achieve basic literacy, Helen asked Bernadine and Sister Ruth Morris to come to Canton and help her establish the Rainbow Literacy Center in 1994.

The Rainbow Literacy Center's mission was to provide basic skills training for illiterate or functionally illiterate children and adults. Helen served as the project's director and Bernadine as its primary fundraiser. All three Humilities served as tutors in the program. A board of directors composed equally of black and white citizens provided active leadership in the project.

**Sister Helen Strohman**

In September 1994, the Rainbow Literacy Center opened. The Center worked closely with the Madison County Literacy Project, which had been in existence since 1990 and was led by Sister Janita Curoe, a BVM sister from Dubuque, Iowa. Janita, who had taught in Mississippi for nearly twenty years, knew first-hand the failing nature of the school system for African American students. According to Janita, many students who graduate from high school in Mississippi have been passed from grade to grade without having learned to read. With a corps of twenty volunteers, Janita, between 1990 and 1994, had already helped hundreds of people learn to read and earn general education diplomas (GEDs). As the unmet need for literacy education emphasizing the basic skills of reading, writing, and math was so great, a cooperative approach by both programs was common sense and quickly forged.

The students of both the Madison County and the Rainbow Literacy programs included poor lifelong workers without any education, children and youth of school age who had dropped out or had fallen behind in school, prisoners from the county jail, and work release program inmates from the Mississippi Department of Corrections. One of the essential elements of both programs was flexibility in the time and place of the tutoring sessions. Essentially, the tutors adapted to the schedules and needs of their students.

For example, Bernadine taught math and science in the public schools and tutored adults at the Canton public library, the county jail, and the work release program. She and the other tutors, including Helen and Ruth, also tutored children who had fallen behind at the Camden Sacred Heart School, Holy Child Jesus School, and public schools. After school, they taught children at the Canton public library.

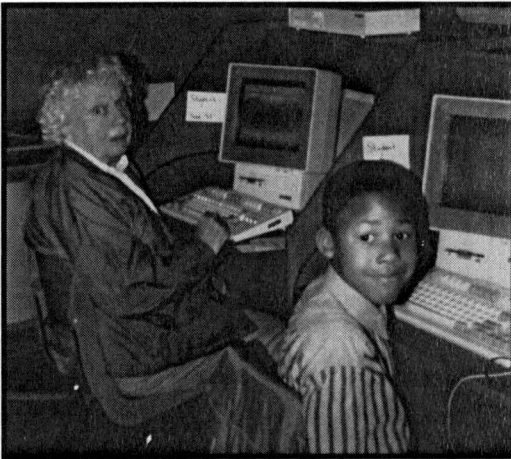

**Sister Bernadine and friend**

The Rainbow Literacy Center students varied widely in the levels of their education and life experiences. For example, Bernadine taught a little girl who had fallen behind in school and needed tutoring to catch up while a grandmother she tutored had never learned to write and wanted to be able to write her own checks and letters. Bernadine also taught an older man who wore shoes that did not fit and whose SSI benefits were being stolen by a Canton employee who claimed to be "administering" his benefits. When Bernadine found out about the theft of the old man's benefits, she pressured the Canton employee to stop stealing from her student.

Another of Bernadine's students was a young woman who was so poor she lived in a house without running water or a stove. After tutoring her for a while, Bernadine asked a Seeds of Hope volunteer to serve as the woman's tutor, as the volunteer could spend more time with her. The volunteer kept in touch with the young woman for years, including returning to visit her in Canton on a number of occasions.

All of the students tutored by the Rainbow Literacy Project had the desire to improve their lives. For many, the GED they secured through the program was one of their most valuable possessions. A young boy who had been told by the public school that he was not "college material" was so defeated that he could not even hold his head up. Bernadine jokingly told him to keep his head up otherwise something might fall on him. She also prepared him for taking the ACT and paid the fee for him to take the test. When he passed it, his self-esteem increased substantially and he kept his head up without any reminder.

Bernadine worked closely with Linda Johnson, a librarian at the Canton Public Library. According to Linda, "Bernadine changed lives while she was in Canton. She was always writing letters for people, giving them money, and doing whatever she could to help them." For example, Linda wanted to begin a master's degree program and was preparing to take the Graduate Record Exam necessary to apply for graduate school admission. When the day came to take the test, Linda didn't have enough money to pay the fee. Bernadine gave Linda the money. When Linda told Bernadine that she had passed the exam, Bernadine smiled and said, "I knew you could do it."

The children at the library loved Bernadine. According to Linda, "When Bernadine drove up in her old car and started walking to the library with her briefcase in hand, the children would run out to meet her shouting, 'Sister B.'" One day, Bernadine came into the library and noticed that three children, who were identical triplets, were wearing post-it notes with their names on their foreheads. Linda explained to Bernadine that she did that because she could not tell them apart. Bernadine told Linda that she just needed to talk to the children and get to know them, and then she would be able to recognize them as separate individuals. Later that day, Bernadine was talking with one of the triplets, and Linda heard him say, "But sister, you are talking about my brother." Bernadine looked at Linda, shook her head and laughed.

In the first year of the combined literacy programs, 1994 to 1995, the programs served 150 students with about sixty percent completing their objectives. As there were more students than tutors, Bernadine put an ad in the church bulletin at Sacred Heart Church, a largely Caucasian church in Canton, soliciting volunteers to tutor African American children. A number of women responded to the ad and offered to help. One, Sis Wohner, a sixth generation Mississippian whose family owned a plantation in Madison County but had a history of supporting integration of the races, began by tutoring a little African American boy. Through the program, she and Bernadine became friends and she later became an associate member of the Sisters of Humility.

In addition, volunteers from Iowa, Arizona, Minnesota, North Carolina, and other states also worked as tutors in the program through the Humilities' Seeds of Hope funding. Some of these volunteers loved the work so much that they returned to tutor in the program a number of times.


Tutoring inmates in the Madison County jail was quite an experience. The jail was overcrowded with up to thirty-two men in a room made for twenty. When Bernadine saw this, she pressed the sheriff to at least get beds for all the inmates. He did, but she quickly sensed that there were limits to pressing him for further improvements in the jail without jeopardizing the inmates' access to the literacy program.

Many inmates of the jail were eager to earn their GEDs and were so proud of themselves when they succeeded they requested five or six copies of their diploma so they could send them to families and friends. Similarly, inmates in the work release program were also receptive to the GED program. As they were on the verge of becoming free citizens, they understood that having a GED was a necessary credential to help them get jobs.

One of Bernadine's most memorable and troubling experiences was tutoring a South African teenager, Azikiwe (Azi) Kambule, in the county jail. Azi was born and raised in the black township of Soweto, outside Johannesburg, South Africa. As a young boy, he excelled in his classes, sports, and sang in the school choir in South Africa. In 1994, when his mother received a scholarship to study psychology at Jackson State University, the family moved to Jackson. His mother believed that Azi would have a greater opportunity to receive a quality education in the United States.

When Azi began high school in Mississippi in 1995, he did well academically, but encountered social problems. As he was a shy young man and had an accent, his peers made fun of him. The social pressures mounted by the time he reached tenth grade. Wanting to be accepted, he became friends with a group of older youth. When Azi's grades fell, his parents raised the money necessary to send him to a respected boarding school for African American students outside of Jackson. Azi was set to begin at the new school when tragedy struck.

When Bernadine first met Azi in the county jail, he was awaiting trial on charges of kidnapping and murder of a young African American woman from Jackson. Azi was arrested a week after the incident. At the time of his arrest, he was seventeen and had no prior criminal history. Although Azi was riding in the car with twenty-one year-old Santonio Berry when he kidnapped and murdered the young woman, Azi did not participate in either the kidnapping or murder. As Azi was afraid of Berry, he did not know what to do. When arrested, Azi cooperated with the police, recounted the events, and tried to lead the police to the place where Santonio Berry had led the young woman into the woods. He also told the police that he neither instigated the kidnapping nor murdered the young woman.

Although a witness confirmed that Berry killed the woman, the D.A. cut a deal with him to dismiss the capital murder charge in exchange for his plea to a term of life in prison without parole and agreement to testify against Azi. The D.A. charged Azi with capital murder and kidnapping and announced he would seek the death penalty.

As added pressure on Azi, the D.A. transferred his case to Madison County, because Madison County juries were known to be more willing to award the death penalty than those in Hinds County where the crimes had occurred. According to the August 24, 1996 brief by the

National Coalition to Abolish the Death Penalty (NCADP) on Azi's case, law enforcement in Madison County was historically racially biased and the county had a history of excluding black people from juries, especially in capital cases.

Because Azi was seventeen at the time of the incident, the prosecutor's election of the death penalty violated his rights under the United Nations Covenant on Rights of the Child, which prohibits capital punishment or life imprisonment without possibility of parole to be imposed for offenses committed by persons under eighteen years of age. Although the United States is a signatory to this U.N. Covenant, the D.A., nevertheless, sought the death penalty against Azi. According to the NCADP brief, at the time the D.A. filed the capital charges, the U.S. was one of only five countries in the world, which executed persons for crimes they allegedly committed when they were younger than eighteen years old. The other four are Iran, Pakistan, Yemen, and Saudi Arabia. Both Amnesty International and the NCADP challenged the charges asserted against Azi on the grounds that they violated both his human and constitutional rights under the U.N. covenant and the U.S. Constitution.

Bernadine worked with Azi in the jail for many months. She had read about him in the paper and knew that he would be under enormous pressure. She asked to see him when she went to the jail to tutor other inmates. She began by bringing magazines for him to read and spent a lot of time just talking to him in order to understand the events that led up to his arrest, and to help him adjust to his circumstances. According to Helen, it took a lot of courage for Bernadine to befriend Azi given the widespread negative publicity about the case and the abiding racial prejudice in the community. Bernadine didn't care. Once she got to know Azi, Bernadine concluded that he was not capable of murder and offered to testify as a character witness for Azi at his trial.

To Azi, Bernadine was "an amazing person." When she first asked to see him at the jail, he wondered if she thought he was the terrible person portrayed on television and in the newspapers. But, says Azi, "Bernadine from the beginning treated me as a human being." Azi was embarrassed about his circumstances and scared. He told

Bernadine that he was afraid to call his parents, both of whom at the time were in South Africa. Bernadine urged him to call his parents. He did, and they stood by him.

Azi's trial was delayed for many months, so Bernadine used the time to prepare him for the GED exam. As he is very bright, he passed the GED easily. After he did so, he asked if he could begin tutoring other inmates for their GEDs.

Shortly before trial, the judge ruled that Azi's sentence could not be tougher than the one given to Mr. Berry, who had actually killed the young woman. The judge's ruling still subjected Azi to a possibility of life in prison without parole.

Prior to trial, Azi's lawyer recommended that he accept a plea to a reduced charge of armed kidnapping and accessory to murder despite the fact that Azi had had no weapon. His lawyer told him that such a plea would avoid a sentence of life without parole and more likely than not would result in a more lenient sentence than the maximum permitted for such charges. He further warned Azi that, given the potential racial bias of Madison County juries, he might well receive a life sentence without parole if he went to trial. Based upon his lawyer's advice and not having an independent understanding of the criminal justice system, Azi entered the proposed plea. Instead of the lesser sentence, the judge in June 1997 imposed on Azi the maximum sentence of thirty-five years in prison. Bernadine was saddened and outraged by the sentence.

Early in her stay in Canton, Bernadine had tried to lessen the obvious racial divide in Madison County. She became active in both the white and black Catholic Churches in the Canton/Camden area. She then began to work with ministers and clergy from churches of every denomination in Madison County to form a ministerial alliance similar to the Ringgold County Ministerial Alliance in Maloy. Her suggestion received broad support in many churches. As the first project for such alliance, Bernadine suggested that the churches jointly sponsor an emergency assistance fund to which the churches could both contribute and refer people requiring such assistance. The members of the

Alliance agreed to take up a special collection at each of their churches to capitalize the fund. As Bernadine established the fund and administered it, the project was quite successful while she lived in Mississippi.

Bernadine also became very involved in the Mission Mississippi Program, whose goal was to "foster unity across racial and denominational lines so that communities throughout Mississippi can better understand the gospel message." This program began in Jackson in 1993. One hundred pastors and civic leaders gathered to discuss how racial issues were negatively affecting the Christian community and all people in Mississippi. In 1994, a "Reconciliation Rally" was held in Jackson. Bernadine, Helen, and Ruth attended the rally.

For the next two and a half years, Bernadine and a Sister of Notre Dame, Sister Jacqueline Mertz, worked hard to organize the churches and the citizens of the Canton/Camden area to get involved in the Mission Mississippi project. But unlike in Jackson where Mission Mississippi has been very successful, citizens in the Canton/Camden area never fully embraced the program. According to Sister Janita Curoe, the Canton church leaders did not commit themselves to racial reconciliation. The longstanding racial divide in Canton, she said, is too deep and wide for Mission Mississippi to take root.

Although Bernadine firmly believed that persistent efforts on the part of people of good will from all races could eventually break down the racial divide, her work in Mississippi was cut short when she was diagnosed with terminal cancer on August 30, 1997. Her cancer was far advanced, so Bernadine had to return to Davenport, Iowa for treatment and never had the opportunity to complete her work for racial reconciliation in Mississippi.

But the Humility mission in Mississippi did not end. With Bernadine's encouragement, Helen continues her work with low-income people in Canton without regard to race. She and Janita continued tutoring inmates in the jail and work release program inmates as well as students at the various schools and adults and children at the public library. However, in 1998, when Helen honestly answered a newspaper reporter's question about conditions in the jail, the Madison County Sheriff barred her from further tutoring at the jail and prohibited any replacement tutor for her position.

Just before Helen was barred from the jail, she had tutored twenty-seven inmates who passed the tests for GEDs and received their diplomas. One of the women released from jail after securing her GED wrote Helen from California thanking her for teaching her. Her letter said, "Getting my GED was the best thing that has happened to me in my whole life."

Being barred from the jail hasn't stopped Helen from teaching both adults and children basic skills and preparing them for GED examinations. Helen currently works with other community-based groups to strengthen families and foster reading by both parents and children.

Since 2000, Helen has worked with Sacred Heart Parish to develop a program to help the seven to twelve hundred Latino immigrants recruited to the area by the owners of a chicken factory. Sacred Heart Church provides religious education and social services as well as a Spanish language mass for the immigrants despite substantial opposition by some people in the community. Helen teaches English as a second language to immigrants from Peru, Guatemala, and México. With jobs in short supply, she has created and supervises a house cleaning service to enable both African American and Latino women to be employed.

As the only Humility presently working in Mississippi, Helen has her hands full. However, at seventy-eight years old and after twenty-three years of serving poor people in Mississippi, Helen has no plans to retire or to change her career soon. Serving poor people is all she has ever wanted to do. She remains committed to the poor people of Madison County.

# Going Out as a Shooting Star

When Bernadine arrived in Davenport in the fall of 1997, she sought an evaluation of her cancer at the University of Iowa Medical Center in Iowa City. After consulting with Dr. Frederick Johlin, Bernadine decided to forego aggressive treatment, which would at most prolong her life for a relatively short period but would probably cause her to become quite sick due to the treatment's side effects. Bernadine chose quality of life over longevity. She and Dr. Johlin agreed upon a treatment regimen that they hoped would preserve her life for sufficient time to allow her to complete a number of projects she had in mind. As Father John Zeitler remarked after Bernadine's death, "She preferred to die with her boots on."

One of the first things Bernadine did was write a no frills summary of her life, which she personally delivered to Sister Jude Fitzpatrick, president of the Humilities in 1997. Bernadine told Jude she wanted this statement read at her funeral with no additional flourishes. In her statement, she explained her approach to life as a religious sister:

> In our culture, people come in pairs. A religious sister, however, makes a decision not to love at all or to love all who come her way, to love without asking to be the first in anyone's life. I chose the second alternative and sought to say and do what would help each person grow in grace and love. I respected the decisions of others and tried "to walk in their shoes." I love many people. The . . . outpouring of concern for me, surprising as it was, convinced me that this love is reciprocal.[1]

Bernadine summed up her life by saying, "I am one among many who have heard the first commandment, 'Love God with your whole heart, soul, mind and strength and your neighbor as yourself.'"

After writing what she hoped would be her obituary, she went right on living. She completed a number of writing projects she had been thinking about, including the history of sisterhoods in the last two hundred years, the spirituality of the Sisters of Humility, and changes in the Catholic Church and religious communities as a result of Vatican II.

Bernadine also wanted to write an essay on a subject close to her heart, care of the earth. Growing up on a farm made her appreciate and marvel at the myriad of animals, plants, rocks, sunsets and stars lighting up the night sky. As Bernadine's understanding about the interconnection of all things in the universe deepened, so too did her faith. But with Bernadine, faith must always be reconciled with science and translated into action. So in June 1998, she wrote the following reflection on care of the earth.

### Care of the Earth: A Reflection on Creation Spirituality

Edited by Elizabeth Thoman, CHM

Like the rest of our culture, we tend to think of "care of the earth" in economic terms. For example, we recycle newspapers and aluminum cans as sources of income. We equate the beginning of heaven upon earth as comfort and possessions rather than union with God.

Religious people can be slow in accepting the findings of scientists, believing that science is the enemy of faith. The Catholic Church has finally officially accepted Galileo's teaching that the earth revolved around the sun after more than four hundred years. However, many of us still hold that humans are the center of the universe and that the planet was made for us to dominate. Yet, we are now in the era in which humans are destroying our planet faster than it is being created. Globally we lose 2.5 billion tons of fertile topsoil annually and our sprawling cities are covering fertile land with concrete.

The central message of the creation story is that God created everything and that all is good. Our universe has been around for fifteen billion years. The sun, soil, the mold producing penicillin, oak tree, and pig are all good *in themselves,* not just in their usefulness to humankind. We are part of the web of life, not the spider.

## Challenge to Consumerism

We live in a culture, which defines its standard of living by how much we consume. Beginning with children's programs, television commercials successfully sell the notion that instant happiness and good looks come only from the products they advertise. Sometimes, even in our efforts to care for the earth, we deceive ourselves. I read about a woman who thought she was simplifying her life when she got rid of the clothes she didn't need. After she did this three or four times, she recognized that she was still an addict of consumerism.

We are increasingly stressed, pulled and pushed in every direction. The antidote is to take time out to contemplate God's creation. Churches today are locked but all of outdoors is available as a place to thank God for the sun, water, marigolds, butterflies. We might start with the hymn of St. Francis in which he called on his relatives – Brother Sun, Sister Moon, fire and wind – to praise God. In Chiapas, México, I was moved when I saw a smiling woman carrying one red gladiola flower up the mountain from the market. Some of us have acres as space for contemplation, others only a flower pot at home.

Conversely we need to see the crucified Christ, not only in the starving child, but also in the eroded field, polluted pond and smog-filled air.

## From Word to Action

From our attitude of appreciation for the Creator and awareness that we are interconnected to all of creation, actions should flow. Here are a few suggestions for individuals, families, churches and parishes. I take it for granted that recycling is already a habit.

There is a slogan, "It is good to recycle, better to reuse and best to refuse." And yet, even more basic is a contemplative attitude of appreciation for our Creator, a deep respect for all of creation and awareness that we are interconnected to everything else in the universe. "Care for the earth" is a taproot that anchors Humility spirituality through all seasons and all the seasons of life.

Every one of us can make conservation a way of life. For example, use as little water as possible to brush teeth and wash face, turn off the lights and television when not in the room, use disposable products such as paper napkins and plastic plates sparingly.

For transportation we might more often car pool, walk, bike and use mass transportation.

We might teach our children the names of the myriad plants and animals which surround us. Many of them can identify the make of every car but scarcely know the difference between a marigold and a rose.

Families and groups might plant trees, native grasses and forbs to celebrate birthdays and other events.

Groups and individuals might make their own environmentally friendly cleansers.

Persons building homes might consider the use of solar panels or at least passive energy sources and the use of wind.

Parish groups might invite inner city children to enjoy a week with them to learn about the earth, plants and animals and their relationship to us.

Youth and adult groups might study the sources of our food. We could buy more food in season instead of imports from another part of the world. We need to realize that our choices influence farmers in poor nations who are forced to raise food for export instead of for themselves and their families or often lose their little plots to mega-corporations.

Homilists might connect appropriate scripture readings with creation theology and care for the earth.

Parishes with farms and farmers might research successful farming using fewer chemicals. Parishes often use proceeds from farms to fund school programs, but saving the soil will benefit generations of children to come.

Groups might use empty lots or unused church property for community gardens.

Individuals and groups might learn more about global environmental issues such as use of nuclear power and bombs, the building of mammoth hog lots, or global warming and respond to such issues even when if we ourselves are not directly affected.


In addition to writing this reflection, Bernadine also helped plan the development of Our Lady of the Prairie Retreat Center, which grew out of the New Horizons of Faith project. For ten years, Joann Kuebrich and Father Vincent Fabula, a Trappist monk from New Melleray, taught New Horizons of Faith courses in forty parishes of the Davenport Diocese. These courses included Genesis II, scripture, the beatitudes, fundamentalism, contemplative prayer, theology, and world religions.

When the Diocese of Davenport assumed responsibility for the faith development and education for adults throughout the entire diocese in 1987, New Horizons of Faith changed its focus to respond to the expressed need by many adults in the diocese for an affordable center for spiritual reflection and renewal. After consulting with Bernadine and the other members of the New Horizons of Faith board, Joann and Vincent began to explore the possibility of establishing a spirituality center in the Davenport diocese similar to Shantivanam, the House of Prayer for the Catholic Archdiocese of Kansas City, Kansas.

In 1987, Joann and Vincent began the search for the perfect place of spiritual stillness in the Davenport diocese. Their primary site selection criterion was that the site must be so beautiful, still, and serene that, by itself, it will attract and serve people seeking solitude, contemplation, and renewal.

After Joann and Vincent conducted site reviews of forty-seven different farms over a five year period, Vincent, using his own funds, purchased the 208-acre Dierickx farm near Wheatland, Iowa in 1992 and named it Our Lady of the Prairie Retreat ("the Prairie"). The spirit of the Prairie was the major reason for its purchase. Tom Fennelly, a

Russell Construction manager, who went out to the Prairie to consult on adding additional space to the Victorian house on the farm, stopped in his tracks when entering the property and exclaimed, "I can't believe the spirit of this place." As Sister Jude Fitzpatrick later observed, "Tom had never met Vincent nor Joann or ever heard of Our Lady of the Prairie until our trip that day but his words captured the essence of the Prairie."

Vincent and Joann, along with a few paid workers and many volunteers that included a number of Humilities, planted trees and returned most of the tillable land to prairie grass and wild flowers. Bernadine served as their landscaping consultant. They also built a pond, and restored and added more bedrooms, a chapel, and a library in the old Victorian house on the property. They also built a labyrinth, which is a sacred circular path for prayer and reflection.

In the spring of 1997, when Our Lady of the Prairie Retreat Center was ready to open, Vincent was diagnosed with a terminal brain tumor. He lived most of the next year at the Prairie and a short time at Humility Center in Davenport. When Vincent died in July 1997, the Prairie retreat became the property of the Trappists of New Melleray. Although the Trappist community supported the Prairie's ministry, they were not in a position to continue it. They approached the Humilities to see if they would be interested in taking over the retreat center.

The Trappists' proposal was intriguing to the Humilities, as it would allow them not only to continue to serve the spiritual needs of adults in the Davenport diocese, but also to promote care of the earth, another Humility priority. Assuming responsibility for the Prairie was also consistent with the Humilities' long tradition of providing spiritual renewal services, particularly for women. However, according to Sister Jude Fitzpatrick, President of the Humilities at the time,

> It was the strong urging of two CHMs, which pushed us to action. Sister Bernadine Pieper, who was instrumental in the establishment of New Horizons of Faith to serve the spiritual needs of the people, and Sister Mary John Byers, who had devoted so many years providing spiritual direction and re-

treats to countless individuals and groups, were the driving forces in moving us to take on this ministry.[2]

The negotiations between the Humilities and the Trappists went on for nearly a year. Jude led the negotiations. Bernadine, a friend of Abbot Brendan Freeman, tried to move the negotiations along by suggesting that the Trappists simply give the Humilities forty acres of the farm and the Victorian house to enable them to carry on the mission since it was a common priority for each community. While some Trappists were open to Bernadine's suggestion, they ultimately decided to sell the entire property. After further discussions, the Humilities and the Trappists agreed on a reasonable purchase price for the entire property. On August 5, 1999, the Sisters of Humility became the owner of Our Lady of the Prairie Retreat.

**Sister Mary John Byers**

For the Sisters of Humility, this property is sacred ground, and they intend to keep it that way in order to allow individuals and small groups who come to the Prairie to hear the voice of God in the stillness. They have deliberately scaled the facilities to small groups of thirty or fewer persons during the day and fifteen overnight guests. The Prairie is available only to adults who are seeking the solitude necessary to renew their spirits. No big weddings. No large scale conferences. No Easter egg hunts. The prairie remains a place of serenity, beauty, and peace.

The Humilities also plan to keep the retreat center affordable for rural and small town people. For the last ten years, Joann and the co-director, Barbara Gross, along with Sisters Cathleen Real, Miriam Ehrhardt, Joan Sheil, Harriet Ping, Dolores Schuh, Marcia Eckerman, Roberta Brich, and Marie Van Horst have provided the administrative supports for the center, as well as the warm hospitality that is the hallmark of the Sisters of Humility to all who come to the Prairie. It is, according to Joann, who has spent thousands of hours at the Prairie over the past ten years, filled with the spirit of Bernadine.

The care of this sacred ground is also a part of rhythms of life and nature so much a part of the Prairie and a charism of the Sisters of Humility. As Bernadine described in her article, "The Spirituality of the Sisters of Humility," the word 'humble' comes from 'humus' meaning 'earth' or 'ground.' Humus is matter essential for fertility of the soil and is integral to the cycle of life.[3] The sisters are grounded in the earth and the care of the Prairie is integral to the cycle of their lives and the lives of those enriched by the Prairie Retreat.

The proper care of the Prairie requires its burning, which the Dixon Volunteer Fire Department does in the spring of each year. In a 1993 article about the prairie that Bernadine recreated in Maloy, "A Year in the Life of the Prairie," she described how periodic fires helped maintain the ancient prairies by suppressing growth of trees and brush, and how the Native Americans set fires to control the grazing patterns of the buffalo herds. According to Bernadine, "the prairie fires of eons ago as well as those of today are integral to prairie. The natural prairies which met our ancestors, no less than the prairies of today are a particular hybrid of nature and culture, fashioned by a cultural gift or blessing, fire." For the Humilities, care of the Prairie allows them to participate in God's mysterious and evolving creation and faithfully carry out their mission, adopted in 1990, to care for the earth itself.


During the last two and a half years of her life, Bernadine spent considerable time with individual Sisters of Humility, who resided at the Center, and other friends who came to visit her. Bernadine, the lifelong learner, took a painting course from Mary John Byers. They spent a lot of time together discussing life and death and became close friends. In reflecting on Bernadine in 2001, Mary John said with a smile, "In 1966, I didn't vote for Bernadine as president of the community. She was so brilliant and talked so fast I couldn't keep up with her. But when I really got to know her, I learned that she was not only brilliant but also a gentle, deeply spiritual woman. I personally and the community as a whole owe her a lot."

When I visited Bernadine a number of times after her terminal diagnosis, she was her same old self. As always, she was intensely interested in what was happening in the world and what our mutual friends and I were doing. The first time I visited her in Davenport in 1997, she had just received a letter from Azi Kambule thanking her for befriending him during his time in the Madison County jail. He told her that he had been transferred to a prison in southern Mississippi to begin serving the thirty-five year sentence. Bernadine was touched by the letter but saddened by Azi's long confinement in prison. For the remainder of her life, Bernadine believed that justice was not done in Azi's case. She asked me to see if I could help him. When I called Azi's mother, she told me that they had already secured a new lawyer for Azi who would seek to overturn the plea agreement and the resulting sentence.

In 2002, when I went to Mississippi to visit Azi, the ward supervisor on Azi's prison unit told me "Azi does not belong here." His lawyer, Cynthia Stewart, filed appeals challenging the plea bargain on the grounds of ineffective assistance by counsel, Azi's lack of understanding about the consequences of the plea agreement, and violations of his constitutional rights. The Mississippi appellate courts, however, rejected Azi's appeals and the U.S. Supreme Court refused to hear his case. Ms. Stewart, however, kept on fighting for Azi. After fifteen years of imprisonment, Azi finally regained his freedom when Mississippi governor Haley Barbour granted Azi a full and unconditional pardon in 2012.

Bernadine never let her illness get in the way of issues and people she cared about. Each morning, she would get up early and read the *Des Moines Register* from cover to cover. She continued to write letters to the editor for publication in the *Des Moines Register* and the *Davenport Catholic Messenger* on social and political issues she cared about. In 1999, Bernadine organized a conference to explore the impact on ordinary Iraqis of the sanctions imposed by the United States and other western countries. This conference featured Brian Terrell, Bernadine's Catholic

Worker colleague from Maloy, who had traveled to Iraq in violation of the sanctions to deliver medicine to very desperate people and saw first hand the terrible economic, social, and medical problems caused by these sanctions.

Approximately six months before Bernadine died in February 2000, a group of Humilities, the "CHM Future, 2000 and Beyond planning group," were meeting at the Humility Center. Bernadine got up out of bed and went down to the meeting. According to Roberta Brich, chair of the meeting, Bernadine in her usual direct manner told them:

> I have a few things to say. Return to the first three hundred years of religious life to see how those women lived. They came together to live, pray, and minister, usually to the poor and homeless. If they had a diversity of ministries, one usually came to the fore. No need to worry about canon law or papal/diocesan approval or permanent vows. A small group of two may do this to see how it works. It may be better to do it in a place where we are not so well known, but needs are great.[4]

Having given the sisters her views, she excused herself and left without another word. According to Roberta, it was as though "the Spirit had just blown in and out." Bernadine's advice sparked a "spirited discussion" and has continued to inform decisions made by individual sisters and the community in the last eleven years.

Before she died, Bernadine also responded to inquiries from a reporter for the *Quad City Times* about her response to learning "her days were numbered." She explained how she reconciled her life as a scientist and her life of faith and described her thoughts about the afterlife. Bernadine said that a "life of service and prayer . . . has helped me to accept mystery" even though "scientists don't like mystery." As for the afterlife, she said, "What the afterlife is, I don't know. We just have to trust in God." But then she adds, "I was told you should love God for God's sake. You don't do it because God is going to give you a bigger piece of heaven."[5]

As a number of sisters said at the time of her death, "She did more in two and a half years than many of us do in our lifetimes. She taught us how to live until we die." A few weeks before she died, Bernadine fell and fractured her hip and had to be moved to a skilled nursing facility. The Humilities maintained a constant presence at the nursing facility and were with her when she died.

Just before she died, Bernadine wrote, "I believe God is creating the universe through evolution. I hope for some kind of existence after death. These ideas have affected who I am and what I do."[6] When recalling the months leading up to her death, I remember her delight in the flashing colors from the sun reflected around her room by a prism hanging in her window and her fascination with stars shimmering in the night's sky. I also think of the quilt block she created with a continuous ribbon of ever widening circles, ending in a star. Explaining the quilt, Bernadine wrote, "The continuous ribbon represents my life on earth with ever widening relationships and experiences as I grow. One of my friends . . . said that I'm going out like a shooting star. The star represents my hope in continued life of love for God."

These star images made me think of Robert Kennedy's quote from *Romeo and Juliet* in his eulogy to his brother, JFK, at the 1964 Democratic convention. I think it is equally applicable to Bernadine:

> When s] he shall die, take [her] and cut [her] out in little stars, and s] he shall make the face of heavens so fine that all the world will be in love with night and pay no worship to the garish sun.

While Bernadine, as a very humble woman, would probably think that equating her to the whole galaxy of stars was too expansive, she would love to be one of the many twinkling stars in the night sky.

# Book II
# The Humilities of Iowa

Bernadine was not the only great woman in the Sisters of Humility. As she always insisted, she was just one among many. When the members of the community were freed up in 1969 to determine for themselves where they might best serve, they took advantage of the opportunity, going where they believed people with the greatest needs could best use their individual talents and skills.

While the adoption of the principle of self-determination was at the time considered radical and precipitated prophecies of the imminent demise of the community, it in fact re-energized and sustained the community over the past fifty years, and a wide diversity of multi-cultural ministries blossomed both here in the United States and in third world countries.

The following stories are about women who are representative of the Humilities and Bernadine's legacy—women who chose to live the gospel message of universal love with simplicity, humility and joy by serving the poor and powerless, seeking peace and justice, and faithfully caring for the earth.

# The Witch Doctor of Chiapas

In September 1968, Sisters Ana María Orozco and Angélica Inda arrived in San Andrés Larráinzar, a small town northeast of San Cristóbal de la Casas in Chiapas, México, close to the Guatemala border. They were delighted to be back to work in their native country.

Ana María had from childhood a fierce desire to become a missionary. As a young woman, she enrolled in medical school at the Universidad Nacional Autónoma de México so that she could become a missionary doctor. In her last year in medical school, she came to the United States to investigate the possibility of transferring to a U.S. medical school. She enrolled at Marycrest College to take some of the preliminary courses she would need to qualify for such transfer.

While studying at Marycrest, she began to think about becoming a sister, but was still intent on being a missionary doctor. After interviews with communities specializing in working in foreign missions, Ana María chose to join the Humilities even though Mother Geraldine candidly told her that if she joined the community, she would teach Spanish rather than serve as a missionary doctor. For the next seventeen years, Ana María taught Spanish language and literature at Marycrest.

When Bernadine announced in January 1967 her plan to establish missions in Latin America, Ana María was among the first to volunteer. In the opening page of the collected letters that chronicle her daily life in "a lost village in the Cloud Forest of Chiapas," Ana María credits Bernadine with helping her achieve her dream of becoming a missionary by starting the mission in San Andrés.[1]

When Ana María and Angélica arrived in San Andrés, 200,000 people inhabited the region, including 120,000 Tzotzil Mayan Indians, who were and continue to be among México's poorest and most deprived citizens. For centuries, these Indians have been rooted in the land, both culturally and as a means of subsistence. They have an almost mystical connection with the earth and a unique sense of their interconnection to the whole universe.

In 1968, San Andrés and the surrounding Indian villages were extremely isolated, with no adequate roads, transportation, or other basic services. Since most of the Indians had no shoes, they had to walk barefoot over unforgiving rocky terrain for three to seven hours depending on the rains to reach the market town of San Cristóbal.

Sister Ana María Orozco

San Andrés and the Indian villages in the region also lacked electricity, potable water, and basic sewer systems. Potable water and electricity that worked "most of the time" arrived in San Andrés in 1972. Sewage systems followed in 1980, all due to efforts of Isidro Orozco, Ana María's father, an engineer and technical advisor to the president of México. After seeing first-hand the living conditions in San Andrés, Mr. Orozco pressed the government to deliver these basic services to San Andrés and to build a safe road between San Andrés and San Cristóbal. He also urged that the same services be extended to the rural Indian villages in the region, but this request went unheeded.

The Indians in the region also lacked adequate income, but had high birth rates and equally high child mortality as they had no real access to health care. In 1968, ninety percent of Indian children in the region died before they were five years old.

The Indians subsisted primarily on a breakfast of corn gruel dissolved in water, coffee made from burnt tortillas, beans, and fruit, when it was available. On All Souls Day, they would share a piece of meat and once a month they put an egg into the maize to make tortillas or mixed it with the beans. This diet caused a high rate of malnutrition, particularly among children. When drought, torrential rain, hurricanes, or volcanic eruptions damaged or destroyed the corn and bean crops, malnutrition to the point of starvation became epidemic.

In the face of these intractable problems, Ana María and Angélica focused on working to improve the health and nutrition of the people. But first, they had to forge a trusting relationship with them. Although both Ana María and Angélica were native Méxicans, they had to prove themselves to the Indians who had been abused for years by citizens of their native land.

To secure the confidence of many of her patients, Ana María knew she would have to be a *curandera,* a natural healer, as well as a practitioner of western medicine. That was not a problem because, as Ana María proudly states, she "comes from a family of doctors, some of whom practiced western medicine while others dispensed traditional medicine, including herbal remedies."

As she had no clinic, no stock of medicines or other supplies necessary to operate a health clinic, Ana María worked to raise money to secure them. She also sought financing to train male Indians as "nurses" so they could provide basic health care and also serve as her eyes and ears regarding emerging medical problems in their villages. Angélica planned to bring Indian girls from remote villages to San Andrés to attend public school and be trained in agricultural techniques, nutrition, and homemaking skills.

A year later, Ana María, Angélica and thirteen young girls moved into the partially constructed clinic. They had raised enough money to stock the dispensary, start training the village "nurses," and begin the educational program for the girls. Ana María and Angélica, with the help of the girls, planted an experimental garden of vegetables, fruits, and herbs to test which varieties would grow best in the climate. They fed the young girls produce from the garden to supplement their basic diet of beans and tortillas and to teach them the nutritional value of these foods so that they would reproduce these gardens in their villages.

The garden produced radishes, carrots, green beans, brussel sprouts, lettuce, zucchinis, potatoes, pears, strawberries and cauliflowers, which they fed to the girls and shared with their neighbors and clinic patients. In one year, the garden produced two thousand heads of cauliflower. Ana María and Angélica also planted herbs indigenous to the region, many of which are used in traditional medicine. They catalogued these herbs and their uses to preserve this cultural resource for the people.

In the first year, Ana María learned that traditional fundraising was so time-consuming that it interfered with her real work of providing desperately needed health care to her patients. Therefore, she secured the funding for the clinic from the Humilities' common fund, individual contributions from nearly one hundred Sisters of Humility, including Bernadine, and donations from 150 other individual benefactors—family, friends, and tourists she'd met in Chiapas. To maintain this support, Ana María wrote periodic letters to these 250 friends describing the lives and culture of the indigenous people, and their critical unmet needs. In an early letter, she explained the nature of her work by drawing upon an article written by her sister, Luz María Orozco:

All of us working here are facing the reality of the third world in all its disturbing and entangled implications. . . .We are answering the call to share in the culture and values of this world, but we brought no panacea, no hygienic package deal, or magic wand.

Our work is a work of centuries, but every effort in the struggle to conquer prejudice and fear, cure chronic injustices, restore the dignity of the weak, downtrodden, underprivileged, and illiterate and understand the intolerable social and political contradictions dramatizes the good news of God's revelation.

Though unique in our tastes and training, these are offered to God. We are united in the firm belief that the central message of Christianity is one of liberation and we see the key to social and cultural development in a basic humanism that affirms the freedom of the individual and the capacity of people to decide their own destiny.[2]

Ana María's friends' generous responses to her pleas for help during her thirty-six years in Chiapas sustained the vital work of the clinic. For example, in the first four years of the clinic, the Sisters of Humility alone financed eighty thousand dollars worth of medication, which Ana María supplemented with free medicine donated by her friends in México and the Catholic Mission Board. In addition, for years Sister Elizabeth Anne Schneider, one of Ana María's colleagues at Marycrest, gathered medications from drug company representatives and doctors' offices, sorted the drugs by type and dosage, repackaged them in small boxes, and sent them to Ana María. Elizabeth Anne sent so many boxes to México that she became friends with a postal employee, who became interested in the project and helped pay the mailing cost of a large shipment.

Her friends' contributions also bought food and milk for impoverished families, *manta* (the cloth for making clothes and burying the dead), and shoes for the barefooted. They also sent money to buy land, cows, or pigs for Indians who had no other means to support their families, and money to repair trucks and loans for innocent persons who had to pay "fines" demanded by corrupt police officers to get out of jail. Through their generosity, Ana María also provided scholarships for indigenous students to attend high school or college, school supplies and prizes for children in San Andrés, and funds for building or restoring homes and roofs destroyed by storms. During her time in Chiapas, Ana María built or rebuilt at least seventy-five homes for poor families.

By February 1971, Ana María had trained seventy male nurses to operate small clinics in their villages. They had learned to recognize symptoms, give shots and other medicines for malnutrition, TB, hepatitis and various abdominal disorders prevalent in the region. In 1975, she trained an additional twenty nurses. Although government clinics lured some of her nurses away by offering uniforms and wages, a substantial number of talented and committed nurses stayed with Ana María's program and continue to provide essential healthcare to people in their villages.

In May 1971, at the request of residents in Chenalhó and Los Chorros, Ana María and Angélica presented a twelve-day course on health care, nutrition, sanitation, catechesis, and home improvement. Five hundred adults and many children from the two villages attended the course and many of the villagers received emergency health care. The Los Chorros villagers, who escorted Ana María and Angélica out of their village after the course, repeatedly thanked them and asked them to come back "to show us how we can improve ourselves and our surroundings because as persons we are unique."[3] Over the years, Ana María returned to Los Chorros and Chenalhó, and offered similar courses to other Indian villages in the region.

Because of this work, word spread about Ana María's clinic. Indians from remote villages walked hours or days to be treated by her. For example, in 1972 a family from Magdalenas traveled four days to have Ana María treat their son's snakebite on the sole of his left foot. When they arrived at the clinic, the bite itself was no longer life-threatening because the father had sucked the poison out of the wound. However, the child was suffering from starvation and a machete wound made by his father so that the child's other leg "would be in sympathy with the sick one." While treating the child's malnutrition, Ana María asked why they had not gone to the clinic in a village next to theirs. The father replied, "I know you and I do not know the people in the closer village."[4]

The importance of being known and trusted was underscored for Ana María when a three-year old child, who insisted he was Pancho Villa, became ill. Ana María went to his home and found him delirious with fever caused by measles. Although Ana María successfully treated this boy's measles, another child died from a measles-induced fever. These children's illnesses were preventable had they been vaccinated, but due to the parents' distrust of the government, many of them hid their children when the vaccination brigade came to town.[5] As the people grew to trust Ana María, she was able to convince them to allow their children to be vaccinated, thereby substantially reducing deaths among children.

For five days a week for thirty-six years, Ana María treated patients by herself in the San Andrés clinic. On weekends, she had the help of two assistants. On average, she and her assistants treated 650 patients a week. Frequent illnesses included amoebiasis, roundworms, tracheal bronchitis, malnutrition, rheumatic arthritis, and alcoholism.

At times there were epidemics of whooping cough, flu, and other easily transmittable diseases. A fair number of children were born with birth defects, which she referred to hospitals in San Cristóbal for more specialized treatment.

But treating acute medical conditions was only part of Ana María's practice. She also instituted prevention programs for maternal and child illnesses. Ana María's gentleness and welcoming smile, not to mention the cookies and candy she offered, eased children's hesitation about "going to the doctor," and she quickly developed a strong following among them. By providing milk, food, vitamins, herbal remedies, and other preventative care, she helped reduce high infant mortality rates.

Through education about contraceptives and referrals to the government clinic to secure them, Ana María helped many women decrease their number of pregnancies and in doing so improved their own health as well as the health of their children. She also taught the mothers, many of whom were as young as twelve years old, how to care for their babies.

But the needs of the women and children at times outstripped Ana María's resources and prevailing customs sometimes prevented her from providing the necessary care. For example, when she began distributing milk, the demand for it became so great she had to temporarily limit its distribution to acutely ill children or orphans until an emergency appeal for money produced a sufficient supply of milk for all who needed it. Ana María generally was not allowed to help deliver babies due to the custom that the woman must deliver the baby directly to the earth and the woman's partner must cut the placenta before anyone else is allowed to touch her or the baby. As a result, many women and children died from untreated complications during childbirth. She was also largely unsuccessful in convincing women subject to domestic violence to move to safety in order to protect themselves and their children.

Far too many times children were brought to the clinic too late for Ana María to save their lives. Sometimes she had to simply watch a child without obvious signs of illness fade away like a candle gradually burning out. She thought that perhaps the burden the child and parents carried was too much for the child. If the parents requested that a dying child be baptized, Ana María performed the baptism. She also anointed the sick and often provided the traditional burial cloth.

Many times, families who could not support all of their children asked Ana María to buy one. By selling one, they could buy food for the rest. Once an Indian mother with four small children appeared at the clinic and said: "Here are your children." When Ana María asked why the children were hers, the woman explained:

> You gave medicine and saved them from worms. You saved them from small pox, from whooping cough, from pneumonia. Now, the harvest has failed and I have nothing to feed them. If you had not saved them, perhaps only one would have lived, and I could feed one. I cannot feed four. They are your children.[6]

Ana María told the mother she would entrust the children to her, and gave her enough seeds, food, and other assistance to sustain her and her family until the next harvest.

In the course of her practice, Ana María became known as the Witch Doctor of Chiapas because of her use of both traditional treatments and western medicine. Sometimes only traditional healing would work. One of her patients presented with spreading wounds on his face that were not responsive to western medicines. Although Ana María referred the patient to a dermatologist at the medical school who hospitalized the patient for treatment, the wounds did not improve. The patient returned to Ana María and reported he had a friend who knew a treatment that might work. A few days later, the patient and his friend brought in some herbs. The friend told Ana María that she should chew the herbs to mix them with her saliva to make a paste to apply to the wounds and then she should cover them with bandages. At first, she looked aghast and then gave the treatment a try. When she took off the bandages three days later, the wounds were completely healed.[7]

In another case, Ana María could not determine the cause of a three-year old girl's severely painful foot that was preventing her from walking. When she examined the foot, she felt what seemed to be an extra bone. She sent the child to three separate doctors for X-rays, but they all reported the foot was normal even though the child continued to cry from the pain and could not walk. A few days later, Ana María saw the child running and jumping. She asked the parents what happened. They told her,

> When the doctors could not help the child, we took her to a witch doctor who told us that evil was the cause of the child's pain. The witch doctor instructed us to pass raw eggs over the foot and crack an egg in the water. If the water was clear, the evil had not yet come out. At the third egg, the water turned cloudy and showed "faces." They then buried this mixture under one meter of earth and sprinkled holy water over the mound so the evil would be contained. The child's foot was cured.

As Ana María had no alternative explanation, she accepted the power of traditional healing as the curative treatment.[8]

In some cases, proper treatment required both traditional healing techniques and western medicine. A young couple sought traditional treatment from Ana María for their daughter after a witch doctor had failed to cure her. They arrived with their child wrapped in a bundle of blankets, apparently bringing her incognito so as not to anger the witch doctor.

Ana María performed a quick examination and determined that the child had pneumonia. To gain the parents' authorization to give the necessary injection to treat the child's pneumonia, Ana María started with traditional incantations while at the same time holding up a lollypop in the child's line of vision but out of her parents' sight. When the child reached for the lollypop, her parents took the child's movement as a sign that Ana María's force was stronger than the witch doctor's and consented to her giving their daughter the necessary shot. To ensure that they kept the child warm, Ana María told the parents to keep their daughter incognito in the blankets until they brought her back to the clinic so that she could make certain that her pneumonia was resolved.[9]

When the parents of a baby whose left eye was inadvertently gouged by a machete refused to take him to the hospital in Tuxtla for treatment, Ana María intervened. She put on her sober face and took the baby's right arm to "listen to his blood." Affecting the singsong cadence used by some witch doctors, she said: "The blood tells me the baby has to take a long trip with the doctor to get better." She also told the parents, "Do not to be afraid. The trip will not cost the family a penny. You will be given food and shelter during the trip and return in three days." She then looked into the eyes of the parents and said: "Be sure to do what the doctor says" and then left. When the couple was later asked why they agreed to hospitalize their baby, the father answered, "Magre has looked into our souls and has talked to our son's blood."[10]

One day an elderly man came to Ana María's clinic asking for medication for his arthritis. She could tell by observation that he was not an ordinary patient. Ana María's assistant told her he was the most venerated shaman in the whole region and had come to consult with her. Ana María and the shaman talked for a number of hours. He told her that his practice had gone down since she opened the clinic, but that was all right because he found out she is a good healer. "But the catechists," he said, "are making me miserable by saying I am evil when in fact I pray to God not the devil." When Ana María asked if he used a chicken over the patient, he said, "Yes, just as you use the stethoscope." "What happens to the chicken?" Ana María asked. "They cook it and we all eat the soup," he answered. When Ana María asked if he used candles and greens, he said, "Of course I do." He looked her straight in the eye and said, "We have to impress on the people the desire to get over whatever ails them." Ana María understood his position perfectly and they parted with mutual respect and admiration. They became friends.[11]

When Ana María herself developed hemorrhaging that was not successfully treated by two separate surgeries, the shaman brought her two irregular hard pods the size of acorns. One he described as male and the other female. He told her to keep these pods with her at all times and the hemorrhaging would stop. Ana María followed his advice; her hemorrhaging stopped and never returned. She continues to keep these pods with her at all times today.

Ana María also served as the jack-of-all-trades for her neighbors and others who sought her assistance. She diagnosed and treated the illnesses of pigs, sheep, and chickens, repaired electrical wiring so an elderly neighbor could have light, fixed flashlights, watches, and batteries, served as the village barber for young girls who needed a haircut, and taught a series of knitting classes for them.

As a respected elder in the community, she also served as an advocate for Indians unfairly treated by merchants or police, and served as a mediator of disputes between Indians and "Ladinos." In the informal caste system of the region, Indians are at the bottom and Ladinos, mixed race people with some European blood, are one rung above them. The conflicts between Indians and Ladinos often involved land disputes. Ladinos at times took advantage of the Indians by moving the boundary markers for their plots of land, thus cheating the Indians out of a portion of the meager land they held.

These conflicts paled in comparison to the major conflict caused by a government policy that benefited rich farmers to the detriment of indigenous people's rights. This conflict was beyond her ability to resolve, because she could take no formal stand against the government's land policies without compromising the safety and operation of the clinic. When asked by Indians or government agents what side she was on in these disputes, she could say only, "I am on God's side."

Often Ana María had no medicine to cure the pain and suffering of some patients, particularly women who were bone-tired from being poor. In the Tzotzil culture, women marry young, often at twelve or thirteen, and bear five to thirteen children. Their daily routine begins around three o'clock in the morning when they make the tortillas. They then take care of the house, the children, and the few chickens they might have; do the family's washing and make their clothes; and on a daily basis find wood and water, which they then carry for miles to their homes. When their husbands are disabled or dead, they must also plant and tend the corn and beans, knowing that if they fail to do so, they and their children will have nothing to eat. At times, these burdens are simply overwhelming and the women lose all hope. In these cases, Ana

María simply listened to them and asked what would make them feel better. The needs they expressed were often quite simple: a blanket, coffee with sugar, some meat, some cloth with which to make a blouse or a skirt. Ana María's ability to meet these simple needs helped restore their hope.

Ana María's clinic succeeded due to her willingness to live among the people, learn about and respect their culture, and treat them as friends rather than simply patients seeking medical services. She planned to stay in Chiapas until she died, but her leg was crushed in a car accident, bitten by a snake, and became so filled with arthritis that she was barely able to walk. After thirty-six years in Chiapas, Ana María had to return to the Humility Center in Davenport. She left her house/clinic to her long-time assistant, Lucas. When her neighbors and some patients learned that she was going to the United States and would never return, they asked to go with her. After all, they said, "We are North Americans too."

For the past seven years, Ana María, who can no longer walk independently, has used her skill at knitting to make bandages for slow healing sores and ulcers caused by leprosy, HIV/AIDS, insect bites and burns. Global Health Ministries has distributed these bandages to health care clinics in Latin America and the Caribbean. She also knits caps, scarves, and blankets for people in need of them. She continues to follow current affairs both in the United States and around the world, and is fascinated by the advances in medicine, technology, and science. But her heart remains among the indigenous people of Chiapas.

# Preserving Mayan Culture/ Empowering its People

Angélica, like Ana María, had a fierce desire to serve poor people in her native land. Her dream was to become an anthropologist and help preserve the culture of the Mayan people in Chiapas. When she joined the Humilities in 1953, Angélica became a teacher rather than an anthropologist. However, when Bernadine founded the mission in the heart of the Mayan region of Chiapas, Angélica saw her chance to study firsthand the Mayan culture and its people.

In 1973, Angélica moved to Chenalhó to work directly with the Mayans just as the newly-elected President Luis Echeverría announced with great fanfare a new program to resolve the longstanding problems in the Indian zones of Chiapas. He promised to (1) establish schools for girls in the rural villages; (2) send social workers to help improve home life; (3) provide agronomists to teach the people better utilization and treatment of the land, and veterinarians to teach control of disease among animals; (4) send out civil engineers to teach and build for the people adequate housing, stables, and latrines; (5) provide sanitation engineers to introduce potable water and electrical engineers to expand electricity to the remote villages; and (6) dispatch industrial engineers to introduce looms and the preservation of fruit as ways to increase income.

The government, however, quickly abandoned these programs when it ran out of money to support them. Similarly, in early 1974, the government promised to restore to indigenous people in Chiapas their land rights by returning to them land that had been taken unlawfully from them. But before this policy was implemented, the government caved to pressure from current landowners and abruptly canceled it.

Frustrated by these developments and the continued deprivation of their property rights, Indians from villages surrounding San Andrés attempted in May 1974 to secure their fair share of land by taking over some farms. The farmers responded with gunfire, which led to bloodshed on both sides. Many Ladino residents of San Andrés temporarily abandoned the town out of fear and the Indians then moved into their abandoned houses, which only worsened the conflict. The government sent in the military to quell the "uprising," but it only exacerbated the conflict.

The same year, the governor of Chiapas, Manuel Velasco Suárez, decided to hold an Indigenous Congress to celebrate the 150th anniversary of Chiapas as part of México and the 500th birthday of Fray Bartolomé de las Casas, the first bishop of Chiapas, known as the "Defender of the Indians." Because of the longstanding conflicts between the government and indigenous people, Governor Velasco asked Dom Samuel Ruiz García, the bishop of the Diocese of San Cristóbal de las Casas (Diocese of San Cristóbal), to co-sponsor the congress. Bishop Ruiz agreed, but only if representatives of indigenous communities planned and led the congress. He argued that such a plan would be consistent with "the spirit and work of Bartolomé de las Casas who promoted respect and recognition of the indigenous peoples and their cultures."[1]

After some discussion in regional assemblies, a majority of the indigenous communities in Chiapas agreed to plan and lead the congress. Representatives from the Tzeltal, Tojolabal, Ch'ol, and Tzotzil peoples—the four largest indigenous communities in the diocese—met for three days to discuss the major problems they faced concerning land, health care, education, and the commercialization of agricultural products.[2] They learned that these problems affected all of them and they agreed to make these issues the focus of their united efforts for systemic change through the congress.

In November 1974, two thousand people attended the congress, with twelve hundred delegates representing more than three hundred indigenous communities. For three days, the Indian delegates passionately detailed in their own languages the specific causes of their poverty and misery. According to historian, Thomas Benjamin:

> Their greatest complaint was the lack of good land. That
> was the primary cause of their hunger, misery, and exploi-

tation. The agrarian reform process was decades in arrears due to corruption and illegal noncompliance with the law . . . Business in the Highlands was controlled by Ladino or Indian *caciques* (bosses) who, aligned with government agencies, bought their produce for little and sold them goods for a lot. Education and health care hardly existed, as high rates of illiteracy and infant mortality demonstrated. Where schools and clinics have been built, they were rarely staffed by teachers, nurses or doctors, or provided with books or medicines. Chronic alcoholism made every problem worse.[3]

The government continued to ignore the indigenous peoples' plight and demands, but as a result of the congress, the Indian delegates nevertheless successfully launched a new social movement that mobilized indigenous communities throughout Chiapas. The rallying cry became, "In our union is our strength."

Angélica attended that First Indigenous Congress with French anthropologist Andrés Aubry, Padre Miguel Chantaeu, and indigenous people from the village of Chenalhó. At the end of the congress, Bishop Ruiz told Angélica and Andrés that he would like to have in his diocese an Institute of Anthropology for the Mayan Area. While continuing to work with the people in Chenalhó, Angelíca and Andrés, with Jan Rus, a Tzotzil speaking Mayan expert working in the Highlands, founded the Institute for Anthropological Assessment Maya Region (INAMERAC). The Institute for many years brought together American and European experts in the Mayan culture to help the Mayan people preserve their culture, oppose the systemic violence perpetrated against their communities, and help them to regain their independence and autonomy.

One of the Institute's first projects was to develop a transcription graph, dictionary, and embryonic literature of the previously unwritten Tzotzil language, and to store it all in a data bank. It also helped local communities organize reflection groups and record their oral histories. The Institute published native language books on the historical struggle for land, labor contracting and coffee plantations, and women's artisan cooperatives.

Angélica also served as the director of the Historical Archives of the Diocese of San Cristóbal. In 1975, she participated in the first diocesan assembly after the Indigenous Congress during which the diocese and its organizations committed to "the preferential option for the poor," which meant taking a stand against the policies and agendas of the government and its powerful patrons who caused the misery of the indigenous people. It also meant transforming pastoral practices, church structures, and the public stance of the Church in support of this commitment. By casting its lot with the poor indigenous people of Chiapas and taking steps aimed at solving the root problems causing their misery, the diocese during the next eighteen years placed itself in direct opposition to both the interests of the Vatican and the Méxican government.

The government responded swiftly to the diocese's challenge by subjecting it to violence and persecution similar to that inflicted on the indigenous people for generations. Angélica, in conjunction with the Fray Bartolomé de las Casas Center for Human Rights, documented over one hundred attacks against the pastoral work of the diocese by the Méxican government itself, militias, and other paramilitary forces funded by the government or the governing party, PRI, between December 1974 and June 1977.

The June 21, 1977 pastoral letter issued by the San Cristóbal Diocesan Council, Bishop Ruiz, and the Adjunct Bishop of the diocese, Vera López, publicized these attacks, describing: (1) false charges against Bishops Ruiz and Vera claiming that they were the cause of violence and political and social instability in the State of Chiapas; (2) physical attacks and death threats against pastoral workers, including catechists, predeacons, and deacons, as well as illegal judicial processes initiated against them; (3) torture and arbitrary executions of many catechists because they refused to sign papers accusing the bishops and priests of providing arms to the rebels; (4) persecution of missionaries from other countries, including repeated interrogation of them by immigration police and deportation of twelve percent of the priests in the diocese; (5) bombing of diocesan property and forced closing or burning of chapels and other religious symbols; (6) deliberate inciting of conflicts within communities by forcing some members of the community to become members of the paramilitary forces; and (7) forcibly displacing Catholics from their homes and communities.[4]

The pastoral letter called upon the Catholic community, other Christian churches, and Méxican civil society to join with the Diocese of San Cristóbal in challenging the government's deliberate actions to undermine the peace process that "could end the massacre and genocide against the Chiapanecan people." It also called upon the government "to revise its present policies and orient its actions towards the solution of the true root causes of the conflicts our country is experiencing."[5]

Although the government's attacks continued, the diocese remained faithful to its commitment to the indigenous people. The Vatican did not support the diocese; instead, on October 26, 1993, the papal nuncio, Monsignor Gerónimo Prigione, informed Bishop Ruiz that the Vatican's Congregation of Bishops requested his resignation. The request to remove the bishop, in fact, came from José Córdoba Montoya, the Chief Advisor to the President of Mexico after Bishop Ruiz, during the pope's August 1993 visit to Mérida, Mexico, handed him a pastoral letter criticizing governmental policy. As reported by Miguel Angel Granados Chapa in his column in *El Financiero* on October 23, 1994, Monsignor Prigione initially stated that the decision to remove Bishop Ruiz "responds to governmental needs rather than to ecclesiastical concerns, and even less to the needs of the social and indigenous ministry in which Don Samuel excels." However, on October 28, 1994, he reversed course by alleging that Bishop Ruiz was being removed because "He has made grave doctrinal, pastoral and governmental errors that clash with the church and offend the pope."[6]

When Monsignor Prigione's action became public, a firestorm of protest erupted from both church and civil society, nationally and internationally. Hundreds of people marched to the papal nuncio's residence in Mexico City and delivered a letter signed by religious communities, civil society, human rights, and international organizations opposing the attempted forced resignation of Bishop Ruiz. Bernadine and Angélica joined in the protest. As the Méxican Bishops' Conference also supported Bishop Ruiz, the papal nuncio finally caved to the pressure and withdrew his demand for Bishop Ruiz' resignation.

During these years, Angélica and Andrés continued to work directly with both the diocese and the various indigenous communities in the region. In these communities, they continued to witness the struggle of the people due to shortage of land, poverty, and high unemployment, but they also witnessed the growing mobilization of indigenous people on issues of mutual concern and forged close relationships with the emerging leaders of this movement.

On January 1, 1994, three thousand indigenous men and women, under the banner of the Zapatista army, Ejército Zapatista de Liberación Nacional (EZLN), seized control of four cities, including San Cristóbal. They resorted to this armed resistance only after many legal attempts to have their voices heard had failed. The EZLN called themselves "Zapatistas," invoking the memory of Emiliano Zapata, one of the leaders of the Méxican revolution in the early 1900s. Their struggle mirrored Zapata's earlier challenge of the corrupt and repressive regime of large land owners and big business that left indigenous people landless and exploited.

In communiqués sent round the world by fax and cell phones, the EZLN explained that its decision to take up arms coincided with the implementation of the North American Free Trade Agreement (NAFTA) because cheap grains from the U.S. would soon pour into México and obliterate any chance for Indian farmers to compete. The EZLN considered NAFTA "a death sentence for México's indigenous people, whom the Salinas government views as dispensable." Their demands were three: land, justice, and greater democracy.[7]

The Méxican government responded by sending seventeen hundred troops, supported by tanks and heavy armaments, to quash the revolt by attacking indigenous communities, as well as the EZLN. The war lasted ten days. While the government's military outstripped the strength of the EZLN, the Zapatistas won the war of ideas. Méxican civil society, the media, and international public opinion supported the justness of the Zapatistas' position. As a result, President Salinas ordered a unilateral cease-fire on January 12, 1994.

On February 21, 1994, in the Cathedral of San Cristóbal, a dialogue for peace between representatives of the EZLN and the government, commenced. Bishop Ruiz, at the request of both the government and the EZLN, served as the mediator at the Comisíon Nacional de Intermediacíon proceedings.

During the three-year negotiation process, Angélica served as Secretary of the EZLN delegation and was one of its strong voices. On February 16, 1996, the indigenous people and the Méxican government reached a partial

Sisters Ana María Orozco and Angélica Inda

agreement set forth in the San Andrés Peace Accords related solely to the autonomy of the Chiapas indigenous communities. They tabled the issues of justice and democracy for later negotiations. However, the Méxican government failed to implement even the limited agreements set forth in the Accords. Instead, it resumed its military occupation of Chiapas and its war of attrition against the indigenous people there.

Between 1985 until Angélica died of cancer in 2001, she and Andrés wrote over thirty articles published in the Méxican daily newspaper *La Jornada,* and in international publications including the *Wall Street Journal.* These articles described the war waged by the Méxican government, the military, public police forces, paramilitary groups, ranchers' private police forces, and militias funded by PRI. Nine of these articles detailed the rise of paramilitary forces in the region and their attacks on rural indigenous communities, thus debunking the government's assertion that the ongoing violence in Chiapas was nothing more than a religious conflict.

Angélica and Andrés also exposed atrocities such as the December 1997 massacre of forty-five Tzotzil Indians in the Acteal refugee camp by the PRI militia called the Red Mask. The Indians were members of the *Los Abejas* who, while sympathetic to the Zapatista cause, were committed to non-violence. Witnesses to the event reported that the public police force, stationed very close to Acteal, heard the shootings but failed to investigate or intervene. The Red Mask paramilitary force not only shot but also brutalized with machetes the victims of this assault—twenty-one women, fifteen children, and nine men. Angélica and Andrés also reported that soldiers forcibly removed villagers from their homes and destroyed or interfered with the villagers' cultivation of crops, which were their basic source of food.

These articles helped to build national and international support for the Zapatista cause, and also sparked retaliation by the government. In mid-1998, the Méxican government subjected Angélica and Andrés to harassment and intimidation, including attempted detention by security forces; theft of their computers, notes, and manuscripts; break-ins and vandalism of their home; and attempted break-ins at the Historical Archives of the Diocese of San Cristóbal. Angélica and Andrés also received death threats and, for a time, had to go underground.

These governmental attacks only strengthened Angélica's and Andrés' resolve to stand in solidarity with the indigenous people of Chiapas and to do everything in their power to liberate and protect them. They did so until they died—Angélica in 2001 and Andrés in 2007.

Since Angélica's death, support for the indigenous people of Chiapas' cause has grown both in the Méxican civil society and throughout the world. Nevertheless, the five hundred year struggle between the Méxican government and its native people continues. The Zapatistas' political and social movement has grown, and the number of Zapatista autonomous communities has increased. While they have tried to improve the health and welfare of their people, they lack the financial resources necessary to provide the full education and health services needed. As a whole, these communities still lack the land and resources necessary to be self-sufficient. The burdens on the indigenous communities have become so great that some of the younger people are beginning to immigrate to other countries hoping to improve their lives.

Nevertheless, the indigenous people of Chiapas have survived with their culture largely intact due to the continuing strong support of the Diocese of San Cristóbal as well as other national and international support developed by the Zapatistas themselves. For that, Angélica would be grateful. Were she still alive, Angélica would be lending her voice to the as yet unresolved but just cause of the Zapatistas. This brave woman was remembered at the time of her death by her friend of fifty years, Luz María Orozco:

### Angélica's Ashes

Gray Silent sands
Once the fiery voice
Of the Zapatistas' just cause
The quick hand and beating heart
Salvaging Historic Maya Lore.
Brave soul! Surviving sacked home
And snipers' guns.
Succumbing only
To that sinister
Fifth columnist: Cancer.
Your memory shines
In each particle of sand
Shouting from above:
"Well Done!"

# Living the "Preferential Option for the Poor"

Sisters Ana María and Angélica weren't the only ones who chose to work in Chiapas. Three other Sisters of Humility, Johanna Rickl, Carole Anne Guckeen, and Penelope Wink dedicated years of their lives to work there. As children, Johanna and Carole Anne had hoped to become missionaries, but after joining the Humilities in the early 1960s, they too became teachers rather than missionaries.

When Bernadine established the mission in Chiapas and encouraged sisters to seek out new ways to serve poor people, Johanna and Carole Anne seized the opportunity to become missionaries there. In 1971, they traveled to Chiapas to experience first-hand the daily life of mission work, including the isolated and primitive conditions in which Ana María and Angélica lived, and the unique people with whom they were working. They saw opportunities within the Diocese of San Cristóbal for learning more about the Mayan culture and working with the people to improve their lives.

In 1972, Johanna and Carol Anne became papal volunteers and joined the Diocese of San Cristóbal, initially serving as members of the southeastern pastoral team serving the parish of La Trinitaria, which covered five hundred square miles and thirty-five thousand people with one priest. The people were mostly mestizo subsistence farmers who like the indigenous people in the Highlands of Chiapas lacked sufficient land to support their families.

As the indigenous people of Chiapas had specifically requested that members of their own communities be chosen and trained to minister to them, the diocese in the early 1970s made it a priority to train both Indian and mestizo people to serve as catechists in their own communities. Initially, the majority of the catechists were men who exercised varying degrees of influence or leadership in the villages. They led the Sunday worship service consisting of prayers, songs, scripture readings, and an interpretation or discussion of the scriptural text. They also held sacramental preparation classes and served as the liaison with the priest in scheduling pastoral visits to their communities. Some of these catechists became community organizers and leaders who helped plan and lead the First Indigenous Congress in 1974.

After the First Indigenous Congress, representatives of the indigenous communities told Bishop Samuel Ruiz about their desire to have their own people serve as priests of their communities, as well as catechists. In response to this request,

> Bishop Ruiz agreed to ordain indigenous ministers, or *tuhuneles* (servants), as the Tzeltal communities called them. The *tuhuneles* were in most cases experienced, tested men chosen by the assemblies of their communities and approved by the bishop. Ordinations of the *tuhuneles*, first as pre-deacons and then deacons, marked the beginning of a new form of incarnated local diocesan church among indigenous peoples, after almost five centuries of domination by the Western forms of church organization. In his 1975 Christmas message, Don Samuel announced with great joy the birth of what he called autochthonous churches in his diocese.[1]

Thirty-five years later, in 2000, when Bishop Ruiz reached the mandatory retirement age of seventy-five, the number of native catechists serving the diocese of Chiapas had grown to more than twenty thousand men and women. In addition to the native catechists, the diocese had also ordained over 350 native deacons, many of whom were married men, with about a hundred more training to become deacons.

On February 1, 2002, after Bishop Ruiz's retirement, the Vatican, in a letter signed by Cardinal Jorge Medina and Archbishop Francesco Pio of the Congregation for the Divine Worship and the Discipline of the Sacraments, ordered the current bishop of the Diocese of San Cristóbal, Felipe Arizmendi, to stop ordaining married native deacons. However, the training of new indigenous leaders continues in the diocese. When asked about the future of the diaconate program, a member of the leadership team at a January 2005 training in the Tzotzil region of the diocese said, "When the ban on ordination is lifted, we will have many indigenous candidates ready for ordination, hopefully even to be ordained for the priesthood."[2]

Johanna and Carol Anne, in addition to training and supporting catechists, also carried out the diocesan philosophy of "helping communities recognize that they are subjects of their own history and providing them with knowledge needed to exercise their power." They taught the people their rights under the agrarian reform law and Johanna teamed with a young doctor and nurse to provide health classes to people from the outlying villages. In many villages, they taught classes on preventative health care and first aid, and worked with the people to develop agricultural skills to increase the nutritional content of their diets.

Sisters Johanna Rickl, Ana María Orozco and Penelope Wink, with Bishop Samuel Ruiz

Johanna and Carole Anne also worked specifically with women in small villages who were eager to learn new skills to help support themselves and their families. Johanna devised a low cost method of baking bread in a large lard can over an open fire and then taught the women how to do it. This new skill allowed the women to make bread for communal celebrations as well as for daily meals. Some women became proficient bread makers and started micro-businesses selling bread in their villages. Carole Anne also taught the women to knit and crochet, which in turn stimulated some women to make and sell baby booties, sweaters, scarves, and hats.

Johanna and Carol Anne helped the women, many of whom did not speak up within the family or in community gatherings, to find their own voices. Over time they began to appreciate that they had wisdom to share and became confident enough to speak up in both family and public meetings. Eventually, some women became catechists and community leaders.

At the completion of her three-year commitment as a papal volunteer, Carole Anne returned to the United States. Although she loved the work she was doing in Chiapas, she decided to give up her vowed membership in the community and focus her work in the United States. When Carole Anne told Bernadine her decision, Bernadine was supportive. According to Carole Anne, Bernadine really listened to her and affirmed her as a person. Carole Anne subsequently became an associate member of the community.

Johanna remained in Chiapas for another ten years. She continued her work in La Trinitaria, but after five years she moved on to work with another pastoral team serving villages in areas surrounding La Independencia, Tzimol and Comitán de Domínguez, which included a zone of Tzeltal speaking people. Although her work varied depending upon the needs of the people, a strong component was still to train catechists to serve as spiritual and community leaders. Johanna found that "the communities were strengthened through increased participation in worship, sacramental celebrations, and resolution of problems through prayerful reflection on scripture and dialogue among the members of the community."

In La Independencia, Johanna also taught the people the requirements for securing additional land under the agrarian reform law and basic health care. She also mediated disputes between members of the various communities, and helped to establish cooperatives.

In Comitán, Johanna teamed with residents to help meet the needs of the people in the barrios, organized celebrations on patronal feast days, and helped to form small Christian communities. In the rural zones of the Santo Domingo Parish surrounding Comitán, she focused on *campesino* (subsistence farmer) communities. In the Tzeltal zone, Johanna, in conjunction with a Méxican sister and a local doctor, helped the people establish a small pharmacy that dispensed medications, including traditional herbal remedies, to health promoters and villagers.

Johanna insists that, during her thirteen years in Chiapas, she learned more from the people than she taught. She studied anthropology to learn more about Mayan culture so that she could promote and assist the people to preserve their culture. Over the years, Johanna and other pastoral workers and priests in the diocese have helped the people incorporate Mayan symbols and culture in their church celebrations.

Johanna also learned the real meaning of community from observing the village assemblies and the interaction among the villagers. She personally benefited from the generosity and sharing which are integral to these communities. Meat for the rural people of Chiapas was and still is a luxury. But when the villagers had meat, they shared it with everyone in the community, including visitors like Johanna.

In 1974, Penelope Wink joined the Diocese of San Cristóbal as a pastoral worker. Initially, Penelope worked with Johanna in both La Trinitaria and La Independencia. However, in 1980, when the southeast diocesan team reorganized itself to better serve villages far away from any parish church, Penelope began serving forty-five poor mountain villages. Forty of these villages were accessible only by foot, requiring between eight and twelve hours to reach them. The other five villages had some form of primitive road access, but were often accessible only by foot during inclement weather.

All of these villages lacked electricity and potable water. The people

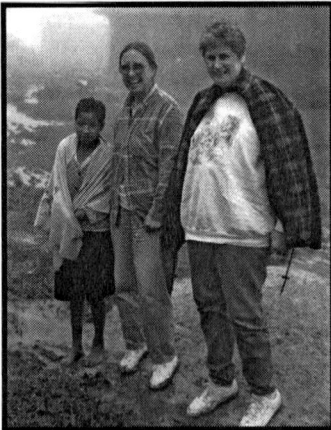

Sisters Penelope Wink and Roberta Brich, and friend

lived in very primitive housing without heat. Teachers assigned to these villages refused to live there due to the lack of basic amenities. They would show up the first day and then disappear for the school term.

Because Penelope and other pastoral team members were the only people who lived with the villagers for any significant period of time, being an attentive presence was their most important function. They still offered scripture and skill building courses as appropriate, but Penelope spent a lot of time sitting with people around the village fire listening to them with "an interested ear." She ate what they ate, slept where they indicated was a place for her, and celebrated with them the little things in life, events that were important to them. She learned from them their cultural values and their deep faith. By listening, Penelope gave them hope and empowered them individually and collectively to exercise more control over their own lives.

In 1982, while Penelope was working in villages near the border of Guatemala, two thousand refugees came across the border over a two-week period. Military operations had leveled hundreds of villages in Guatemala, killing thousands of innocent peasants. The refugees were primarily poor agricultural workers who had little to no education. Many of them, especially the women, did not speak Spanish. A large number of them had hidden in the mountains or the jungle for months waiting for the military to leave their villages before fleeing the country. As a result, many suffered from poor health, malnutrition, and emotional trauma. For six months, Penelope, other pastoral team members, and local people helped the refugees secure basic food and shelter.

As tens of thousands of Guatemalan refugees ended up in a camp along the border in Chiapas, the Diocese of San Cristóbal established a special pastoral team to work with them thus freeing Penelope to turn her attention to the remaining twenty-eight villages for which she was responsible. For ten years, she worked in these villages as an attentive presence as well as offering courses in scripture, health, and agricultural practices. She also helped people in some villages develop cooperatives. According to Penelope, "This experience changed my life. I learned so much from the people that I became a more developed, well-rounded person strongly committed to the people with whom I work."

In 1992, the diocese reassigned Penelope to the Tzeltal zone, where she lived in Ocosingo, the county seat, and worked in surrounding villages. Since many of the Tzeltal people supported the Zapatista movement, the Méxican military literally encircled the village of Ocosingo harassing and traumatizing the people. In one month alone, the military killed over a thousand civilians. Villagers requiring urgent medical care had to be accompanied through rows of tanks to get it.

After Penelope had worked three years in this war zone, the

Diocesan officials suggested that she work in a quieter place, Venustiano Carranza in the South of Chiapas. The "quieter place" turned out to be fraught with conflicts among the people themselves, which dated back to the 1960s and 70s. Penelope and other members of the parish team had to become healers of conflict.

In 1999, Penelope began a graduate program in psychotherapy through the Guadalajara Institute while continuing her pastoral work. After completing a master's degree in Gestalt psychotherapy, Penelope began to provide psychological counseling to people in the parish as well as others in San Cristóbal while continuing to serve as a pastoral worker. Her counseling work is rooted in the theory of social psychology of liberation articulated by Father Ignacio Martin-Baro, a renowned pioneer in the field, who believed that the primary work of a psychologist is to raise consciousness about one's relationship with society and the world. In 1989, Father Martin-Baro was executed along with five other Jesuits and two members of their household by the Salvadoran military in response to their human rights work on behalf of poor Salvadorans.

Like Father Martin-Baro, Penelope has lived for years in a society where the power and wealth of a privileged few is maintained by military might. Some of her clients have been victims of the systemic violence perpetrated against the indigenous people by the Méxican military and paramilitary forces. Others have been hurt and have lost loved ones or homes as a result of natural disasters such as earthquakes, mudslides, and floods. Like Father Martin-Baro, Penelope tries to raise the consciousness of her clients, colleagues, and people in the broader society regarding their relationship to the world in which they live where social inequalities dominate.

In 2007, Penelope and a small group of colleagues applied to serve as the host site for the Ninth International Congress of Social Psychology of Liberation. They believed that the theory and practice governing much of the work and movements in Chiapas could have an important impact on the congress. In turn, the Congress would bring new experiences from other parts of the world to the people of Chiapas.

When Chiapas was chosen as the site for the 2008 congress,

Penelope and her colleagues organized and hosted the event without a single person getting paid for their work. As the logo and theme for the Congress, they chose the image of a Mayan weaver accompanied by the words, "We weave new visions and the paths to them, highlighting the flowers and the colors proper to each culture so that life flourishes."

The congress attracted over two thousand participants from twenty-two countries and even more cultures, representing universities, popular movements, church groups, and non-governmental organizations. It focused on raising consciousness among participants regarding their responsibility to help men and women liberate themselves from the bonds of the social-cultural, spiritual, and material ties holding them prisoners.[3]

Although Penelope has lived and worked in Chiapas far away from the Sisters of Humility for over thirty-five years, she remains strongly committed to both the sisters of the community and its mission. According to Penelope,

> The community's commitment to the poor and its mission to ensure justice with dignity for all people, its history of creatively responding to the reality in which the sisters live, the sisters' continual searching out the needs of the time in order to focus their service among those most in need, and the words of Mary's Magnificat, which has become so ingrained in all of us, has been and continues to be a primary motivation for my work among the poor people of Chiapas. Needless to say, the support of Bernadine, the community in general and other individual sisters has certainly helped me in hard times.

Another Sister of Humility, Nancy Wooldridge, lived and worked in three different Méxican states from 1972 to 1977. When Bishop Ruiz asked Nancy, who is a licensed practical nurse, to go to Tumbalá high up in the north-central mountains to help organize a dispensary for primarily Ch'ol Indians and to train native nurses to staff the dispensary, she went.

After establishing the dispensary and training the native nurses, Nancy then moved to San Juan Aragón, a very poor area of México City. For two years, she ran the parish clinic, which served a population of nine thousand people, visited elderly and sick people in their homes, and started a parish choir. When two nurses in the parish volunteered to staff the clinic, Nancy turned the clinic over to them and moved to Cuernavaca, when the Nuestros Pequeños Hermanos orphanage recruited her to serve as a nurse.

**Sister Nancy Wooldridge**

The philosophy of the orphanage was to care for entire families. When Nancy arrived, fourteen hundred children and young adults lived at the orphanage and the facility needed a purchasing agent to secure the food and other supplies necessary to feed and care for these young people. Nancy took on this responsibility even though she was totally unfamiliar with the markets. After a local woman taught her how to successfully barter and bargain, Nancy, for a year and a half, scoured the markets making the deals necessary to secure sufficient food to feed fourteen hundred children and adults each day on the orphanage's extremely limited budget. When a Mexican woman who worked with Nancy was ready to assume the purchasing responsibilities, Nancy turned the job over to her and returned to Ottumwa, Iowa to take care of the retired sisters.

# Forging Friendships and Improving Lives in Latin America and Africa

In September 1968, three Sisters of Humility, Maxine Lloyd, Irene Muñoz, and Delphine Vasquez headed to Ecuador as papal volunteers. When Delphine volunteered for the Latin American missions, she was young, had not yet developed confidence and was, therefore, somewhat fearful about going to Ecuador. In fact, according to Delphine, she would not have had the courage to go without Bernadine's encouragement and support. But, when Delphine underwent the psychological screening for volunteers, the psychologist wrote on her evaluation, "This sister should go." When Bernadine saw the note, she met with Delphine, showed her the note, and said, "I think you should go, too." So she did and the experience opened up a whole new world for Delphine.

Maxine and Irene, on the other hand, needed no nudging to go to Ecuador. Irene was eager to respond to Bernadine's call for sisters to serve poor people in third world countries. She thought she could contribute to such a mission with her fluency in Spanish and her training as a nurse. The opportunity to work with *campesinos* in Ecuador also drew Maxine to volunteer. The opportunity to use her fluency in Spanish to help poor people and at the same time experience a new culture was an opportunity too good to pass up.

When these three Humilities arrived in Ecuador, they explored the towns and villages of the Ambato diocese to determine the needs of the people. But before they decided where and with whom they would work, Irene was called back to the United States because of her father's terminal illness.

Delphine and Maxine remained, and elected to work with Father Alonzo Peréz, an Ecuadorian priest with a passion for working with rural people. He invited them to join him in serving *campesinos* in small mountain villages around Ambato, Patate, and Pelileo as well as indigenous people in villages located in the northern part of the diocese. Social justice was one of his passions. He taught his parishioners that Jesus intended them to have a better life and educated them about their rights under Ecuador's agrarian reform law. He also helped them track their applications for land under the reform act when they got "lost" in the municipal office responsible for implementing the law. As he had a holistic approach to his pastoral work, he also helped the people organize their fiestas and village celebrations and often leant his ability to play the accordion to help make the music at these celebrations.

Delphine and Maxine lived in the parish house in Patate so they would be close to the mountain villages in which they worked. In Ambato, they used the social center as their home base, as it was the gathering place for the poor people there.

The *campesinos* were subsistence farmers whose small plots of land were insufficient to feed and support their families. Their basic crops were lima beans and corn. They lived in small homes with dirt floors that sheltered not only themselves but also their chickens and other small animals they might have. Their children often had no shoes and inadequate clothing.

When Delphine and Maxine learned that forty percent of preschool children in Ecuador suffered from malnutrition, they, in conjunction with Catholic Relief Services (CRS), initiated a health and nutrition program focused on two hundred *campesino* women with children under five years old. Through this program, they distributed vitamins and milk to supplement the diets of the children. In addition, they arranged for a baker to use surplus flour and oil to make bread for the women and their families, a program so popular among the women that it continued for years.

Delphine and Maxine taught the women basic nutrition aimed at keeping their children healthy and helped them determine how to allocate their limited resources to provide more nutritious foods for their families. The CRS nurse weighed the children each session to make certain they were benefiting from the supplements and evaluated their overall health. When necessary, the nurse treated children for worms often caused by a lack of clean water in the villages. Maxine obtained second-hand clothing and taught the women how to tailor the clothing to fit members of their families. Delphine teamed up with a Peace Corps volunteer with an agricultural background to start a number of community gardens to train people in basic agricultural skills and to encourage them to start community gardens in their own villages.

Another focus of their work was health education and literacy.

**Sister Maxine Lloyd**

Maxine and Delphine traveled a circuit of ten schools in small villages in the Patate parish to teach basic health and religion classes. When the government initiated a national literacy campaign, they taught literacy classes for middle school children by day and adults at night to supplement the minimal education the one-room schools were able to provide.

In her third year in Ecuador, Maxine taught English at night to high school students who had dropped out of school, since they needed it to receive the basic educational certificate signifying completion of classes equivalent to a sixth-grade education. Possessing this certificate increased the students' prospects for getting jobs.

Delphine and Maxine also performed more traditional pastoral work. As Father Peréz was the only priest for many villages, they trained catechists as substitute ministers to conduct Sunday worship services in their villages when Father Peréz was in other parishes. Maxine, a trained musician, led congregational singing at masses, and at times she would accompany the children singing hymns. According to Delphine, the people loved Maxine because she was a blonde, blue-eyed woman with a marvelous smile and great personality, who was very fluent in Spanish and demonstrated that she cared about the people.

When Bernadine visited the sisters in Ecuador, a native band greeted her. She described the warm welcome to the community saying, "It was a tribute to Maxine and Delphine rather than to me—one bit of evidence of the good rapport between the sisters and the people." She further reported to the community that at the First Inter-American Conference of Major Superiors in Mexico City in 1971, the work and the style of life of the Humility sisters in Latin America, who lived simply, practiced poverty, and made themselves readily available to the people, was seen as the model for the future.

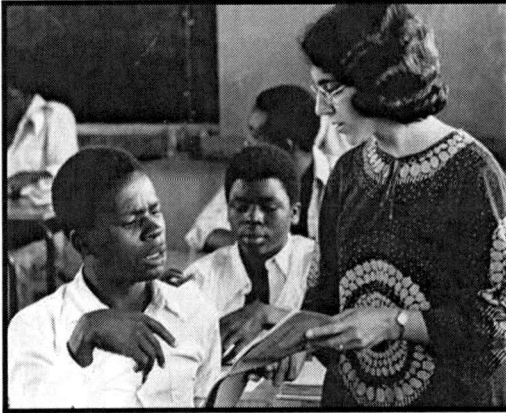
Sister Delphine Vasquez

When Maxine completed her three-year commitment as a papal volunteer and returned to the United States, Delphine joined Father Peréz in establishing a leadership-training program for seventy village catechists, including both men and women. They taught them basic leadership skills applicable to their work in the parishes and the villages at large. Some of these catechists later became leaders of their villages.

Forty years later, both Maxine and Delphine still remember the welcoming nature and generosity of the poor people of Ecuador despite the grinding poverty in which they lived. Their strong sense of family and their determination to improve their lives also remain etched in Maxine and Delphine's memories.

After four years as a papal volunteer in Ecuador, Delphine joined the Peace Corps and taught English as a foreign language to high school students and sex education to nurses in the Congo (Zaire), Africa. According to Delphine, the English class was an "open forum for discussion of the students' problems, conflicts, and opinions. They learned the meaning of injustice and how it affected their lives. They also learned how to work against injustice in the classroom, school and villages."

After four years in Zaire, Delphine returned to Ecuador as a Peace

Corp volunteer to teach high school. While there, she again worked in the leadership-training program for *campesinos*. She then moved to Panama and taught in multi-cultural schools for ten years. Her students included not only Panamanian students and children of Department of Defense and Diplomatic Corps personnel, but also students from Korea, Japan, and the Philippines.

From all of these experiences, Delphine gained a broadened understanding of the world, a greater sense of her own talents, and the opportunity to make a difference in the lives of the people she served. Delphine is a passionate teacher who believes that education is the key to lifting people up, whether they are *campesinos* in Ecuador, high school students in Zaire and Panama, immigrants in Washington, D.C., or the students she is now teaching in Davenport, Iowa. Delphine still thanks Bernadine for giving her the nudge and support to become a missionary in Ecuador.

# Caring for the Sick and Visiting the Imprisoned

While the Latin American missions were being established in the late 1960s and early 1970s, sisters in the United States continued or initiated new projects to serve low-income and other disadvantaged persons.

For 133 years, the Humilities have cared for the sick and dying in Ottumwa, Iowa. Shortly after arriving in Ottumwa in 1877, they opened their convent to mentally ill patients who had been discharged from the state hospital because of overcrowding. In 1880, they opened Tally Hospital to care for these patients and others who required general inpatient medical care. During the typhoid and smallpox epidemics of the 1880s, the sisters also served as home health workers, caring for the sick and comforting the dying in their homes while raising money for the medications necessary to treat these illnesses. In commenting on the sisters' work, the *Ottumwa Courier* in its December 19, 1890 issue wrote:

> The Sisters of Humility have been with us for twelve years. During that time, how many homes in the hour of their affliction have felt the benign effects of their presence? Race and creed are not considered when duty calls. Contagious diseases have no terror when duty calls them. They only seek to alleviate suffering under whatever form it may be, absolutely without money or price.[1]

In 1892, Tally Hospital closed when Wapello Country opened its own hospital. But in 1912, at the request of Ottumwa leaders, the sisters remodeled their convent and reopened it as St. Joseph's Hospital to relieve overcrowding in the existing community hospital. They replaced this small hospital with a modern one hundred-bed facility in 1926, and expanded it again in 1957 at the request of the Ottumwa community. In 1923, when she announced the fund drive for the one hundred-bed hospital, Mother Mary Liguori Ketterer, then the General Superior of the Sisters of Humility, said to the *Ottumwa Courier*, "We hope to build a hospital that will be a credit as well as a source of pride to Ottumwa. Our lives are short and uncertain, but the life of the community is permanent. We must build for the community and not ourselves."[2]

For seventy-five years, seventy Sisters of Humility staffed St. Joseph's Hospital before the merger in 1987 with the city hospital and its re-emergence as the Ottumwa Regional Health Center (ORHC). Even after the merger, seven sisters continued their work at ORHC until they retired. Two of them, Sisters Suzanne Wickenkamp and Kayleen Heffron, provided health care to the people in Ottumwa for a combined 114 years. Suzanne, a nurse and director of the school of nursing and chief executive officer of St. Joseph's hospital for forty-eight years, was one of the founders of ORHC. She remained in its leadership for twenty-two years to ensure that the regional health center continued the mission of caring for poor people without regard to their ability to pay and providing pastoral care for the sick and the dying. Kayleen served as a nurse at St. Joseph Hospital and ORHC for a total of forty-four years and currently provides pastoral care to people in Ottumwa at the Pennsylvania Place "retirement community."

Sisters Pat Miller, Kayleen Heffron and Suzanne Wickenkamp

Beginning in the early 1970s, other sisters trained as nurses served in other parts of the United States, as well as in Tunisia. For example, Sister Kathryn Doyle worked with the United Farm Workers in Calexico, California for two years before moving to Phoenix, Arizona where she served for sixteen years as a community-based nurse for migrant families who have babies with potential for developmental disabilities.

Sister Kathryn O'Meara served as a Project Hope nurse consultant at Charles Nicole Hospital in Tunis, Tunisia from 1971-72 when the country, which had achieved its independence in the mid-1960s, was in the early stages of developing schools of nursing. Kathryn helped develop a program for continuing education of nurses at the hospital, as well as established a model hypertension medical unit. In subsequent years, Kathryn served as a public health nurse for the Navajo Nation Health Foundation in Ganado, Arizona and as a family nurse practitioner in rural Georgia.

When she graduated from St. Joseph's School of Nursing, Kay Holland headed to Appalachia, where she worked at Mount Vernon Rock Castle County Baptist Hospital. Since joining the Humilities, she has served as a home health care nurse in Haver and Lewistown, Montana as well as in Davenport, Iowa. These women, like the Humility nurses who helped sustain St. Joseph's Hospital for seventy-five years, have responded to the needs of the communities in which they worked without regard to patients' ability to pay.


In addition to caring for the sick, other sisters in Ottumwa have cared for poor families and visited people who were incarcerated. Sister Matilda Herber for decades operated a one-person social work department among poor families. She quietly made her rounds visiting poor families to assess their needs and solicited donations from friends, family members, individual Sisters of Humility, and the community as a whole to meet their needs. She performed this service for years even when she held full time jobs, including serving as treasurer of the community.

At times, Matilda would take younger sisters with her on her visits. They delivered food, clothing, household goods and medicine, or provided money for rent. On one occasion, Matilda asked Sister Irene Muñoz to go with her to visit a poor, elderly woman in her home. They collected some blankets the woman had requested and when they arrived at the home, the woman was in bed looking very sick. Matilda pulled back the covers to put on the new blankets and found a large wound on her leg covered with maggots. Irene was shocked. Matilda gently assured the woman that she would send someone over to take care of the wound and that she would be all right. When she returned to the Heights, Matilda, true to her word, arranged for a home health nurse to evaluate and ensure proper treatment for the elderly woman's wound, saving the woman's life.

Another younger sister, Sister Mary Hilary Veith, a quiet, gentle woman who had served as a driver for the retired sisters at Ottumwa Heights for ten years, approached Matilda with a plan for starting her own ministry visiting prisoners at the county jail and disabled persons in halfway houses, nursing homes, and group homes in Ottumwa. Matilda went with Hilary to the county jail and introduced her to the sheriff, who agreed to the visitation plan.

Like Matilda, Hilary has quietly carried out her ministry of visiting prisoners and other poor persons in the community. Each week for forty-five years she has visited anyone in the four wards of the Wapello county jail who wished to talk to her. She treats the prisoners with respect as she listens to them and encourages them without judgment. In essence, she brings a bit of humanity into a dehumanizing penal system. When she visits the prisoners, she also gives puzzles, rosaries, and crosses and/or other gifts to any prisoner who wants them. A female inmate once reported to Hilary that she had seen some of "her boys" wearing crosses in court. Hilary just smiled.

On one of Hilary's visits to the jail, a large man named Chris approached her and told her he was not doing very well as he had just received a long sentence. Hilary asked him why he got such a long sentence. He replied, "I spit at the judge." Without skipping a beat, Hilary told him, "Chris, I have great hope for you and I will keep you in my prayers, but please stop spitting at the judge." Chris stopped spitting at the judge and was eventually released from jail. When discharged, he left a tribute to Hilary on the walls of his cell, "Sister Mary rules."

Many of the prisoners respond in kind to Hilary's gentle support of them. She has never felt at risk in the jail because she knows that the prisoners will always protect her. Not long ago, and to Hilary's surprise, the inmates collected money among themselves and gave her a gift of twenty dollars, quite a bit of money for them, to show their appreciation of her kindness. The City of Ottumwa has also declared her to be one of their outstanding citizens based upon her work in the jail.

In addition to her visits to prisoners confined in the Wapello County jail, Hilary keeps in touch with prisoners she met in the county jail, but who were subsequently transferred to the Fort Madison penitentiary or other prisons around the country. For nearly forty-five years, she has written on average thirty to thirty-five letters each month to these prisoners. Many of them write back or use their limited telephone privileges to call her. For many, she is their primary support.

Sister Mary Hilary Veith

But not everyone appreciated Hilary's work when she began her jail ministry. One of the sisters at Ottumwa Heights College complained to Bernadine about Hilary's visits to the jail. Bernadine took Hilary aside and asked her whether this was appropriate work for her. But Bernadine did not order her to stop and Hilary continued her work because she had been taught as a child that visiting the imprisoned is one of the corporal works of mercy. Years later, when Bernadine gave a talk to the community about her own experience tutoring prisoners in the Madison County jail, Hilary asked if she remembered advising her that her jail visiting program might not be a proper ministry. Bernadine candidly replied, "I was wrong and did not understand the value of jail ministry at the time."

When recently asked why she has continued to visit prisoners for forty-five years, Hilary replied, "I believe that God loves everyone no matter what they have done." After a pause, Hilary then explained how she describes this to her friends in the jail. "The bible," she said, "states that Jesus descended from the line of King David. But King David was not such a good man. According to the bible, he impregnated a married woman and then sent her husband to the front lines to be killed in battle."

Bernadine started tutoring prisoners in 1984 when she learned that women at the Iowa Correctional Institution for Women (ICIW) in Mitchellville needed tutors to help them complete a beginning algebra course offered by the Des Moines Area Community College. She and four other Sisters of Humility, Donna Schmitt, Alberta Ann Scott, Helen Strohman, and Cathy Talarico became tutors for the women, visiting them once a week for three months and helping sixteen women complete the class. When one of the inmates interviewed Bernadine for the prison newsletter about what she had learned from working with the women at the ICIW, Bernadine replied,

> We human beings impose punishment on people without realizing that the person is suffering enough already. Prisons are very punitive and some people are more fragile than others. I think we should realize that we are all sisters and brothers and treat one another accordingly.[3]

This 1984 tutoring program led to a long-term commitment to the women at ICIW by a number of Sisters of Humility who continue to live and work in Des Moines. For over fifteen years, Sisters Donna Schmidt and Cathy Talarico have taught a course on art and spirituality to the women at ICIW. The course allows the women to explore their own spirituality by giving it expression in their artwork. A variety of women, including those with life sentences or who suffer from drug addiction or mental illness, have participated in the course. Normally, between twelve and twenty-three women participate in each class and on some nights, Donna and Cathy have had to turn women away because the classroom was too small to accommodate them.

During their fifteen years teaching at Mitchellville, Donna and Cathy have observed the very different governing styles of four wardens. In more recent years, the state has focused the majority of its resources on modernization and expansion of the physical capacity of the prison to the detriment of programming and rehabilitation. As the state has decreased program staff, it now relies heavily on volunteers like Donna and Cathy to provide rehabilitative services to the women.

The number of mentally ill women imprisoned has also dramatically increased. Iowa, like many states, generally operates under a "lock them up" mentality rather than a "care and treat" philosophy. In this environment, Donna and Cathy's art and spirituality class has been one of the few opportunities for free expression and rehabilitation for many women confined at ICIW.

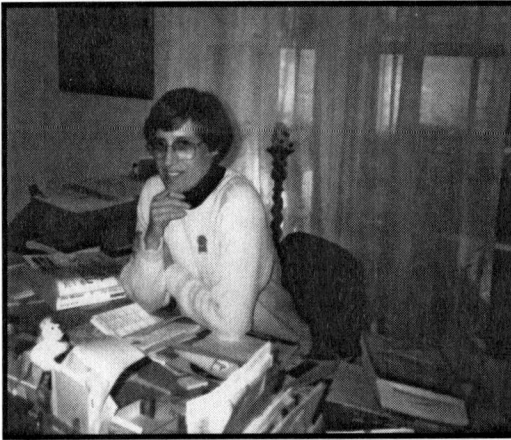

**Sister Cathy Talarico**

Recently, Cathy has joined another artist in offering a more traditional art course that is focused on helping the women develop their artistic talents. The class meets once a week and the students commit to completing the entire course, giving Cathy a greater opportunity to work with them over a longer period of time and increasing her ability to form a more personal relationship with them.

In 1989, Sister JoAnne Talarico, Cathy's sister, began to visit a young woman at ICIW who was serving a mandatory life term based on charges that she had been an accomplice to murder when she was only seventeen. As the story published in the *Des Moines Register* poignantly describes, JoAnne has continued to visit this woman, Christine Lockheart, for the past twenty-two years. Just as her relationship with Christine has deepened over the years, so too has her determination to change the Iowa law which authorizes life sentences without the possibility of parole for Class A felonies committed by youth fourteen and older.

## Nun seeks to free youths destined to die in prison

Twenty years ago, Sister JoAnne Talarico stepped inside a women's prison to visit someone she didn't know, and embarked on a journey and a relationship that would become driving forces for her life's work.

Talarico, 72, of Des Moines, is a nun with the Sisters of Humility of Mary in Davenport. Her commitment to social justice has taken her to El Salvador, seen her marching and speaking out for civil rights and advocating for homeless veterans.

But the relationship with a young female inmate named Christine Lockheart made her work personal, challenging basic assumptions about crime and punishment and giving her "the daughter I never had."

Talarico met Lockheart when she took over visiting the Mitchellville inmate after a nun who had been doing it moved away.

**Sister JoAnne Talarico**

She had never before been in a prison or known a criminal, and assumed whatever the young woman had done warranted the life sentence she got.

Lockheart was convicted of murder four years earlier at age 17. The victim was a man for whom she had cleaned house. Talarico says Lockheart hadn't anticipated the outcome when she accompanied her boyfriend to the victim's house to ask for a loan. They left when he said no, but the boyfriend went back in the house and stabbed him.

Lockheart didn't directly participate but also didn't immediately turn her boyfriend in. Iowa law permits accomplices to be charged and punished the same as the killers. It also requires mandatory life sentences for Class A felonies committed from age 14 on.

Twenty years of weekly visits to Lockheart, now nearly 42 years old, have convinced Talarico that's wrong. People under 18 can't even vote or drink or sign contracts, she notes. "They are children and should be treated as children in the criminal-justice system. They don't always see the consequences of their actions and are highly susceptible to peer pressures." And they can be reformed.

There are 44 people serving life sentences in Iowa who were under 18 when they committed their crimes. That's out of 2,225 in the 42 states with such laws. Amnesty International says 59 percent were first-time offenders. Many of those laws were passed in the 1980s by lawmakers responding to gang violence and wanting to be tough on crime, says Talarico.

She has watched an uncertain young woman mature into an articulate, creative mentor to others, getting scholarships and taking courses through the University of Iowa. "I'm inspired by the fact that she stays so positive. Sometimes I think maybe she does it just for me, but I see all the beautiful things she does ... I don't know that I could be as positive."

She adds, "My heart aches for her that one mistake just ruined her whole life." So Talarico is determined to get the law changed.

Nearly three years ago, she attended an Amnesty International conference in Des Moines and met others who shared her concerns. They formed the Iowa Coalition to Oppose Life Without the Possibility of Parole for Youth. Talarico spent most of the last session at the Capitol lobbying for a bill (HF 43, SF 74) that would allow work or parole releases for Class A felons who committed their crimes before turning 18. They'd have to serve 15 years before the parole board could consider, among other things, their age, maturity and susceptibility to outside pressures when the crimes were committed.

The bill never made it out of committee. Talarico believes lawmakers fear being seen as soft on crime when they're up for re-election, and 2010 is an election year.

Phyllis Stevens is the coalition's board president. "She's fabulous," she said of Talarico. "She's conversational. She brings a nice personal style to it, but she's also knowledgeable, not just a 'bleeding heart.'"

As a nun who believes in redemption, Talarico offers a compelling dimension to the debate, says Stevens. You wouldn't know it to see her, since she doesn't wear a habit. One legislator discovered it after his rather forceful outburst at a committee meeting, then apologized, red-faced, Stevens said. But Talarico wasn't bothered.

Asked whether her faith drives her to this cause, Talarico says, "It's a justice issue. In a way, I'm acting on my own but in accordance with our laws and beliefs and our mission to the world."

She answered the call to service at a time when people were drawn into lifetime commitments, she says. "I said 'forever' at one time, but I don't know that we live in a society where people want to do things forever."

So, ironically, someone who pledged a lifetime commitment to a calling has found her cause in helping undo a lifetime commitment imposed on someone else.

For Lockheart, the only way out of prison now would be a grant of clemency by the governor. She applied, unsuccessfully, in 2003.

But she's not giving up, and neither will Talarico, who hopes that as the coalition grows broader—especially with neurologists, psychologists and experts in the youthful brain —more lawmakers will listen.

"You just have to keep repeating over and over that we're dealing with children," says the former teacher. "Children sometimes do horrible things, but we cannot dispose of them."

Call it idealism, call it spiritual, call it the instinctive, compassionate response of an older person to a younger one in trouble. Or call it the Lord's work. Whatever you call it, Talarico's message is both profound and profoundly simple: Our youth are our future. We cannot afford to give up on them.

Basu: Dreamers & Doers series, by REKHA BASU. July 10, 2009. Copyright ©2009. All rights reserved. Printed with the permission of the *Des Moines Register.*

Across the state in the Quad Cities, Sister Nancy Schwieters in 1983 became a volunteer chaplain in the county jail after being confined for a week in a halfway house for a federal misdemeanor conviction arising out of her anti-war protests at the Moline, Illinois Arsenal, a major supplier of parts for tanks and other implements of war. Her experience with the people confined with her at the halfway house convinced her that they were the kind of people she wanted to serve.

In addition to her job as a fifth grade teacher at Holy Trinity School, Nancy served as a volunteer chaplain for ten years through a program sponsored by Churches United of the Quad Cities. She spent most of her time visiting prisoners, male and female, who chose to speak with her. She offered them friendship and encouragement.

**Sister Nancy Schwieters**

According to Nancy, she has a "lot of friends with pretty bad records." However, she believes it is important to refrain from judging them because "so often prisoners have been burned in life and need someone who believes in them to trust." Nancy's primary objective as a jail chaplain was simple: "To support the prisoners and let them know that they are worthwhile people."

One man Nancy encountered in the jail was considered so dangerous that the deputies would not transfer him to the regular visiting area. So Nancy went into the men's section of the jail, sat on the floor in front of this man's cell, and visited with him through his meal slot. She was not afraid of him, nor was he threatening in any way to her—they connected as human beings.

Many of the women in the jail were serving time for prostitution and drug use. Most of these women had a history of sexual or physical abuse, lacked education or training to secure alternative employment, and suffered from poor self-images. Nancy and Churches United established a shelter, as well as weekly support groups to help the women develop confidence and get jobs necessary for them to succeed in the community.

While these three examples of jail ministries in Ottumwa, Mitchellville, and the Quad Cities are different in form, they reflect the Humilities' core belief that prisoners, considered by many in society to be "the least among us," are worthy of the support and care they need to improve their lives.

# Training Med Techs to Care for
# Their Own Communities

In the early 1970s, Sister Marie Vittetoe substantially changed the course of her life. She had for twenty years served as a medical technologist and laboratory supervisor at St. Joseph's hospital and taught at the hospital's School of Nursing and the Ottumwa School of Medical Technology. But in 1971, she set out to develop programs to train and provide incentives for health professionals to provide care for their own people in rural, underserved communities. Over the next forty years, Marie developed and implemented such programs in rural areas of the United States and in the Caribbean.

Marie knew that she had to upgrade her professional credentials to carry out this plan, so she pursued both a masters and PhD degree in Education at West Virginia University. She then became an Assistant Professor and Division Chair of the Health Occupations Teacher Education Program (HOTEP) at the University of Illinois. From 1973 to 1978, while administering the division and teaching a regular on-campus class load, Marie traveled the state teaching night classes to prepare health professionals as teachers who, in turn, trained local practitioners to improve health services in their rural communities.

At the University of Kentucky College of Allied Health Professions, where she served as Professor and Department Chair of Clinical Laboratory Sciences from 1978 to 1994, Marie helped implement a multi-disciplinary Area Health Education System. This system provides state-wide off-site clinical experiences for medical, dental, nursing, pharmacy, and allied health students, including mandatory clinical rotations in rural or underserved communities. These mandatory rotations have both improved health care in rural communities and encouraged students to serve in these communities after completing their degree programs.

In addition, Marie and her colleagues established a medical technology program within the Allied Health Education Center in Hazard, a small isolated mining community in the mountains of Kentucky. The Center allows students and existing health care providers living in the rural area surrounding Hazard to access on-site educational programs and participate in distance learning courses being taught at the main campus in Lexington. Over the years, the University of Kentucky has added seven more AHEC Centers in other rural or underserved areas of Kentucky. These regional programs have substantially increased access to health care services in underserved areas of the state and empowered rural people to provide the necessary health care services to citizens of their own communities.

**Sister Marie Vittetoe at Hôpital Sacré Coeur in Milot, Haiti**

In 1985, Marie spent several months of her sabbatical year volunteering for Project HOPE in Haiti as a consultant to the University of Haiti Medical Technology programs in Port au Prince and Cap Haitian. While she found Haitian students eager to learn, the University lacked the equipment necessary to teach basic laboratory skills. The Medical Technology program had no laboratory, no microscopes, and no books for its students. To remedy this intolerable situation, Marie bought books for the students and secured donated laboratory supplies and equipment from St. Joseph's School of Nursing and colleagues with whom she had worked in the United States. Marie also worked with the new pathologist at the University of Haiti to organize a small laboratory using the equipment and supplies she secured.

Marie's consultant role at the University ended in 1987 when a coup destabilized the country and prevented her from traveling to Haiti. During her flight back to the United States, Marie described her work to a fellow passenger who was doing film work in Haiti. When she explained that the medical technology students at the University of Haiti still lacked the equipment necessary to study blood cell and microbial organisms, he donated a projector.

During her 1992 sabbatical, Marie again worked in the Caribbean. This time she volunteered in laboratories and taught medical technology in St. Lucia, Barbados, Guyana, and Jamaica. Based upon her assessments of the four programs, Marie chose Guyana and Jamaica as most in need of instruction and mentoring to upgrade their programs. Both countries lacked the equipment and trained medical technologists needed to properly operate hospital laboratories, so she concentrated her efforts in these two programs.

In December 1999, five years after she retired from the University of Kentucky, Marie received a telephone call from Dr. Ted Dubuque, a surgeon in St. Louis who in 1986 was the first medical volunteer to arrive at Hôpital Sacré Coeur (HSC) in Milot, Haiti after construction of the hospital. The Brothers of the Sacred Heart, as part of their Center for Rural Development of Milot mission, built HSC near Cap Hatien, seventy miles north of Port au Prince. In the same year, Dr. Dubuque and his childhood friend, Carlos Reese, formed the CRUDEM Foundation, a 501(c) 3 organization to provide financial and other support for HSC. For sixteen years, Dr. Dubuque served as a volunteer surgeon at the hospital. He stayed six months that first year, but in subsequent years he made at least four visits a year, performing surgeries for weeks or months at a time.

In his initial telephone conversation with Marie, Dr. Dubuque said, "This is Dr. Ted Dubuque from CRUDEM and I wonder if you could come and help us improve our laboratory in Haiti? The lab results at the hospital are so bad they are incompatible with life."

As Marie had never met Dr. Dubuque nor heard of CRUDEM, she wondered how Dr. Dubuque found her. He explained that when he had unsuccessfully sought assistance from various religious communities to improve the functioning of the HSC laboratory in Milot, he contacted Project HOPE. He learned from the director that Marie had taught medical technology to students at the University of Haiti in Port au Prince in 1985 and might be willing to volunteer to help improve the laboratory at HSC. Marie, while listening to Dr. Dubuque, thought, "Is this God calling?" She answered the call.

In early spring 2000, Marie made her first trip to HSC in Milot. The hospital at the time was a forty-bed inpatient facility with outpatient clinics serving thirty thousand patients per year. The CRUDEM Foundation then and now recruits teams of volunteer medical specialists, including dentists, orthopedists, urologists, surgeons, gynecologists, nurses, and other clinical specialists like Marie who travel at their own expense from the United States and Canada on a scheduled basis throughout the year for weeks or months at a time to provide specialty care and to educate the local practitioners. One of the founding principles of the hospital is that it must empower the Haitian people to care for themselves. As a result of this program, today the hospital is administered and staffed primarily by trained Haitian personnel and provides the full array of public health services to the region's population of 225,000 people.

HSC also provides extensive community health services in the five "communes" in the Milot region, and in the spring of 2005, it began operating a Red Cross blood bank which serves patients at the hospital, area dispensaries, and at a smaller area hospital. At the time of the earthquake in 2010, the blood bank was a life-saving resource for hundreds of severely injured patients.

At the time of Marie's first visit in 2000, HSC's laboratory was located in an old house on the HSC property. The lab was much too small and lacked essential basic equipment: not even a functional refrigerator or a distilled water source. It was also cockroach infested, had a compromised sanitary environment due to dust blowing in open windows, and other substandard hygienic conditions.

Marie performed a complete evaluation of the laboratory and the skill levels of the staff, which she reported to Dr. Dubuque. When asked by the laboratory technicians what she would be doing, she told them that she would first evaluate the laboratory's needs before setting forth a complete plan. But she also told them that a central focus of her work would be to help them develop the necessary knowledge and technical skills to correctly do the required laboratory tests.

Marie found the original group of nine laboratory technicians easy to teach. They were eager to learn and extremely appreciative of her efforts. She began by teaching formal classes on hematology, chemistry, and serology as well as techniques at bench side. In the subsequent decade, Marie made approximately twenty-five trips to Haiti and executed her philosophy "to teach and go so that the students can implement what they have been taught." Using this method, she upgraded the skills of the original technicians and trained six additional laboratory technicians hired by HSC in subsequent years. To this day, one of the technicians always greets Marie with the question, "What new technique or laboratory test are you going to teach us this time?"

Based in part on Marie's evaluation of the laboratory, Dr. Dubuque secured a $100,000 grant from the Flatley Foundation to construct a new laboratory and an architect to work on the plans with Marie. The architect knew of another lab that was getting all new cabinetry, so HSC inherited their old cabinets. With newly fabricated counter tops, the lab was ready for occupancy, but had nothing of value to move into it. Just then Marycrest International University closed and Marie secured from the college free equipment and furniture necessary to equip the HSC lab. She also bought from the University of Iowa Surplus Store two refrigerators and other lab furnishings, including chairs, desks and white boards, at a very low cost. Through her contacts in clinical laboratory science programs, she obtained donated books, slides, teaching materials, and a dual-headed microscope. A manufacturer of automated cell counters donated an old counter, which greatly increased the volume and accuracy of cell counts, and she purchased semi-automated chemistry instruments with donations from several sources.

After gathering the equipment and furnishings for the laboratory, Marie rented a truck in Iowa and with another Sister of Humility, Rebecca Dobbels, drove the equipment and furnishings to the Port of Fort Lauderdale for shipment to Haiti. Once the equipment and furnishings arrived in Haiti, Marie went to Haiti and organized the lab.

On October 25, 2002, the HSC community held a dedication ceremony for the new laboratory, a nutrition center for poor children, and a "mission house" for guests. Consistent with Haitian culture, the day was filled with a blessing ceremony conducted by the Chancellor of the Cap-Haitian Catholic Archdiocese followed by tributes to Marie and Dr. Dubuque, other speeches, a great feast, and singing and dancing.

By 2008, the HSC laboratory had the basic equipment and trained staff necessary to meet the needs of the hospital's mission at the time. The volume of laboratory testing had increased from twenty thousand tests in 2000 to seventy-eight thousand tests in 2008. At age eighty-one, Marie thought her work at HSC was finished. But no successor had yet been found, so she continued her work on behalf of HSC. The laboratory could not function without a knowledgeable person in the U.S. to order supplies and to do onsite consults in Haiti to follow up on many facets of the laboratory's operations.

During the years that Marie served as a consultant to HSC, she also provided similar services for ten other labs in northern Haiti and was an International Training Center for Health (I-TECH) curriculum consultant for the Med Tech Education project at the National Public Health Laboratory (NPHL) of Haiti.


The earthquake, which struck Haiti on January 12, 2010, severely tested the quality of HSC, including its laboratory. The hospital, a sixty-bed facility when the earthquake hit, became a major trauma center of four hundred-plus beds within a week. Because HSC was one of the few existing Haitian hospitals standing after the earthquake, the CRUDEM Foundation board members, Caritas Christi, Project HOPE, and individual volunteers, including Marie, sprang into action to secure the additional medical, nursing, rehabilitation, and allied heath staff, supplies, and equipment necessary to respond to the horrific disaster.

Marie called her cousin, David Vittetoe, MD in Des Moines, Iowa and asked him to go to Haiti to provide emergency orthopedic care. Within two days of Marie's request, Dr. Vittetoe and another orthopedic surgeon from Des Moines, Dr. Matthew De Wall, were on a plane bound for Haiti. A third surgeon, Dr. Jon Gehrke and a surgical tech, from Iowa Health, Damir Mujic, followed two days later. As soon as they arrived, they started work immediately as the number of people with very severe injuries was overwhelming.

Two hours after doctors from the French government field hospital in Port au Prince and the U.S. Navy evaluated the HSC facilities and staff capabilities, helicopters transporting ten patients each began arriving and continued to deliver patients injured by the earthquake for months. According to Dr. Gehrke, HSC received the most severely injured patients because it had the surgery and rehabilitation system necessary to handle the severe injuries.[1]

The local residents of Milot did everything in their power to support the hospital. They organized triage areas outside where patients were lined up by the dozens, transported patients from helicopters to the hospital, turned over two schools to the hospital to accommodate the increasing number of patients, and performed necessary tasks such as cooking, washing, and comforting patients who had no relatives.[2]

HSC treated over five hundred earthquake victims transferred from Port au Prince and volunteer doctors performed seven hundred major surgeries in the first three months of the year, compared to 1316 the entire previous year. Throughout these three months, one thousand volunteer medical providers came to HSC from all over the US and Canada to help.

One of the real crises was how to expand the bed capacity at HSC from sixty to four hundred to meet the demand. Caritas Christi, after failing to get military tents to meet the need, found a commercial tent supplier who provided the necessary tents at a forty percent discount and delivered them in a week's time. In addition, Philips Healthcare donated new monitors for the OR, ICU, PACU, the ward/floor, and all the ancillary areas as well as C-arm X-ray machines, twenty respirators, an ultrasound machine, and eight full ventilators. On top of that, Phillips sent technicians to set up the equipment. Angelica, a healthcare linen supplier, provided the clean hospital gowns, bed linen, and towels to ensure that all the patients were treated in a sanitary and dignified manner. Siemens sent water purification systems, blood gas instruments, ultrasound, and laundry equipment. Sanyo donated two new refrigerators for the blood bank, lab reagents, and an upright freezer.[3]

One of the most touching contributions came from a group of homeless people at the St. Patrick Center for the Homeless in St. Louis. When they heard about the earthquake in Haiti, they wanted to do something to make a difference. One of the homeless persons suggested holding a bake sale, and Helping Hearts Cookies for Haiti emerged. A local baking company contributed the dough and supervised the homeless people, who mixed the dough and baked the cookies. The homeless people and community volunteers packaged and sold more than thirty thousand cookies. Volunteers from several local companies passed out more than fifteen thousand Helping Hearts Cookies at a St. Louis Blues game, with all donations given to Haitian earthquake relief efforts. On February 22, 2010, homeless persons from St. Patrick Center gave fifty-seven thousand dollars they helped raised to the CRUDEM Foundation for HSC.[4]

During the first three months following the earthquake, Marie was busy raising money and soliciting medical volunteers for HSC through the CHM website, speeches, and direct contacts with colleagues. She pointed out in all these appeals the hospital's significant need for money to feed eight hundred people a day, pay the freight costs to transport the food to Haiti, secure medical supplies, and cover the payroll for the Haitian HSC staff. Marie purchased mattresses and bedding with donations to meet the needs posed by the quickly expanding hospital population and secured additional donated equipment for the laboratory.

The hospital laboratory, with its existing staff plus one additional person, handled all the required laboratory tests and blood transfusions during the three-month peak of the medical emergency caused by the earthquake. The laboratory staff worked long hours, sometimes through the night, to meet the very high demand for a broad spectrum of tests because they felt it was better to do the work themselves than trying to teach others how to do all the procedures properly. As they reported to Marie, they worked together as a team drawing and cross-matching blood for transfusions, searching the hospital, the auxiliary hospital tents and schools to find the patients on whom tests were ordered, determining which tests had priority, and doing them competently as doctors waited for results. In the first three months of 2010, they performed 29,648 tests on 7,255 patients, 7,107 more tests than they had performed in the first quarter of 2009. According to Marie, "They proved in this time of crisis that their laboratory was in fact the best little laboratory in all of Haiti."

In June 2010, Marie returned to Haiti to check on the status of Haiti generally and the laboratory staff at HSC in particular. She listened to the laboratory technicians' stories of the heroic efforts they and others at the hospital made to save the lives of hundreds of earthquake victims. She told them how proud she was of their ability to function as a competent, committed team in a period of enormous stress and trauma.

In addition, the laboratory had received more donated equipment during the crisis and the staff had not had time to integrate it all into the laboratory. Marie helped to organize the new equipment and recycle the old. She also reviewed the construction plan for expansion of the laboratory to accommodate the new tests for the HIV/AIDS program, which had commenced several years before the earthquake. She found the plan deficient in many ways and redesigned it to guide the reconstruction of the laboratory.

Marie returned again to Haiti in May 2011 to make certain that the expansion of the laboratory was constructed consistent with her design and that it would in fact advance the hospital's new role in Haitian society as a laboratory reference center, a trauma and HIV/AIDS treatment center, as well as a community hospital. Prior to this 2011 trip, Marie recruited a highly qualified medical technologist, Treasa Smith, as her possible successor in Haiti. To protect the progress made in the HSC laboratory, Marie knew that she would have to find a person committed to the mission and possessing the values and skills necessary to help the HSC laboratory continue to improve. Treasa accompanied Marie on the May trip, spending several weeks at HSC meeting the staff and experiencing the milieu of the hospital and lab. During this trip, Marie and CRUDEM President Dr. Peter Kelly concluded that Treasa was the appropriate successor for Marie. Treasa has now spent many months working with the laboratory staff in Haiti and will return on a regular basis. So, Marie, in the tradition of the Humilities, turned over to Treasa the "best little laboratory in Haiti."

Many of the volunteers who treated patients at the HSC immediately after the earthquake and during the many years Marie worked in Haiti refer to their experiences as "life changing." Marie's ten years in northern Haiti were for her a whole series of life changing experiences. According to her, every day presented reminders of life's true meaning and the opportunity "to meditate on one's own purpose and how to fulfill it, to thank God for one's gifts and the ability to use them, to praise God for the beauty of the people and all creation, to admire the poor and their acceptance of dire circumstances . . . and to ask God's blessing on this poor traumatized nation."

But Marie also experienced great joys in Haiti. Through the years, she has met hundreds of Haitians who have demonstrated dignity, resilience, great faith, and strength in the face of enormous adversity. One such person is the young man she befriended when he served as her guide in Port au Prince in 1985. As a result of the earthquake, he lost the home she had helped him to build. For the past year, he and his family have been living in a tattered tent. But after receiving the money she sent him to help buy water and food for his family and those in nearby tents, he wrote to Marie in his self-taught English on December 3, 2010:

Dear Sister Vittetoe,

Dear shepherd,

Thanks full for this spiritual love.

I thank God for loving me because is only Him who can do that.

Your contact is something for me who from right away to God and I'm sure is an amazing grace.

I'm really can't explain me to say thank you dear Sister, like I'm usually said my vocabulary is to poor that I'm really can't find the right, the correct word to say thank you.

Let me tell you, shepherd that thanks to God I'm still be, I'm still living. I take much precaution to avoid the Cholera because I know many people who are already have it and some of them are die.

As you know it the life is so very wrong for us down here but as you and I know and believe it—Jesus never leave his children by themselves.

Thanks a lot shepherd for your prayer, your psalm, your deep support so keep praying for me because the thing is no good at all and I'm really need you close, specially your prayer. May God in his abundant love bless you abundantly shepherd. I love you much.

Sincerely, Jerry

During her years in Haiti, Marie also had the privilege to work side-by-side with Christians, Jews, Muslims, and agnostics who put cultural and religious differences aside in order to work together to better the lives of the people of Haiti. The motto "Live simply so others may simply live" became a daily reality to her and her coworkers in Haiti and she continues to live by it today.'

# Making Values the Heart of Education

Throughout her ten years in office, Bernadine urged the sisters to think globally when determining how they might use their talents and resources to help shape the future of the world. She believed that to become an effective force in changing the world, you had to become informed about emerging issues throughout the world. To stimulate interest in these issues, Bernadine's letters to the community highlighted war and peace in various parts of the world; the crises in India, Pakistan, and Africa in which millions of women and children faced starvation; the effects on third world countries of the energy crisis in 1974; the need for structural reforms in both developed and developing countries to advance peace and justice, and ecological disasters caused by unchecked industrial development. She also set aside funds for continuing education of the sisters and urged them to utilize the community's seed grant fund to develop new methods of teaching to make ethics and values the heart of their educational process.

Since the community's renewal in the 1960s, the majority of the sisters have continued to serve as teachers, but they have broadened the focus and methods of their teaching as well the diversity of their students. Understanding that their students in the twenty-first century will live in a world with far fewer boundaries and operate in a global economy, the sisters have created educational environments to help students understand their place in the world, have the skills to navigate a more complex world, and become citizens who strive to make the world a better place for all people.

Some, like Sister Micheline Curtis, have made issues of justice and peace integral to the school curriculum on a par with traditional subjects. For twenty-five years, Micheline taught at Montini High School in Lombard, Illinois, a Christian Brother's school that combines a rigorous college prep curriculum with a strong emphasis on social justice.

Although the majority of the Montini students are from more affluent families, lower income students constitute ten to fifteen percent of the student body. Their education is subsidized by proceeds from an annual fundraiser and contributions from benefactors, including more affluent parents of other students in the school. Like many metropolitan area schools, a significant number of Montini students are members of single parent or blended families and many also have problems with drugs or alcohol.

During her tenure at Montini, Micheline served as the justice coordinator for the school. One of the programs she helped create, Rainbows for All God's Children, was a support group for students in single parent or blended families, which allowed them to share their stories and learn from other students in similar families. In addition, the program offered parents interactive forums on issues common in single parent or blended families. To provide drug and alcohol addiction prevention for the at-risk students at Montini, Micheline established a cooperative program with a local hospital.

**Sister Micheline Curtis**

When Micheline first arrived at Montini, she noticed that the school provided more programs for boys than girls, with virtually no athletic programs for girls. Although all students took college prep courses, the girls often had no real career plans other than getting married and having children. Micheline and the other women on the faculty decided to remedy these problems by establishing competitive sports programs for female students and a counseling program that helped them appreciate each other more, gain confidence in their own abilities, and plan professional careers.

Micheline taught history and chaired the combined social studies, economics, and history department. In consultation with the teachers in the department, she developed a four-year curriculum with core courses in global studies, geography, history, and economics. She also developed a course for junior and senior high school students called "Justice in the Modern World," in which students explored issues such as the disparity of wealth among nations and peoples, how consumption of natural resources affects developing countries, the criminal justice system, issues of war and peace, and race relations in the United States.

With a Humilities seed grant, Micheline developed a community-based program, which allowed students to study justice issues in real life. The students went to court hearings, halfway houses, poor inner city neighborhoods, and an Illinois prison. As many students had never been in central Chicago before, let alone poor inner-city neighborhoods, they had to learn how to find and transport themselves to these places. Once they mastered navigating the city, they began to learn first hand the substandard conditions in which many low-income residents live, as well as the problems in the criminal justice system. To facilitate the students' understanding of their experiences in the inner city as well as other justice issues, Micheline developed a Justice Resource Center of books, periodicals, and other resource materials with more seed grant funding from the Humilities.

Through Micheline's leadership, the school also offered programs to encourage students to become contributors to their city. Montini held hunger awareness events in concert with the annual Campaign for Human Development sponsored by the U.S. Bishops' Conference. The students also sponsored food and clothing drives for a Chicago inner city parish. Student weekly collections yielding five to six thousand dollars a year supported direct service projects for poor people. Every year, the Montini students provided inner-city families Christmas celebrations, including food and gifts for each member of the family. Students were able to meet people they would not otherwise have known and learned the value of reaching out to help others. As a result of these experiences, some students began volunteering in other projects serving poor or disadvantaged people.

While many parents appreciated the school's emphasis on social justice, some did not. One parent unhappy with Micheline's emphasis on social justice stated on a parent survey that the school should "get rid of that history teacher." When told of this comment, Micheline said, "I must be doing this job right."


Another Humility sister, Roberta Brich, set out to change the entire educational structure in which children are taught. With a seed grant from the Humilities, Roberta researched alternative education systems in the United States. Through her research, Roberta identified an experimental program, Individual Education, in its implementation phase at a Catholic elementary school in Wahiawa, Hawaii on the island of Oahu. She went to Hawaii to learn about the program and, in the process, received a two and a half year internship to help implement it.

As Roberta explained to the community, Individual Education is a philosophy of life as applied to education. One of the primary goals of this system is to help students on an individual basis develop a sense of belonging, which allows them to live a cooperative life. It does so by providing a supportive environment for each student to learn and become a more responsible, respectful, responsive, and resourceful person.

The following principles underlie this system:

- Students learn responsibility by making choices, including about whether to learn or not and when, where, and what they will learn. Students also learn responsibility by making choices regarding their teachers, counselors, and friends. By making these choices, they also learn from experiencing the consequences of such choices.

- Students learn respect by being allowed to make decisions that are rightfully theirs to make and by being trained to recognize and accept the decision areas belonging to others. Clear agreements and consequences set up ahead of time and consistently adhered to are essential for the development of this mutual respect.

- Students become resourceful when they develop a sense that they can do what is necessary in a situation and that they have the ability to control their own lives. Resourcefulness is also fostered by a challenging academic curriculum presented in an exciting and creative learning environment, which gives each student an opportunity to operate in a more unstructured environment.

- Responsiveness develops when a student experiences being heard and, in turn, is encouraged and trained to hear others.

After working with the program in Hawaii for two and a half years, Roberta received a call from Father Lawrence Beeson in Neola, Iowa, Roberta's hometown. Neola is a small town in southwestern Iowa with

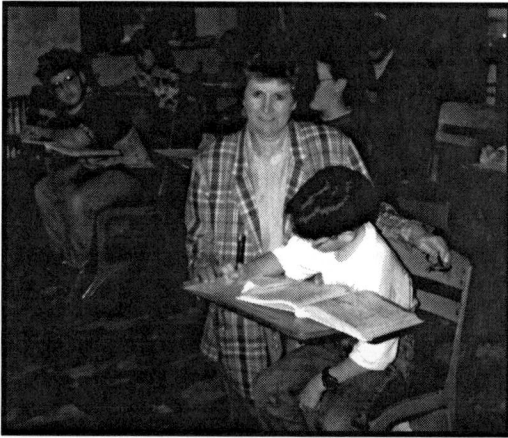

Sister Roberta Brich

a population of fewer than a thousand people. The Sisters of Humility had taught at St. Joseph's school in Neola since the school's founding in 1891. Father Beeson told Roberta that St. Joseph's was on the verge of closure and asked her to become the principal of the

school in order to save it. Roberta, believing that Neola would be a good place to test out the Individual Education program, wrote to Father Beeson, the Des Moines Diocesan Education Department, and St. Joseph's school board explaining the Individual Education system and describing her interest in bringing it to Neola. Father Beeson invited Roberta to come to Neola to describe her proposed change in the educational system offered at St. Joseph's to the parents and students.

In February 1977, Roberta conducted a series of parent, student, and teacher study groups in Neola in which she described the philosophy, theory, and practice of the Individual Education system. In her discussions with parents, Roberta explained that they would be essential participants in this educational system, and some or all of them may be required to change their way of interacting with their children in order to comply with the basic agreements which underlie the program. While some parents initially expressed concerns about this new system of education, their initial resistance dissipated as their understanding of the program grew.

Roberta also described the proposed educational system to existing students at St. Joseph's. She emphasized to the students the following basic agreements, which serve as the foundation for the program:

- Each student will do nothing that could harm him/herself, others, or school property;
- Each student will at all times engage in his/her own individual educational program, either in his/her homeroom, an alternative classroom, or library and
- If a student violates either of the first two agreements, the teacher will give the student the "go signal" by pointing at the student and then at the door. The student must then quickly and quietly leave the room.

The student's exit from the classroom avoids power struggles and signals to the student that he or she has breached one of the basic

St. Joseph School in Neola

agreements. After the student has left the room as directed, he or she may return and resume his/her program in the same classroom, or may go to another classroom, or to the library. If the teacher in another classroom refuses the student admission to the classroom, the student has to find another classroom or go to the library. Any student who wishes to dispute the basis for being required to leave the class has the opportunity to do so individually with the teacher when he/she returns to the classroom or during their weekly meeting.

Roberta also explained to the students that, prior to becoming a participant in the Individual Education system, they would each also have to agree to the following system of progressive consequences for breaching any of the three basic agreements:

- If a student breaks any of the agreements three times, the student and the homeroom teacher meet to review the agreements and see if there is something that the student does not understand about the agreements
- If a student breaks any of the agreements three more times, the student, teacher and principal meet to discuss the agreements and any problems the student may have in complying with them
- If a student then breaks any of the agreements three more times, the parents will be called and informed about the student's pattern of behavior. During this call, the parents are reminded that if the student breaks any of the agreements again, the consequence will be that the student will be sent home and he/she is to go to his/her room and remain there for the rest of the day, except for meals and bathroom breaks. The parents are not to punish the student or talk about the reasons he/she was sent home. The student then returns to school the next day
- If a student continues to break any of the agreements, he/she is sent home and the same procedures apply.

Roberta emphasized to the students the importance of the individual weekly meeting between each student and his or her teacher. At the initial meeting, the student and the teacher develop the student's individual education plan and, at subsequent meetings, they continue to review the plan and make any changes necessary. They also have the opportunity at these meetings to give and receive feedback from one another regarding the actual implementation of the plan.

Roberta also spent time in February 1977 educating the school's existing teachers about the Individual Education program, determining their interest in and ability to work in such a program, and their willingness to undergo the necessary training to effectively implement the program.

As a result of these meetings, the Board of St. Joseph's School voted unanimously to implement the Individualized Education program. The board hired Roberta as principal of St. Joseph's school and Sister Rosalind ("Rosie") Restelli, a trained Individual Education teacher, to help implement the program in Neola beginning in August 1977. While most students chose to regularly attend their grade level classes, a few opted to study individually in the library or to study in alternative classrooms. The teachers tested all students in each of their subjects every Friday to determine whether they were progressing at the level expected in each subject. If a student was not progressing, the teacher and student decided jointly what additional teacher assistance or changes by the student were necessary for the student to improve his or her mastery of the academic subjects or behavioral goals.

The Individual Education program created the peaceful environment that allowed students to learn and develop individual responsibility, respect for themselves, responsiveness to others, and increased resourcefulness. During the seventeen years of its operation, students were seldom sent home more than once. In the few cases in which a student was sent home more than once, Roberta usually discovered that the parents were not keeping their part of the agreements by talking to the student about the reasons why he/she had been sent home or punishing the student for his/her breach of the agreement(s). Except for these few cases, parents abided by and appreciated the Individual Education system. Some of them implemented the agreements and consequences system in their homes as well. During those years, the Individual Education program formed the core of St. Joseph's educational environment and both students and the school thrived.

From their teaching experience in Neola, Roberta and Rosie learned to appreciate the determination of parents in rural communities to ensure that their children learn discipline and receive a good education. Their experience in Neola also deepened Roberta and Rosie's belief in the importance of the Humilities' commitment to provide students in rural areas the same innovative educational opportunities available in larger towns and cities.

In 1994, when St. Joseph's school closed due to the lack of sufficient numbers of school age children to maintain both the Catholic and public schools, Rosie remained in Neola to continue serving the people of Neola as a pastoral minister. By doing so, she is continuing the tradition of 102 Humilities before her who have served the people of Neola for the past 121 years.

Another gifted teacher was Sister Camille Clark, whose specialty was helping "those who get lost in the shuffle of life." For sixteen years, she cared for and taught children at the St. Vincent's Home in Davenport, Iowa, an orphanage and school renowned for excellence in education.

**Sisters Camille Clark and Luz María Orozco**

St. Vincent's at the time was a laboratory school in which Camille helped train Marycrest and St. Ambrose students to become teachers.

In the 1970s, Camille became an alcohol and drug abuse counselor for troubled youth, unwed mothers, and adults down on their luck. In 1977, she helped establish New Hope Lodge for women with addictions and in 1985 began working at Beacon House, a halfway house for men addicted to drugs or alcohol. She was the lead counselor at both facilities. In the late 1980s, she became the addictions counselor for the Mercer County Addictions Office, a treatment program for persons found guilty of driving under the influence of alcohol. Camille was herself a recovering alcoholic with over thirty years of sobriety, so she understood people who simply need someone to help them understand that

185

"their worth comes from inside."

An optimist by nature, Camille spread cheer wherever she went. Through her special affinity for persons suffering from addiction and her ability to connect with almost anyone, she raised the spirits and improved the fortunes of hundreds of her clients. Her clients recognized and responded to her magic touch. One of her clients at Beacon House painted her portrait with a magic wand in her hand. Another resident who could not accept her alcoholism said of her, "Camille reached out and grabbed hold of my heart. And no one had ever gotten that close to me before."[1]

At an age when most teachers retire, Camille joined the faculty at Black Hawk College in Moline, Illinois. She started teaching education courses, but when the college needed someone to help prepare students who had never completed high school to take the General Education Diploma tests, she volunteered. She also volunteered to facilitate the Student Development Workshop, a one-to-one tutoring program for students who read at between the first and eighth grade levels and were on a waiting list for the regular tutoring service at the college. Camille formed such a bond with these students that they often remained in the workshop even after being accepted in the regular tutoring program.

During her years at Black Hawk College, Camille also taught English as a second language and citizenship classes to new immigrants. She did so, she said, in order "to be the cheerleader for those who want to get their General Education Diplomas and those who want to become citizens of this great nation." According to Camille, "The immigrants were among the most motivated and hardest working students I ever taught. They were focused on improving their own lives and the lives of their families."[2]

In recognition of Camille's five decades of work as an educator, including her work promoting literacy among immigrants and people without high school educations, the Bi-State Literacy Council for Iowa and Illinois created the Sister Camille Clark Award for Exemplary Service. This award is given annually to educators demonstrating a continuing dedication to promoting literacy and being a role model for others.

# Taking Back the Church through
# Non-Violent Resistance

In the early 1970s, two Humility educators, Sisters Caridad Inda and Kathryn Bissell, while working in Washington, D.C. identified the need for increased bilingual and multicultural staff in hospitals, churches, jails, courts, and government offices to deal with the growing number of non-English speaking immigrants. To respond to this need, they established the Center for International Resources, Inc. (CIRIMEX) in Guadalajara, México.

CIRIMEX is a one-on-one, total immersion Spanish language and culture-training program for U.S. professionals, especially those in "confidence professions" such as priests, lawyers, doctors, nurses, and counselors. The program provides not only intensive Spanish language training but also immersion of students in the Hispanic culture by integrating students with Spanish speaking families in Guadalajara and using the city of Guadalajara as its language laboratory.

During the past forty years, seminarians, priests, and other staff of Catholic churches in the United States have made up the majority of the CIRIMEX student population. While studying at CIRIMEX, they become involved in the sacramental life of Guadalajara Catholic churches as well as outreach programs through these churches to the surrounding community. Through this experience, they learn how Spanish-speaking people experience the church in their homeland and thus become better able to serve their Hispanic and Latino parishioners in the U.S. They also develop an understanding of and compassion for the plight of immigrants as well as the skills necessary to help immigrants integrate into parish and/or community life in the U.S.

While CIRIMEX is an effective training program for church personnel who minister to Hispanic and Latino persons, the numbers of such staff sent by the Catholic Church to CIRIMEX or similar Spanish language training programs do not begin to prepare enough Spanish speaking church personnel to meet the needs of the large numbers of immigrants and other Catholics in the church whose primary language is Spanish. According to the U.S. Conference of Catholic Bishops (USCCB), almost half of the members of the U.S. Catholic Church are Hispanic or Latino people, and their numbers are expected to increase. However, according to the 2011 report of the Hispanic Affairs Division of the USCCB, only twenty percent of the Catholic parishes in the United State have Hispanic/Latino ministries. Although Caridad, Kathryn, and other advocates for Hispanic and Latino Catholics have repeatedly advised the leaders of the U.S. Catholic Church of the need for more Spanish-speaking ministers, they have largely been ignored.

In 1972, Caridad, an experienced linguist and translator, served as the official English translator of the Position Papers and Conclusions promulgated at the 1968 Second General Conference of Latin American Bishops in Medellin, Colombia. These documents grew out of the longstanding inequalities in Latin American societies, the emergence in the 1950s and 60s of popular movements seeking justice for poor people, and the bishops' theological reflections on these events. Caridad's translation facilitated the broad dissemination of these documents, which are considered the *Magna Carta* of the liberation theology movement in the United States and other English-speaking countries.

In these documents, the Latin American Bishops explore the church's responsibility for social justice through the perspective of poor and oppressed people. They specifically condemn unjust social structures within societies, denounce as sinful institutionalized violence that oppresses poor people, and call on all Christians to become involved in the transformation of society to liberate poor and marginalized people from economic, political, and social oppression. They also critique the Church's alignment with the ruling class as part of the structural injustice in their own countries and urge the Church to adopt structural and social change as part of its essential mission.

In 1974, Caridad also translated into English Gustavo Gutiérrez' seminal treatise, A *Theology of Liberation: History, Politics and Salvation*,[1] which contains the fundamental principles of liberation theology relied upon by the Latin American Bishops at Medellin, which they reaffirmed at their 1979 conference in Puebla, México. Traces of these liberation theology principles are also reflected in Vatican II documents, including the 1971 decree, Justice in the World and the 1974 decree, Evangelization of the Modern World.

Gutiérrez' treatise calls for a dialogue within the Catholic Church on these principles, including the need for institutional reform of the church. But the Congregation for the Doctrine of the Faith (CDF), the Vatican agency that sees itself as the "truth squad" for the Catholic Church, has not been receptive to such dialogue and has attempted to squash further development and teaching of liberation theology. Further, CDF has clearly signaled that it considers reform of either the hierarchical structure of the church or what it considers to be other "immutable truths" of the Catholic Church unnecessary.

While not totally banning liberation theology, CDF has silenced or otherwise censured several proponents of liberation theology and other theologians who have challenged the CDF and the

Sister Caridad Inda

pope's claim of absolute authority to declare the eternal truths of the Catholic Church. Hans Kung, who served as a theological adviser to the members of the Second Vatican Council, was in 1979 stripped of his license to teach as a Roman Catholic theologian when he publicly challenged papal infallibility as being a man-made doctrine rather than one instituted by God.

In 1983 and 1984 Joseph Cardinal Ratzinger, then the Prefect of CDF and now Pope Benedict XVI, issued instructions criticizing liberation theology's alleged Marxist analysis of history and theology and its call for reform in the Catholic Church. Consistent with these views, the Vatican over the past thirty years has been slow to implement Vatican II decrees that call for institutional reform and emphasize the social justice mission of the church. In addition, conservative bishops supportive of the hierarchical structure of the church and the pope's claim of absolute authority in matters of doctrine have been appointed to replace progressive bishops who emphasize the right of all members to fully participate in the life of the church.

These and other actions by the CDF and Pope Benedict XVI aimed at preventing reform of the hierarchical structure of the church and limiting implementation of the decrees of the Second Vatican Council have sparked the beginnings of a grassroots movement to reform the Catholic Church. In the wake of the Vatican's condemnation of theologians Hans Kung and Edward Schillebeeckx, a group of lay people and clerics formed the Association for the Rights of Catholics in the Church (ARCC). Caridad became a member of ARCC and has served on its board for fifteen years. ARCC's mission is to democratize the church.

Over the past thirty years, ARCC and other reform organizations have attempted to negotiate with both the Vatican and the USCCB on a range of issues including full implementation of the decrees of the Second Vatican Council, reform of church structures to allow all members to participate in ministry and decision-making in the church, recognition of the rights of both women and married men to participate in the priesthood, a comprehensive resolution of the sexual abuse by priests scandal that has precipitated an international crisis for the church, and the need to focus more of the church's resources on the needs of poor people, including immigrants. These attempts to resolve issues by honest dialogue and collaboration have largely failed.

Based upon her experience in negotiating with the USCCB, Caridad believes that the only way progress will be made in resolving these issues is to cause a shift in power. Gene Sharp, professor emeritus of Political Science at the University of Massachusetts at Dartmouth, researcher at the Harvard University Center for International Affairs, and pioneer in the use of strategic nonviolent resistance, stated in *From Dictatorship to Democracy:*

> When the issues at stake are fundamental, affecting religious principles, issues of human freedom, or the whole future development of the society, negotiations do not provide a way of reaching a mutually satisfactory solution. On some basic issues there should be no compromise. Only a shift in power relations in favor of the democrats can adequately safeguard the basic issues at stake. [2]

Caridad, who has collaborated with Professor Sharp as a translator of a number of his books, including *From Dictatorship to Democracy,* believes the time for negotiating with the Vatican and the USCCB is over. Rather, she asserts, it is time to use active nonviolent resistance as a method to achieve basic reforms in the Catholic Church. As an ARCC representative to the American Catholic Council (ACC), a coalition of organizations, communities, and individuals that seek to reform the governing structures of the Catholic Church, Caridad wrote one of the preparatory documents for the ACC's representative assembly held on June 11, 2011. In her paper, "Nonviolent Struggle and the Public Witness of a Believing Community to the Radical Demands of the Gospel," she suggests the strategy of gospel-based nonviolent resistance as a method to reform the Catholic Church and underscores three basic premises of active nonviolent resistance:

> All hierarchical institutions depend on the obedience of the governed,
>
> The governed can choose to obey or not, and
>
> If the governed resist in large enough numbers and for a long enough period of time, policies and institutions change.

Caridad also suggests that teaching large numbers of church members how to internalize these principles and use nonviolent resistance will shift the balance of power from the Vatican to the members of the church and empower them to achieve the reforms they seek. But she also cautions that change through nonviolent resistance takes time, patience, and perseverance. Most importantly, it requires common agreement on clear goals, careful organizing, and a well thought out strategy to achieve such goals.

In June 2011, over eighteen hundred people from every state except Wyoming participated in the ACC representative assembly. Caridad and Sister Christine Schenk, founder of another reform group, FutureChurch, led a workshop at the assembly about creating nonviolent responses to common abuses of authority in the U.S. Catholic Church.

When asked whether she thinks that these efforts to shift the balance of power within the Catholic Church will succeed in her lifetime, Caridad says, "Maybe not, but that is not a reason to stop trying." She points out that all of the important campaigns for reform through the strategic use of nonviolent resistance have started with a small group of highly committed people. She sees potential for such a group from leaders emerging from the June 2011 ACC representative assembly as well as others who are currently leading resistance efforts in parishes around the country.

Caridad also believes that the numbers of groups and parishes challenging the Vatican's hierarchical structure and resistance to democratic reform of the church will continue to grow. Eventually, opposition forces within the church, she says, will reach the critical mass needed to achieve reform. For Caridad, the important task now is to educate people about gospel-based nonviolent resistance and organize them around a common strategy and clear achievable goals of reform. In consultation with Professor Sharp, Caridad and other members of the ACC are planning a workshop on nonviolent resistance that they plan to offer in parishes around the nation.

When challenged whether the large number and diversity of Catholics in the U.S. may make reform of the church impossible, she points to the recent success of the nonviolent resistance movement in Egypt in which millions of very diverse people came together and unseated an autocratic ruler who held a tight grip on power for thirty years. Just as the people of Egypt deposed a dictator through the use of non-violent resistance, Caridad believes that members of the U.S. Catholic Church can take back their church using similar methods. She further states that members of the church have the power to transform the church into an institution that respects the right of every Catholic to proclaim the Gospel, allows members to participate fully in the life of the church, including electing and holding accountable all leaders in the church. In the end, the real issue is whether the members of the church will rise up and enforce their rights as members of the "People of God" through nonviolent resistance or succumb to the demands of obedience issued by the current members of the church hierarchy.

# Shaping Culture through Media Literacy

Humility Sister Elizabeth Thoman pioneered the field of media literacy education beginning in the mid-1970s. Elizabeth, or "Liz" as her friends call her, did not create the foundations for this field overnight or by herself. Rather it grew out of her fifty-year personal journey, aided by others, during the United States' transition from a print-based to a global multi-media culture.

Two influential forces in Liz's journey were Bernadine and the Annenberg School for Communication at the University of Southern California. According to Liz, Bernadine's early recognition of and trust in her talent in photography and journalism spurred Liz to move from Iowa to California in 1970, just as the media revolution was getting underway. Bernadine's support also sustained her during her decades-long quest to gain experience in and understand the potential of media and technology to transform all aspects of modern life. Liz's studies at Annenberg expanded her understanding of the potential of developing technology and provided her the intellectual foundation and organizational management skills that proved to be critical in her work as a leader of the media literacy education movement in the United States.

Liz's journey began in Nashville, Tennessee, where she grew up. Nashville was a segregated city rooted in the entrenched cultural belief that black people are inferior to white people. There were few black Catholics and Liz never had the opportunity as a young person to get to know and develop relationships with black children or their families. When the Nashville Christian Leadership Conference in 1960 launched a sit-in campaign to desegregate lunch counters in the central city, neither Liz nor her all white Catholic schoolmates were encouraged to learn about or support these civil rights efforts. Their teachers instead specifically warned them to "stay away" from the Nashville sit-ins.

It was about this time that two experiences during high school strongly influenced the course of Liz's life. One was a part-time job in a neighborhood camera shop where Liz quickly learned how cameras worked and where she purchased her first professional 35-mm camera. Liz had a good eye and over time gained the skills necessary to be a gifted photographer. She also learned to appreciate how photographs "create the myths in our heads and shape the values we use to make choices day in and day out."

The second experience occurred in Liz's senior year, when the sister-principal recommended Liz and other students for scholarships at Catholic colleges. Liz had not been planning to attend a Catholic college, but she sent in the scholarship application anyway to keep peace with the principal. Liz was quite surprised a few months later when the principal pulled her out of the lunch line to give her a letter that offered her a full tuition four-year scholarship to Marycrest College in Davenport, Iowa. Liz recalls that the principal said, "You will love the nuns at Marycrest."

After accepting the Marycrest scholarship, Liz and her father drove to Davenport to enroll her in the college. Sister Jane Francis Hanrahan welcomed them to the campus. Liz recalls that when Jane Francis left the room for a few minutes, her father remarked, "I have never seen nuns like her before. She has such life." During the course of the next two years, Liz learned that Jane Francis was typical of the Humilities who taught at the college. She admired the fact that these highly educated sisters who taught them by day were friendly, warm, and willing to talk and counsel students late into the night.

Due to her interest in photography, Liz joined the Marycrest camera club. Bernadine, the faculty sponsor for the club, spent a fair amount of time with Liz in the dark room teaching her how to develop and edit her own photos. Liz found Bernadine funny, easy to work with, and very supportive of her desire to combine writing and photography in her career plans.

Early in her first year at Marycrest, Liz and a few other students attended a program sponsored by Davenport's Catholic Inter-Racial Council (CIC). Afterwards, they were invited to dinner by CIC president Charles Toney and his wife, Ann, an African American couple who were pioneers in the civil rights movement both in Davenport and nationally.

The dinner at the Toney's home was a watershed event for Liz, who had never in her life been a guest in an African American home. The interchange among Charles and Ann Toney and their guests—both black and white—exposed the fallacy of the myth she had grown up with, that black people are inferior to whites. Shaken to her core about her racist upbringing, she reached out to Father Marvin Mottet, a renowned social justice advocate in the Davenport Diocese, who encouraged her to become active in social justice issues on campus and in the city. She did, and that involvement and her growing friendship with sisters at the college led Liz to join the Humilities in January 1964.

In 1966, when Bernadine was elected President of the Sisters of Humility, Liz was a newly professed sister. As Bernadine was keenly aware of both the importance of documenting the history of the community and Liz's gift for photography, she said to Liz, "We will have to get you a good camera so that you can record the future development of the Sisters of Humility." The opportunity to do that came during Liz's second year of teaching. After consulting with Bernadine, Liz used a stipend from a short-term contract job creating study guides for a Catholic magazine to purchase a Pentax Spotmatic camera, which she used for many years both in her role as community photographer and in her other professional work.

Liz's short-term contract became a full-time job the following year. She moved to Minneapolis to become an editor for *Catholic Miss/Catholic Boy* at Winston Press, a position that allowed her "to sprout her wings as a professional writer, photographer, and editor." Through the publisher at Winston Press, Liz was introduced to the executive producer at Franciscan Communications Center in Los Angeles, who hired her to work in public relations and marketing at the Center.

During her five years at Franciscan Communications, Liz traveled extensively around the United States conducting seminars on the use of media in religious education programs. She learned creative uses for various forms of media and saw the impact visual storytelling could have on values education and the faith of young people.

In 1972 and 1973, Liz wrote, photographed, and edited a series of "periodic bulletins" for the CHM community under the title, *"Women in Love . . . With Life."* Each one spotlighted through photography and text the spirit and values, ministries, and style of living of the Sisters of Humility. Taken as a whole, these periodic bulletins constituted a sophisticated publicity portfolio, which won a 1973 Golden "Lulu" Achievement Award in the Los Angeles Advertising Women's annual competition for public relations and advertising materials prepared by women.

As other religious communities came across *Women in Love . . . With Life,* Liz's reputation as an effective communications professional with a religious sensibility grew. Convinced that professional communications media could help change the stereotypical "image" of religious life, she accepted an invitation to work with the Sisters Council of New Orleans on a city-wide public relations campaign to support the movement of sisters from their traditional roles as teachers and nurses into urban ministry, prison reform, and other emerging social ministries. The campaign theme—*1200 Sisters: Working Where the Needs are Greatest*— was used on billboards, video spots for television, and in press releases and publications. It did not, however, change things much for the religious of New Orleans who continued to struggle for years to integrate their schools and respond to their growing awareness of poverty and injustice in the city.

Only later in graduate school did Liz begin to grasp that effective societal change requires a much deeper process than a public relations campaign alone could provide. This insight drove her intellectual inquiry for more than a decade. How could media be used to bring about new understandings of race, class, and gender? What impact could it have on changing traditional opinions about societal issues such as poverty, militarism, or the death penalty? Could media be used effectively to reduce stereotyping and create acceptance for women—not just Catholic sisters, but all women? Might justice and peace be effectively promoted through creative use of media?

Over these years, Bernadine and Liz had many conversations

about the limits and potential of communications to transform social structures. Bernadine recommended that Liz read Paolo Freire's *The Pedagogy of the Oppressed* and Gustavo Gutierrez' treatise *A Theology of Liberation: History, Politics and Salvation.* Liz studied these books carefully and read word for word Bernadine's prolific letters to the CHM community about emerging trends in Church and society. She also counted on Bernadine to critique her ideas and her projects because Liz knew Bernadine would give her an honest and thoughtful response. As she began to learn the techniques of social analysis reflected in the writings of Freire and Gutierrez, as well as from social justice advocates such as Sister Marjorie Tuite, O.P., Liz began to better grasp the importance of such analysis for achieving constructive change in media as well as the society at large.

One of the outcomes of the New Orleans project was a forty thousand dollar Lilly Endowment grant, which she used to set up the National Sisters Communication Services (NCSC) in 1975 to help religious communities develop communications and public relations skills to clarify the image of nuns as they modernized after Vatican II. Through her work with NSCS, Liz gained an appreciation for the general lack of awareness among women religious about the significant influence of the media in shaping U.S. culture in general and the lives of the millions of students taught by these communities. Even though women religious were among the most educated people in the field of education at the time, their lack of understanding of media's role in U.S. culture signaled to Liz a need for raising the awareness of *all teachers* about the role of media in society. This insight led to Liz's groundbreaking work in media literacy education.

While she was a Master's candidate at the Annenberg School for Communications & Journalism from 1975-77, Liz was exposed to new communication technology and foresaw that such technology would transform media from being only one aspect of the culture to becoming the very fabric of our lives. But she also knew that to take advantage of the potential positive benefits of the multimedia world of the future, children and adults alike would have to develop new analytic skills and new ways of learning.

As a culminating project at Annenberg, Liz created a magazine for teachers to explore how new technology would "transform schooling, health care, family life, indeed all of social and cultural reality." *Media&Values* became, in effect, the laboratory Liz used to test and refine methods for raising consciousness about the impact of media on our lives and teaching people how to independently interpret the images conveyed by media. In a 1986 article titled, "Blueprint for Response-Ability," Liz introduced the principles of social analysis as a method for interpreting the impact of media on individuals and society. Each subsequent issue of *Media&Values* focused on helping readers learn and apply a four-step process of awareness, social analysis, reflection, and action.

The issues analyzed by the magazine between 1986 and 1994 were wide-ranging, with many of them affecting our society still today. Some were "hot button" issues such as the stereotyping of minorities, women and older people in the media, the mythical presentation of war and the arms race, bias in the news, and media's depiction of violence. But the magazine also explored other issues such as the dangers of centralized control of content presented by media, television as a driver for the consumer culture, sexism and hype in the broadcasting of sporting events, gender bias in the media, how profit motive limits the content of television, television's effect on politics and participatory democracy, and the selling of addiction on television. As Liz indicated in the Summer/Fall 1987 issue of *Media&Values,*

> Whether a group is two people over breakfast, a dozen children in middle school, a college seminar class, or eight teens in a church youth group, we all have media experiences to share! Stimulated by the articles and ideas in *Media&Values,* we can reflect on these experiences and gain deeper insight into how we use the media, how the media uses us and what steps we can take, individually or as a society, to keep our media values in a healthy perspective.

Howard Rosenberg in an April 8, 1986 *Los Angeles Times* article, "*Media & Values* Quarterly Corners Common Sense," described the magazine as "the only one of its kind in the United States . . . simply terrific . . . and just plain smart." The magazine not only educated its subscribers but also provided the basis for hundreds of media literacy workshops that Liz and her colleagues conducted throughout the U.S. *Media&Values*, according to Liz, became "a beacon for guiding media literacy education in the United States."

But Liz also recognized that media literacy would have to become an integral part of the educational system in order to give young people the skills they would need for the twenty-first century. So, in 1989, Liz expanded the magazine into the Center for Media and Values in order to develop and distribute curriculum and train teachers to use it. In 1994, CMV became the Center for Media Literacy (CML), which Liz saw as the base for creating a media literacy movement with a sufficient public profile and political clout to make media literacy education a priority and eventually a reality in the United States.

As the executive director of CML, Liz became one of the leading voices to promote media literacy education in the United States. In 1989, she participated in the UNESCO New Directions in Media Literacy Conference in France, and in 1992 was one of thirty leaders invited to participate in the Aspen Institute's Leadership Conference on Media Literacy. In 1994, she served on the faculty of Harvard University's first U.S. Media Literacy Teaching Institute. In 1996, Liz was among fifty media and educational leaders invited to participate in the White House summit on children's television.

When the depiction of media violence and its impact on society, especially on children, became a national controversy in the mid-90s, Liz and her CML colleagues devoted the final two issues of *Media&Values* to the topic and, with grants from the Carnegie Corporation and other foundations, developed *Beyond Blame: Challenging Violence in Media*, the first comprehensive teaching resource on the topic. Invited to testify before the Senate Commerce Committee investigating media violence, she urged Congress to support media literacy programs in order to enroll millions of citizens in locally-based "national conversations" to resolve the issue of violence in their own lives and ultimately in our common society.

Throughout the decade, Liz and her colleagues also initiated a broad media campaign to educate the public about the importance of and need for universal media literacy education. By the mid-1990s, the media literacy education movement had penetrated the consciousness of various sectors of society but required both a broader and more structured base to ensure ongoing professional growth and to promote the long-term development of a universal system of media literacy education in the United States. Liz and three other leaders of the media literacy movement, Lisa Reisberg, Renee Hobbs, and Nancy Chase Garcia founded the Partnership for Media Education (PME), a non-profit corporation whose purpose was to promote professional development in the field through national media education conferences. Between 1997 and 2000, PME brought together dozens of media literacy experts with new and experienced teachers of media literacy to exchange information about developments in the field and to plot a course to make media literacy a core component of educational systems throughout the country.

In 2001, PME became a national membership organization, the National Association for Media Literacy Education (NAMLE), in order to link the thousands of media literacy practitioners across the country and harness their collective passion and energy to fuel the growth of media literacy. Liz served as an officer and board member of NAMLE for many years.

With the arrival of the new millennium, Liz stepped down as executive director of CML and devoted the next few years to writing. She co-authored with her partner, Tessa Jolls, a significant policy paper, *Media Literacy: A National Priority for a Changing World,* and developed a K-12 framework for media literacy entitled, *Literacy for the 21st Century— An Overview & Orientation Guide to Media Literacy Education.* These publications, along with the classroom activity book, *Five Key Questions That Can Change the World,* continue to guide the development of media literacy education in the United States.

In 2002, when Liz received the Daniel J. Kane Lifetime Achievement Award from the University of Dayton's Institute for Pastoral Initiative for her work in media literacy education, she credited the educational tradition of the Sisters of Humility and their important support for her work over three decades. She said:

> Our sisters have always been pioneers in the field of educa-
> tion. We have a history of innovative projects—moving into
> something new, getting it started and moving on. That's
> one of the charisms of our community. I was encouraged all
> along by the sisters of my community to explore and provide
> leadership in media. Getting into media education was a real
> blending of my community's commitment to education and
> their willingness to embrace my personal gifts and talents in
> the media field.

In 2007, Liz participated in the 21$^{st}$ Century Media Literacy Impact
Conference at the University of California, at which representatives
of twenty corporations, including Apple, Microsoft, and Verizon, plus
executives of dozens of national education organizations for teachers
of English, social studies, math, science, geography and others gathered. The conference's call for young people to be taught media literacy skills, Liz says, "gave me goose bumps." The leading educators
of the U.S. backed by the top corporations in today's global economy
were talking about an educational agenda that she had only vaguely
envisioned in 1977 when she started asking how new technology and
media would change the very nature of schooling. Now, nearly a half
century later, media literacy education was finally being recognized as
the means to teach young people skills necessary for the twenty-first
century, including "knowing how to think critically, solve problems,
work collaboratively, and more importantly, think globally, act ethi-
cally, be socially responsible and provide leadership in one's community and world."[1]

The call throughout the conference for "multimodal literacy" made
Liz smile. She thought about the Sisters of Humility pioneering where
the needs are greatest but when the work is done, leaving it to others
and moving on. Liz thought, "My work in media literacy education is
finished. Amen and alleluia."

While Liz has moved on from her role as one of the founders of media literacy education in the U.S., her creative juices have not stopped
flowing. She returned to her roots as a photographer after an experi-

ence with breast cancer in 2005. As a side effect of her cancer treatment, she lost the ability to concentrate. Prayer eluded her until one afternoon when she opened a book of nature photographs. "I was overwhelmed by the beauty of God's creation. My spirit came alive and I could pray again," she recalls. As she recovered her strength, she started taking photographs of flowers in full bloom. "The pictures seemed to take themselves," she says. "The lens allowed me to see right into the heart of the flower. To me, the act of photography is itself a prayer."[2]

In 2008, Liz embarked on a new project, *Healing Petals: Images for Prayer & Reflection*, which promotes the placement of her photographs in hospital rooms, nursing homes, and at the bedside of cancer patients and others who are chronically ill. One of her goals is "to bring affordable beauty to those in physical or emotional pain and to inspire new ways to image the Divine." Liz also believes that Healing Petals is a deeper and more spiritual approach to visual literacy and she takes inspiration from a quote by Henry David Thoreau: "It's not what you look at that matters; it's what you *see*."

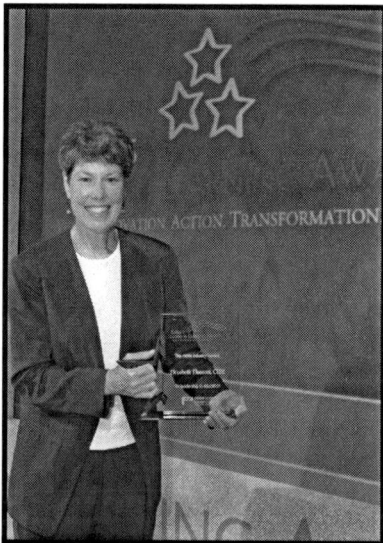

**Sister Elizabeth Thoman**

The beauty of Liz's photos depicted on the Healing Petals website (healingpetals.org) and the many requests she has received from people for framed copies of them demonstrates their universal value. The attraction of such beauty transcends not only health and sickness, but cultures as well.

As an ancient Hindu proverb aptly states, "If you have two loaves of bread, give one to the poor, sell the other and buy hyacinths to feed your soul." Liz's photographs will permanently nourish your soul.

# Serving Hispanics and Latinos
# & Enriching all our Lives

Sisters Irene and Molly Muñoz have spent fifty years caring for and advocating for the rights of immigrants and migrant workers. Born of an immigrant mother and first generation father, they grew up in a multicultural neighborhood in Valley Junction, Iowa, near Des Moines. While fluent in both English and Spanish, they also learned sufficient Italian and Slavic words to be able to greet all their neighbors in their native languages. From their neighbors, they gained an appreciation for the richness of diverse cultures.

Molly and Irene as children also learned to care about people. Their parents took into their home an elderly homeless man who was suffering from cancer and cared for him until he died. Their father, a union organizer who became president of the union at the Marquette Cement plant in Des Moines, declined a management job because he wanted to represent the workers. Because caring for people and advocating for their rights were in Irene and Molly's DNA, joining the Sisters of Humility and working with poor immigrants and migrant workers came naturally to them.

In the summer of 1967, Molly and Sister Maxine Lloyd, with Bernadine's support, went to Muscatine, Iowa to work with migrants arriving in great numbers from Texas to pick tomatoes in southeastern Iowa. They volunteered for the Muscatine Migrant Committee, an ecumenical group headquartered at St. Mary's Parish, and were warmly welcomed by the Muscatine community.

Early in the summer, Maxine and Molly were part of the committee that met the truckloads of migrant farm workers and their families. They invited them to participate in Spanish language masses , arranged for baptisms, and helped them to get connected to the limited health care and other supports available to them. Throughout the summer, they visited farm worker families in the labor camps, saw the substandard conditions in which they lived and learned about the grossly inadequate wages they were being paid for their backbreaking labor—twelve cents per basket of tomatoes. They also observed the significant gap between their health care needs and available services to meet these needs.

**Sisters Irene and Molly Muñoz**

At the end of summer, Molly entered nursing school to secure the training and license necessary to provide health care to farm workers and their families. When she returned to Ottumwa to start her training, Molly told Irene, who was a registered nurse, "Go to Muscatine and take care of the farm workers." Because of Irene's other commitments, she was unable to begin working with the farm workers immediately.

When Irene arrived in Muscatine in the summer of 1969, she witnessed entire farm worker families arriving from the Rio Grande Valley of Texas packed like cattle in the back of open trucks. As they had been on the road for several days without adequate food or water, many of them were sick when they arrived. While talking with these families, Irene found that many of them suffered from untreated, debilitating health conditions. In response to this obvious need, Irene, in conjunction with other staff of the Muscatine Migrant Committee, opened a small health clinic for farm workers.

Over the next few years, Irene's work at the migrant health clinic gave her a front seat view of the endless injustices faced by the workers and their families. Subjected to overcrowded, substandard housing and poor sanitation, they developed bacterial diseases and parasites. Due to grossly inadequate wages paid to the workers, migrant families lived on subsistence diets, which caused chronic health problems. Workers, including pregnant women, suffered poisoning and rashes as a result of aerial pesticide spraying.

Although the migrant health clinic treated emergency health care needs of the migrant families, it lacked the resources necessary to provide the broad spectrum of health services they needed. So Irene and her colleagues approached the University of Iowa School of Medicine and requested that medical students under faculty supervision be sent to Muscatine to provide more comprehensive health services for the farm worker families. The medical school administration agreed to expand the existing farm worker clinic's services by sending medical students and faculty. The clinic became a favorite assignment for both students and faculty. As students learned about medical conditions they would not encounter at the University clinics and treated many conditions for farm worker families that would have gone untreated, both the students and the families benefited.

The clinic treated farm worker families whether they had insurance or not. As these families had not had access to general medical services for a long time, they flooded the clinic. The medical school students, faculty, and existing clinic staff provided pre-natal care, while the Medical School's obstetrics department delivered farm worker babies at the University of Iowa hospital. Over the years, other departments of the University sent students and faculty to help, including the dental school and the nutrition department. The clinic forged lasting friendships between farm workers, their health care providers, and other community supporters.

Irene's work with the farm workers also taught her to speak up and challenge the systemic injustices she observed on a daily basis. She was so shocked and angered by the squalor of the camps that she began reporting the substandard conditions to the state health department and housing inspectors. When the inspectors came out to the camps, they often told the camp owners that they were there to investigate complaints made by Sister Irene. The "good nun" quickly became the "damn nun" to some owners.

Irene was not deterred by this response and continued to do what she believed the gospel demanded—provide health care and other basic services to the farm worker families and join with others to seek justice for them. In 1971, Irene served on a committee that helped enact legal standards for child labor and migrant housing in the state of Iowa. This sparked a backlash among some Muscatine residents who did not think the church should be working with migrants.

When Irene began helping the migrants re-settle in Muscatine, conflicts with Anglo residents arose. The migrant families, however, stood their ground and, with Irene's help, gradually integrated into the church and community. When the migrants asked Irene to speak for them, she encouraged them to speak for themselves. Before Irene left Muscatine, strong leaders among the resettled farm workers had emerged.

In reflecting on her fifteen years in Muscatine, Irene says that she felt like she was on a journey and "it was in Muscatine that God became real to me." According to Irene,

> God was with us and our cause was just. The people had a lot of faith. The leaders of both the diocese and the local Catholic Church stood with us. The farm workers taught me a lot about suffering, celebration, and sharing.

When she returns to Muscatine, Irene still gets the chills because her work there was such a life changing experience.


In 1969, after graduating from nursing school, Molly moved to Laredo, Texas to serve as the coordinator of "Food for Millions." Through this program, Molly distributed soybean flour and other commodities to barrio families plagued with nutritional deficiencies and educated them about the benefits of such food. Molly also became active in other issues affecting poor people.

When the city of Laredo announced that a low-income housing project would be torn down to make room for luxury condominiums, low-income residents asked Molly for help. Dressed in her habit, Molly and other advocates marched to the Laredo City Building to protest the proposed destruction of low-income housing. When the local bishop learned about Molly's involvement in the demonstration, he called Bernadine to tell her that he did not want any Sister of Humility like Molly in his diocese. Bernadine called Molly, told her about the bishop's call, and encouraged her to continue her advocacy for low-come people.

The bishop's view, however, did not represent the view of all Texas church officials regarding the role of sisters. A few months later, Molly attended a Catholic Charities statewide conference, which focused on developing strategies for opposing abortion and promoting the right to life. Molly, after listening for some time, stood up and gave a passionate speech in support of the conference taking a stand against the Vietnam War instead, saying, "It was killing more people than abortion." This time a Texas monsignor called Bernadine and said, "If the community has more sisters like Molly, I want them to work with me."

At the Humilities' 1969 assembly, Irene and Molly presented a workshop describing their work and urged the sisters to support United Farm Worker (UFW) boycotts and other collective actions to redress the injustices faced by farm workers on a daily basis. They were surprised and disappointed by some members' response to their pleas, but continued educating community members regarding the plight of farm workers. Later that year, members of the community's senate, with Bernadine's strong support, adopted a resolution in support of the UFW grape boycott and urged other members to join them. As more sisters became educated about the plight of farm workers, support for their cause within the community substantially increased and more sisters became involved in their campaigns.

In 1970, Molly returned to Muscatine, where she and Irene worked together to provide health care to farm worker families, support the UFW in their various campaigns, and challenge the living conditions in the labor camps. Molly was a constant presence at the camps voicing the farm workers' needs and rights to farmers and government agencies.

As part of her nursing responsibilities, Molly often went out to the fields to follow up on medical conditions of her patients. One day, she went to a farmer's field in Rock Island County, Illinois to find out whether a worker's child was allergic to penicillin. The farmer called the sheriff, who arrested Molly for trespassing and put her in jail. When a Chicago reporter published the story of Molly's arrest, the sheriff immediately released her. The farmer's wife, however, called Bernadine to complain about Molly's support of the farm workers. According to Bernadine, the farmer's wife said, "The sisters should be supporting the farmers rather than the workers." Bernadine politely told the woman, "Since the farmers have more power and support than farm workers, Molly's advocacy for them simply levels the playing field." She also told the farmer's wife that she "supported Molly's advocacy for the workers because their cause is just." With Bernadine's support, Molly continued to assert the rights of farm workers in Muscatine for over ten years.

In the early 1980s, Molly moved to Mexico to staff a dispensary in a remote mountainous village, San Isidro Tepetzitzintla, Puebla. She fell in love with the place. According to Molly, "The Spirit was alive in the people as they lived from day to day with God's help." In contrast to the severe poverty of the people, the surrounding mountains and valleys were breathtaking. She thought, "With all God's beauty surrounding us, how could we forget his presence?"

As the dispensary had been abandoned for some time, Molly sent a plea for assistance to University of Iowa doctors with whom she had worked in Muscatine. Five doctors came to San Isidro. They examined patients and taught Molly how to suture wounds and perform other common procedures. A Méxican doctor came on weekends to check on patients and review the treatments Molly had given during the week.

Patients came to the dispensary from all over the region, sometimes traveling long distances. She averaged thirty-five or more patients a day with diverse medical needs. Common conditions included malnutrition, rashes, and parasites due to unsafe drinking water, and severe burns caused by children sleeping too close to open fires. One patient was carried a long distance to the dispensary on a ladder with padding placed on the rungs to support his body. His friends thought he was dying from drinking homemade alcohol. Molly induced vomiting, gave him Valium and IVs, and he walked home. Another patient, a six-year-old girl, was carried into the clinic on her mother's back. Her mother counted three hundred worms coming out of her child's ears, mouth and nose while Molly was treating her. Molly successfully drew out the parasites, gave her vitamins, and the young girl recovered.

Molly routinely made house calls to patients, so she kept a backpack for obstetrical cases and a separate one for general medical problems. Herminia Marin, a former nun who was teaching Spanish as a second language in the village, took Molly to a very primitive shack where they found a baby with her umbilical cord still attached and her eyes filled with gunk lying in a hammock that was suspended from the ceiling. The family allowed Molly to take the baby to the dispensary to care for her temporarily. She removed the umbilical cord, bathed the baby, made some clothes for her, and took care of her for a few days.

During this time, Molly determined that the child's safety was at risk in the family. She went back to the home with an interpreter who spoke the family's dialect and told the family, "If you wish, La Madre will take care of the baby, feed her, and send her to school." After some time, the family agreed to let Molly keep the baby. To ensure a good home for the baby, Molly arranged for the adoption of the child by a friend in Brownsville, Texas, and personally transported the baby to the border where the prospective mother was waiting. At first, Molly felt sad that she was taking the child from her family and village, but decided it was the best option for her. The child thrived in her new home and developed into a very bright, well-educated woman.

After fifteen years in Muscatine, Irene took some time off to think about her future. While attending a pastoral program at the Méxican American Cultural Center in San Antonio, she met other Hispanic and Anglo people who, like her, had come to San Antonio to deepen their own understanding of how to be effective pastoral ministers for the Hispanic community. In 1987, Irene moved to Denver, Colorado where the Hispanic population had rapidly increased during the 1980s. Irene had what she called "a little rumbling in her heart" concerning the need for female leaders in the Church to serve Hispanic people, so she enrolled at St. Thomas Seminary in a two-year pastoral ministry program.

After completing the program, Irene joined the Archdiocese of Denver as the Assistant to the Director for Hispanic Ministry. Despite the large increase in Hispanic Catholics in the Archdiocese, only 8 out of 141 parishes offered masses in Spanish. So Irene and other staff began urging pastors who had large numbers of Hispanics in their parishes to increase the availability of Spanish language Masses. Only a few priests responded favorably.

Given the paucity of Spanish language masses and other services for Hispanics in the archdiocese, Irene with other Hispanic Ministry staff began to form small base communities similar to those that arose in the 1960s and 70s in Latin America. In these communities, the members studied and reflected on scripture and applied their scriptural interpretations to the circumstances of their own lives. While these base communities were effective in energizing their members to find new ways of living their faith on a daily basis, the Diocesan Office of Hispanic Affairs lacked the personnel and other resources necessary to expand these base communities to other Hispanics in the archdiocese.

Although the Denver Archdiocese was relatively wealthy, it allocated in the 1990s only a small percentage of its own funds to support programs for poor and marginalized people, including Hispanics. After Irene struggled for years to increase services to Hispanic Catholics within the limited Office of Hispanic Affairs budget, she met with Archbishop Chaput and described the need for a greater financial commitment to make ministry to Hispanics real rather than simply an empty slogan. She pointed out that, despite concerted efforts to get parishes to offer Spanish language masses and other programs for Hispanic people, her requests had largely fallen on deaf ears. Irene further suggested that, for Hispanic ministry in the archdiocese to succeed, the Archbishop would have to accord it greater priority. As the Archbishop was not receptive to her concerns, Irene subsequently resigned.

In 1999, Irene moved to Iowa, which was experiencing a great influx of Latino immigrants. Churches in both Marshalltown and Ottumwa recruited her to serve as a multi-cultural pastoral minister. The Catholic parishes in these communities pledged to commit the necessary resources to help integrate the Latinos into the full life of the parishes and surrounding communities. In late 1999, Irene became a multi-cultural minister at St. Mary of the Visitation Church in Ottumwa and continues to work there today.

During Irene's first four years in Ottumwa, the Latino population grew 170%. Expansion of the Cargill meatpacking plant and its vigorous recruiting of immigrants contributed to that growth. The "New Iowans," as town leaders called them, came from Mexico, El Salvador, Guatemala, Honduras, and Columbia.

Ottumwa has worked hard to integrate Latinos into the community. Town leaders started a diversity task force and a workforce center to help them find English classes, jobs, and housing. St. Mary's Church held annual clinics staffed by Ottumwa Public Health Nursing that provided health screenings and medical care. Public Health Nursing also arranged for a bus to periodically show the "New Iowans" the location of city agencies, schools, clinics, the hospital, and other essential services.

Soccer became a vital means for integrating Latino and Anglo communities. When Latinos began to play soccer in the park on Sunday mornings, Anglos gradually joined them. The soccer games helped overcome the initial fear and distrust in both groups, and over the years, the Anglo-Latino sports collaboration expanded to a church softball league, which has fostered a new vitality in the Ottumwa Catholic community. Interracial marriages have also helped improve race relations and the apparent racism is gradually fading.

But, despite Ottumwa's efforts to welcome the immigrants with genuine hospitality, problems still arose. Some landlords took advantage of the Latino immigrants. There were initially no bilingual school staff to register Latino children, elementary grades became overcrowded with Spanish-speaking children, and there was a high drop out rate of Spanish speaking students in the high schools. Irene became a member of the Human Rights Commission and worked with other members of the Commission, town officials and school personnel to help find workable solutions to these problems.

Shortly after Irene arrived in Ottumwa, she partnered with the Central College Service Program to coordinate an English as a Second Language (ESL) program for immigrants staffed by college students. The program served both children at Wilson Elementary School and immigrant families. For Irene, learning the language of the country is an important way for immigrants to claim ownership of the country. According to Central College Service program administrators, the program also benefited the college students by introducing them to the Latino culture and helping them to increase their Spanish fluency.[1]

In her work with Latinos, Irene has focused on developing their leadership skills to help them take their rightful place in the church and the community. She recruits and trains Latinos to serve as ministers in church liturgies and to participate in the music ministry of church. Attendance at the Spanish language mass has continued to grow with both Latinos and Anglos attending.

Many parishioners came to a parish-wide *posada* the Latinos organized. The Latinos also are the core leaders of a charismatic group that meets after the Sunday Spanish language mass. According to Irene, "The Latinos are learning about their faith and claiming ownership of the church, which I think is a good development." As more of the four thousand Latinos in Ottumwa become involved in the Church, the multi-cultural programs continue to expand and the integration of the Latinos and Anglos in the parish is gradually increasing.

Irene also encourages the Latinos to become active members of the broader community. When the issue of Ottumwa's application for ICE 287 funding to train local police officers to enforce federal immigration laws arose, Irene helped organize the Latino community to go to the public hearing and speak in opposition to the proposed application. Although the Council voted to submit an application, it was not funded. The Latino leaders' public challenge of the program was still important because they learned that they had a right to speak up on issues of concern to them.

While Irene works with Latinos in Ottumwa, Molly continues to serve migrant workers and their families in Colorado in conjunction with a church-based coalition called United With Migrants. This coalition aids and advocates for migrants in Denver and surrounding counties. In addition to providing emergency assistance to migrants, United With Migrants is working to develop a full service migrant center, which they intend to call Sister Molly's House, to help migrants learn the skills they need to become economically self-sufficient.

Molly is the consummate advocate for the migrants—she works seven days a week, travels hundreds of miles a month, and is on call twenty-four hours a day. Throughout southeastern Colorado, she is affectionately known as the "Mother Theresa of the Latinos." She distributes food and clothing, and provides nursing care at the migrant camps. She also provides transportation, helps with processing legal documentation necessary for migrants to work in the U.S., accompanies them to court proceedings, secures legal representation for them when necessary, and visits them when they are jailed for immigration violations. She attends to their spiritual and emotional needs by arranging for Spanish language masses, sacramental preparation and baptisms, and serves as the godmother for numerous children of migrants. She is also the convener of celebrations for the migrant community and is the person who consoles them in times of trouble, sickness, and death. In short, she is their friend and the person they trust.

In 2005, Molly received the Cesar Chavez Leadership award from the Denver Cesar Chavez Peace and Justice Committee. Over fifty migrants attended the ceremony. When Molly received the award, she turned to the migrants and said, "This award honors you as well as me."

Molly's mother taught her children, "Don't forget where you came from." Molly has not forgotten. The migrants to Molly are not only friends, but as she often says, "They are like family to me. When they suffer, I suffer. We help each other." Although much of her work is focused on meeting the immediate needs of individual migrants and their families, she also focuses on systemic injustices that continue to deprive migrant families of basic necessities of life and their fundamental rights. Advocates and other persons who seek to understand the needs of the migrants, including conditions in the camps, seek her out. By teaching advocates and others about the plight of the migrants, Molly hopes to build a sufficient political force capable of making changes in public policy necessary to improve the lives of the peaceful and hard working people who nurture the crops, pick the harvest, and put food onto our tables.

# Standing Up and Paying Up Personally

Bernadine's call to the community in 1972 to "speak out on issues of peace and justice and work with others to organize an effective voice for such issues" resonated with many sisters, including Sister Joanne O'Brien who felt liberated to pursue her passion—community-based social justice advocacy.

Like many other Humilities, Joanne had participated in social action campaigns while working full time as a teacher. Through such work, Joanne met and became friends with Elizabeth (Liz) Loescher, a single parent with three children who was teaching poor children and their families how to prevent and resolve conflicts without violence. When Liz invited Joanne to become part of the Loescher family, Liz consulted with Bernadine, who encouraged her to do it. As a result, Joanne and Liz have raised the Loescher children together and have supported each other in their respective passions, pursuit of non-violence and social justice for over thirty years.

In 1979 when the Metropolitan Organization for People (MOP) started its work in Denver to empower poor people to strengthen and transform their communities, Joanne became one of its first organizers. She went door-to-door in a low-income neighborhood in Northwest Denver getting to know people and learning about their problems and concerns. Joanne, a gifted listener, quickly learned the most pressing problems in the neighborhood, including the high cost of utilities and the resulting shut-offs of electricity and heat to many low-income families, the high incidence of violent crime, lack of adequate traffic control signs, inadequate lighting around the community center and public housing units in the neighborhood, and the lack of adequate services in all the low-income housing projects. In these initial discussions, Joanne also identified potential leaders of the neighborhood, who she encouraged to join MOP.

With Joanne's help, these leaders worked with the community at large to devise solutions to these problems. Then they organized public demonstrations and privately persuaded company executives, landlords, government agencies, and police to help. They testified at utility shut-off hearings at the Public Utility Commission (PUC) and supported the establishment of the Low-Income Energy Assistance Program (LEAP), which has provided energy assistance payments to low-income citizens for the past forty years. They also secured safer street signs, better lighting and maintenance for the community center and low-income housing projects, and worked with the police to reduce crime in the neighborhood. After a sustained effort by neighborhood residents, the Denver Housing Authority began improving the conditions and services provided in public housing.

Joanne and neighborhood leaders also investigated Martin Marietta's drainage of toxins into the Denver water supply. This campaign turned out to be a David and Goliath struggle and although the neighborhood residents did not have the financial resources to challenge Martin Marietta successfully in court, they, by joining with others, generated enough public pressure that the company stopped polluting the water supply.

In addition to her work with MOP, Joanne joined Liz in teaching the Loescher children a practical course in representative democracy. As their home was a precinct headquarters, the Loescher children became the unpaid staff for precinct processes and also participated with Joanne and Liz in peace and justice rallies. Joanne helped care for the Loescher children while Liz was establishing the Conflict Center in Denver to teach children and adults how to civilly resolve disputes and avoid violence. The Center became a national model for violence prevention programs and Liz became a leader in the movement to replicate such programs in other parts of the country.

In 1984, Joanne moved to Davenport to care for her mother. While there, she worked with Father Marvin Mottet, who had just been appointed the pastor of Sacred Heart Cathedral. Joanne helped Marvin implement a philosophy of social action—the "Two Feet of Christian Service," as he called it, that paired direct service with societal change.

Joanne concentrated her efforts in the neighborhood of the Cathedral parish close to downtown Davenport. Historically, Irish and Germans had populated the neighborhood, but at the time, substantial numbers of African American and Hispanic people had also moved into the area.

Initially Joanne and Marvin focused on breaking down the divisions among these ethnic groups. Then, using MOP organizing principles, Joanne worked with the residents to identify the issues they cared about. They identified high crime rates, drugs, the deteriorating conditions of many homes, and the threat of a supermarket moving out of the neighborhood as their primary issues.

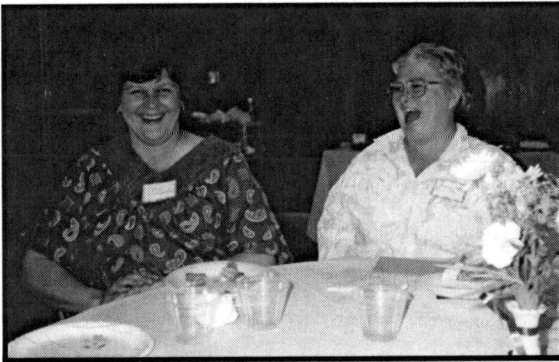

Liz Loescher and Sister Joanne O'Brien

Because the neighborhood was old with a substantial number of homes requiring repair, Marvin, in conjunction with churches in the Quad-City Interfaith Coalition, founded Interfaith Housing, Inc. During the past twenty-four years, Interfaith Housing has served as one of the primary housing repair and refurbishing contractors in the region, particularly in low-income neighborhoods.

In conjunction with community leaders, Joanne established a working relationship with the police and developed mutually agreed upon approaches for reducing drug and crime problems. Over time, those approaches improved both. As for the supermarket, Safeway left the neighborhood, but another grocery store moved in and continues to serve the neighborhood today.

In addition to her community organizing work, Joanne also served as director of the St. Francis Home, a shelter that housed primarily African immigrants who had come to Davenport to study at the Palmer College of Chiropractic Treatments.

After Joanne's mother died, Joanne moved back to Denver and then to Georgia with Liz, where Liz established the Georgia Conflict Center. While blindness prevented Joanne from continuing her community organizing, she never lost her passion for advocating for justice on behalf of poor people. In Georgia, Joanne served as the Spiritual Director for the St. Vincent de Paul Society, a regional association of ten Churches. Although the society focused on providing emergency assistance to poor people, Joanne worked hard to broaden its mission to being a force for justice and systemic change as well.

Other Humilities over the past fifty years have lent their voices to justice and peace efforts while keeping their "day jobs." Elaine and Marilyn Jean (Jeanie) Hagedorn, for instance, have remained full-time educators while serving as grassroots organizers for such issues as the rights of women in church and society, war and peace, a just resolution of the Israeli/Palestinian conflict, and immigration reform.

In 1970, Elaine and Jeanie joined with other women religious to establish the Sisters Council for the Des Moines Diocese to promote the rights of women in the Catholic Church. One of the Council's first projects was to organize women to speak at churches and other events throughout the diocese about their experiences in the church and the contributions they and other women could and should make in their faith communities. These speeches had a substantial impact. For many church members, it was the first time they really thought about the role of women in the church.

Over time, Jeanie, Elaine and other members of the Sisters Council have broadened their focus to include the roles of both men and women in the church and have joined the effort seeking democratic reform of the Catholic Church. For years, they have supported ordination of women and married men to the priesthood. They have also consistently spoken out at the local and diocesan church levels regarding the need for increased participation in the governance of the church by all members. In June 2011, Elaine and Jeanie joined eighteen hundred reform-minded Catholics at the ACC assembly in Detroit to begin forging the national alliances necessary to create a cohesive, broad movement to reform the church.

For forty years, Jeanie and Elaine have also worked with a variety of peace organizations, including Catholic Peace Ministry, American Friends Service Committee, Des Moines Area Catholic Social Action Committee, parish peace and justice groups, and the Des Moines Area Ecumenical Committee for Peace. During their decades of work with these organizations, they have helped organize and participated in petition drives, prayer services, and rallies concerning such issues as the U.S. involvement in the wars in Afghanistan and Iraq, U.S. support of and sale of military equipment and weapons to Central American countries that victimize their own citizens, and the Palestinian/Israeli conflict. Through this work, they have gained a deeper understanding of how war exacerbates global problems and drains resources necessary to create a just and caring society, and have committed themselves to the long-term, day-by-day effort to raise the consciousness of others regarding these issues.

Each year for the past twelve years, Elaine has helped organize the annual Bishop Dingman Peace Award Dinner where the Iowa equivalent to the Nobel Peace Prize, the Dingman Peace Award, is given. Through this event, Iowans are given the opportunity to hear directly from peace and justice activists who have first-hand experience with current justice and peace issues and demonstrate by their lives both the struggles and the rewards of lives committed to peace and justice.

Jeanie and Elaine have also helped organize and publicize a variety of citizen actions to promote peace. For example, on the sixty-fifth anniversary of the bombing of Hiroshima and Nagasaki, Elaine and Jeanie joined other peace activists to celebrate the 1959 airlift by Iowa farmers of hogs to Yamanashi, Japan after two typhoons destroyed the hog population there. Three years after the hog drop, the hog population had grown to five hundred and the Yamanashi citizens began celebrating Iowa Day every year. This exchange fostered a fifty-year cooperative relationship between Japanese and Iowa farmers, proving that hog diplomacy is saner than nuclear bombs and a culture of death. During the 1993 floods in Iowa, Yamanashi farmers reciprocated by sending three hundred thousand dollars in flood relief to Iowa farmers.

But a major focus of Jeanie and Elaine's peace work has been the conflict between the Palestinians and Israel. Their concern about the decades-old Israeli/Palestinian conflict grew out of their trips to the West Bank and Jerusalem, where they saw for themselves the high separation walls and check points blocking Palestinians from their jobs, land, schools, families, and holy sites. They also visited the Israeli settlements on the West Bank in which five hundred thousand Israeli citizens now occupy Palestinian land. In both Jerusalem and the West Bank, they witnessed the gross disparity between living conditions of Israelis as compared to the Palestinians.

**Sisters Elaine and Jeanie Hagedorn, foreground**

Jeanie and Elaine, who believe that Israel's continuing expansion of settlements in both the West Bank and in the Palestinian sectors of Jerusalem has only broadened the conflict, continue to work with the American Friends Service Committee and the Churches for Middle East Peace to educate citizens about these issues. With these organizations, they put pressure on the U.S. government to more actively oppose expansion of Israeli settlements and to push for a roll back of existing settlements on Palestinian land. They also support humanitarian and diplomatic efforts but oppose sending U.S. military equipment and dollars that prolong the conflict between Israel and Palestinians.

Through their work with immigrants at Visitation parish in Des Moines and through Jeanie's work as a teacher of English as a Second Language for immigrants, they have also befriended many immigrants and learned from them their hopes and the problems they face in becoming accepted as citizens in this country. Their personal connections with these immigrants have made them fierce advocates for the rights of all immigrants.

Like the war and peace issues, immigration issues are not easily solved. In 1986, Jeanie and Elaine worked hard to help enact the Immigration Reform and Control Act of 1986, which allowed 2.8 million undocumented immigrants to become citizens of the U.S. But since 1986, public discourse and policy regarding immigrants has become more punitive and the present immigration system more dysfunctional.

So Jeanie and Elaine have redoubled their efforts to build support for immigrants in Iowa and to lobby for immigration reform on a national basis. They have joined other immigrant advocates to fight the unlawful roundups of immigrants by the Immigration, Customs and Enforcement Services (ICE) in meatpacking plants in Iowa and have challenged ICE's indiscriminate round-ups of Hispanic and Latino people in other parts of the country. They have also opposed bills authorizing state and local governments to enforce federal immigration law, and protested unlawful, unlimited detention of immigrants in private detention centers in both Des Moines and nationally.

While engaging in these defensive actions, the Hagedorn sisters have also joined the Justice for Immigrants campaign to press for enactment of comprehensive immigration reform to bring the twelve million undocumented immigrants out of the shadows and give them a fair path to citizenship. During the past five years, they have also organized lobbying efforts in support of the Dream Act, a bipartisan effort to give young immigrants—who arrived in the U.S. before they were sixteen years old, have worked hard to complete their education or served in the military, and have demonstrated good moral character—a conditional path to citizenship. But both of these positive agendas have been stalled due to the culture wars about immigrants that have raged during the past ten years.

Nevertheless, Jeanie and Elaine have not given up. Day by day, they continue to remind Iowans that we are a nation of immigrants and they do everything in their power to ensure a fair and just immigration system. In 2010, they helped the CHM community adopt a strong corporate statement supporting immigrants and comprehensive immigration reform and publicize the statement broadly in hope that the good will the Humilities have generated in Iowa over the last 143 years might entice their fellow Iowans to join the effort to create a just and fair immigration system.

During their forty years of work on peace and justice issues, the Hagedorn sisters have learned the importance of rallying the support of citizens through persistent, targeted educational efforts. In 2004, Jeanie became the Peace and Justice Coordinator for the CHM community. In monthly letters to the sisters, she summarizes current justice and peace issues and provides contact information for organizations that have more detailed information and that are organizing particular actions concerning these issues. She also sends out email alerts to members regarding impending votes on legislation or other decisions by local, state, or federal government officials requiring immediate action.

In 2011, the Catholic Peace Ministry presented the Dingman Peace Award to women religious throughout the nation but with particular emphasis on the communities of sisters in the Des Moines diocese, including the Sisters of Humility. According to the Peace Award Committee, these women "have a record of being open to the Spirit and needs of people, especially the poor" and are "instruments of peace through their non-violent opposition to war and oppression and their promotion of peace and cooperation among all people."[1] Two years earlier, Jeanie and Elaine individually received the Msgr. Marvin Mottet "Footsteps" Award from the Iowa Institute for Social Action for their long-term involvement in causes of peace and justice.

Other Sisters of Humilities and associates are equally passionate advocates for justice and peace. For example, when Sister Roberta Brich learned that sex traffickers were transporting young girls through Iowa and forcing them into prostitution, she and State Senator Maggie Tinsman decided that they would take action to stop it. When police and other officials claimed that human trafficking was not a problem in Iowa, Roberta collected evidence to the contrary. She interviewed truckers at truck stops along Interstate 80 from the Quad Cities on the east to Neola on the west side of the state. The truckers confirmed that I-80 is a significant corridor for trafficking of women and young girls and provided specific examples. Roberta, with this information in hand, worked with Senator Tinsman to draft a bill making human trafficking a crime in Iowa and developed the necessary support to enact this legislation. In 2006, the Iowa legislature outlawed human trafficking within the borders of Iowa. Since the enactment of this legislation, law enforcement has established human trafficking working groups, 125 victims of sex trafficking in Iowa have been identified, a pimp who forced two ten-year-old girls into prostitution has been convicted and given a twenty-five year sentence, and the first annual Conference on Human Trafficking in Iowa was held in 2011. Although much work remains to educate Iowa citizens about this issue, and more resources are needed to adequately enforce the law, the effort of Roberta and Maggie Tinsman in 2006 was the spark that ignited the movement to shut down human trafficking in Iowa.

In 2008, when Roberta was president of the community, the Humilities also joined the Banners Across America initiative organized by the National Religious Campaign Against Torture. They hung a sign that declared "Torture is Wrong" at the entrance to their headquarters in Davenport and publicized the campaign in the Quad Cities, stating:

> Torture is a moral issue. It violates the basic dignity of human persons that all religions, in their highest ideals, hold dear. It degrades everyone involved. By hanging this banner, we hope to inspire people to think about and discuss what many would rather ignore.[2]

The Humilities' support of the campaign rallied many citizens in the Quad Cities to protest continued use of torture by the U.S. military in the wars of Iraq and Afghanistan.

Roberta and other Humilities in the Quad Cities also conducted witness events whenever violent action causing death or serious injury occurred in the community. With the agreement of the family of the victim(s), the sisters went to the area in which the violence occurred, talked to the neighbors about the event, and invited them to join them in prayers in remembrance of the victim(s). These witness events, according to Roberta, were one of the more effective methods for raising the consciousness of the community about violence, and also helped bring neighborhood people together to counter the violence in their communities.

Sister Pat Miller, who has been a nurse for over fifty years, is a passionate advocate for health care for all people in our country. During the

Sister Pat Miller in a meeting with Peter VeKock, district director for Congressman Bruce Braley, seeking the Congressman's support for HRCA

past three years, she has worked with Progressive Action for the Common Good in the Quad Cities to help develop the support necessary to ensure passage of the Health Care Reform Act (HCRA) and to defend the Act both before and after its enactment. Initially, Pat spent much of her time speaking to individuals and groups to explain the benefits of HCRA and counter the argument made by the bishops and various Catholic organizations that the Act should be rejected due to its provision of federal funding for abortions. Pat patiently pointed out that existing law already prohibited the use of federal funding to pay for abortions and that HCRA does not modify this legal prohibition.

But Pat, a no-nonsense advocate for access to necessary health care for all citizens, continues to challenge the broader "Right to Life" opposition to the Act. After first stating that she is a nurse and a Catholic sister, she candidly affirms in her speeches her belief that women have a right to make medical decisions about their own and their children's health. She also points out that millions of people in this country lack access to medical care and that substantial numbers of them die each year because of this. Given these clearly established facts, she says, "Support of HCRA, which will save lives by ensuring access to necessary medical care, is the real 'Right to Life' position." Even though HCRA is now law, the battle for universal health care is not over—so Pat and her colleagues continue to organize against current efforts to repeal the Act while promoting changes to improve it.

The Humilities, individually and as a community, have also demonstrated their willingness to live simply and share their financial and other resources with those in need. They have personally and financially supported victims of civil war and natural disasters, as well as other poor persons throughout the world. For example, in 1971, when an individual sister's personal funds were very small, Bernadine brought to the community's attention an emergency food shortage in a refugee camp filled with Bangladesh children who were at risk of severe malnutrition. She asked the sisters to contribute whatever they could to alleviate the crisis. Ninety-one sisters contributed an average of ninety dollars each to help alleviate this crisis.

As noted earlier, for thirty-six years over one hundred sisters provided consistent funding to Sister Ana María's clinic in Chiapas. More recently, the sisters have responded to calls for financial aid and other support for the victims of the 2004 earthquake and tsunami in Indonesia, of Hurricane Katrina in 2005, and of the 2010 earthquake and cholera epidemic in Haiti.

The Humilities have also provided financial support for many smaller, lesser-known projects. For example, over the past four years, Pat Miller has raised funds within the community to build wells providing clean drinking water for small villages in Honduras and in Tanzania. These wells have decreased typhoid, cholera, and other infections by eighty percent. The project has also provided irrigation water for farmers' crops, taught people in the villages how to build and maintain the wells, and has helped unify the people in these villages.

To support Heifer International, an organization whose mission is to end hunger and poverty and to promote care of the earth, Sister Elizabeth Anne Schneider has each year for many years spearheaded a Christmas fund-raising drive within the community. Heifer International provides livestock, seeds, and training to low-income families throughout the world paid for by contributions from donors like the Sisters of Humility. These gifts improve the families' nutrition and generate sustainable ways of increasing their income. The animals given to the families are considered "living loans." Each recipient of an animal pledges to give the first female offspring to another family in need. The program

**Sister Elizabeth Anne Schneider**

by design creates an ever-expanding network of hope. The Sisters of Humility have, through Heifer International, provided heifers, water buffalos, breeding sheep, breeding llamas, goats, pigs, rabbits, and flocks of chickens, honeybees, tree seedlings, and much needed training to poor families throughout the world. In poor developing countries, these seemingly small contributions often have an exponential effect in improving poor people's lives.

# Caring for the Earth

In 1990, the Sisters of Humility officially adopted the care of the earth as part of their mission. But since the community's founding nearly 160 years ago, care of the earth has always been an integral part of life in the community. From 1890 until 1979, the community had a working farm at Ottumwa Heights. Even though men cultivated the fields and milked the cows, the sisters planted and harvested produce from a large garden, grapes from the vineyard, pears and apples from the orchard, and corn from the fields. All the food produced on the farm was used to feed the sisters, St. Joseph Academy and Ottumwa Heights College students who lived on campus, and poor people in the community. Nothing was wasted.

In 1957, a fire destroyed the buildings at Ottumwa Heights, which housed both the headquarters of the community and the college. After the reconstruction of these facilities, the members in the novitiate under the direction of Sister Helen Marie Heller, who was the crew boss, landscaped the property. They laid sod, planted trees, bushes and flowerbeds, cut down overgrown brush, and built a bridge over the lake on the property. When Ottumwa Heights was sold in 1980, the community built a new headquarters in Davenport, and once again the sisters did much of the landscaping themselves. Through farming and landscaping, the sisters developed an understanding of what caring for the earth means in a practical sense.

In an October 1974 letter to the community, Bernadine stimulated the community's study of the relationship between humans and nature. Quoting Rachel Carson's warning from *Silent Spring*, she said, "I truly believe that we in this generation must come to terms with nature, and I think we are challenged as humankind has never been challenged before, to prove our maturity and mastery, not of nature, but of ourselves."[1]

As both a scientist and a woman of faith, it was important to Bernadine to reconcile science and faith in order to clearly understand our responsibility as human beings to care for the earth. Through science, she said, we have learned that our world is not the center of the universe and that humans share physical characteristics with other living things, including the earth itself. She pointed out that we are simply part of the web of relationships that make up the universe. In order to understand our proper place in the universe, Bernadine said, we have to relinquish the belief that we humans were meant to dominate the earth, and instead see the universe as continuing to evolve as part of ongoing creation, accepting that we are mere kin or partners in a cosmic journey.[2]

Sister Adrienne Marie Savage, beginning in the 1980s, also quietly but persistently urged the sisters to study the inherent relationship between nature and human spirituality. Adrienne Marie grew up in Montana and as a young person joined the military during World War II. When she completed her military service, she had a deep longing to do something significant with her life, so she joined the Humilities and became a teacher of both children and adults for over twenty-five years.

Spurred by Bernadine's personal encouragement and her writings on the earth-human relationship, Adrienne Marie discovered her true calling in life—exploring in depth the earth-human relationship and the revelation of God through nature. She spent the remainder of her life studying the leading spiritual ecology scholars and organizing a library of their books and video lectures at the Humility of Mary Center in Davenport. She also conducted workshops and one-to-one sessions about the interrelationship of human beings and nature, and the importance of respect for and care of the earth in the development of one's spiritual life. As Sister Kathleen Hanley, one of the Humilities in Montana, said of Adrienne Marie, "She became our conscience regarding our mission to care for the earth."

The Sisters of Humility have lived their lives consistent with these values. The sisters' practice of simple living reflects their belief in the sacredness of nature and the mutual relationship between humans and the earth. At the Humility of Mary Center in Davenport and other places where Sisters of Humility reside, respect for the earth through energy efficient lighting and appliances, recycling, conservation of water, organic gardening, investments in preserving the earth such as the development and maintenance of the Our Lady of the Prairie retreat, and advocacy for environmental causes is commonplace.

More recently, however, the Sisters have taken a more public role in raising consciousness regarding the importance of a beneficial relationship between human beings, the earth, and the universe. Their support of the Earth Charter—a declaration of fundamental ethical principles for building a just, sustainable, and peaceful society—is one way the Humilities have chosen to express these values.

The Earth Charter is the product of a decades-long cross-cultural dialogue in which hundreds of organizations and thousands of individuals throughout the world participated. It grew out of the global ethics movement that gave rise to the Universal Declaration of Human Rights adopted by the United Nations General Assembly in December 1948. Its mission is to facilitate the transition from wasteful lifestyles to sustainable living and to foster a global society founded on a shared ethical framework, which promotes respect and care for the community of life, ecological integrity and universal human rights, respect for diversity, economic justice, and a culture of peace.

Unlike the United Nations' Declaration of Human Rights, the Earth Charter is a civil society initiative approved by the Earth Charter Commission at the UNESCO headquarters in Paris in 2000, but it has yet to be adopted by the United Nations. Thus much work remains to build the necessary support across the entire world to make the Earth Charter, like the Declaration of Human Rights, an obligation for all members of the international community.[3] As warned in the Preamble of the Charter, the stark choice facing this generation is "to form a global partnership to care for the earth and one another or risk the destruction of ourselves and the diversity of life."[4]

At the beginning of her term as president of the Sisters of Humility in 2004, Roberta Brich convened a group to plan an Earth Charter Summit in the Quad Cities to educate people in the region about the Earth Charter and to encourage actions to implement its mission and principles. In 2007, the Humilities hosted the first annual Quad Cities Earth Charter Summit, which attracted 250 participants. It focused on the core principles of the charter and on securing commitments from various community-based organizations to help achieve ratification of the charter by the world community.

The Sisters of Humility have continued to raise public conscious-ness regarding the importance of taking collective action to preserve the earth, emphasizing the connection between preserving the earth and promoting justice and peace. In April 2008, Roberta brought to-gether the mayors of Davenport and Bettendorf, Iowa, East Moline, Moline, and Rock Island, Illinois to discuss mutual concerns about the care of the earth and its people in the five communities comprising the Quad Cities. One purpose of the meeting was to publicize the cur-rent and future green initiatives taking place in each of these cities and to rally support for them. While at the Humility of Mary Center, the mayors joined the Humilities in dedicating the internationally recog-nized Peace Pole bearing the message "May Peace Prevail on Earth" in seven languages as a way of highlighting the interconnection between peace and care of the earth.

In October 2008, the Humilities hosted the Second Annual Quad Cities Earth Charter Summit, which drew even more participants than the first. Since the United Nations had designated 2008 as the Year of Planet Earth, this Summit focused on climate change, sustainable sys-tems for identifying and reducing environmental contaminants, and the changes in lifestyle that individuals can make to reduce ecological harm.

At the time of the conference, Sister Cathleen Real, who had chaired the 2007 Summit, was in Nashville, Tennessee as she had been selected by the Climate Project to participate in the first training of 135 faith-based community leaders to teach people in their communities about the perils of climate change and the moral imperative to do something about it. She returned to the Quad Cities and sounded the alarm regarding the dangers to the earth, the biosphere, and all people posed by climate change. Cathleen today continues to educate individuals and groups regarding the immediate actions required to prevent future destruction of the earth and the biosphere, making clear the important choice facing us, "Will we have the moral courage to act now to resolve the looming crisis caused by climate change?"

Cathleen also works with other organizations committed to supporting sensible and sustainable policies to preserve the earth. For example, she serves on the board of the Iowa Interfaith Power and Light (Iowa IPL), a statewide organization that mobilizes church communities to educate their members about the dangers of climate change, helps people reduce their carbon footprints, and advocates for sustainable environmental policies. One of Iowa IPL's current initiatives is to organize people in faith communities to raise awareness of global warming, energy conservation, and renewable energy in forums and discussions with candidates for local, state, and federal offices during the current election cycles.

Sisters Cathleen Real and Joann Kuebrich

In 2009, Progressive Action for the Common Good in the Quad Cities stepped forward and announced that it would take the lead in hosting the 2009 and 2010 Earth Charter Summits. The Humilities and other community-based organizations and businesses served as cosponsors. The goal of the 2009 Summit was to promote and assist in the development of a healthy, safe, sustainable, local food supply for the Quad Cities and local sustainable agriculture. The 2010 Summit focused on the economic justice principles of the Earth Charter. Labor unions, representing thousands of people in the Quad Cities, signed on as co-sponsors and actively participated in this Summit.

In October 2011, the Sisters of Humility, Progressive Action for the Common Good, and Augustana College sponsored the Fifth Earth Charter Summit, which explored ways to sustain and strengthen communities by building local food production and distribution systems. To broaden the participation in the Summit, the proceedings were carried online.

In addition to these efforts, the Humilities in Davenport have also in the past seven years supported practical care of the earth projects, including the annual community-based cleanup of the Mississippi river. For decades, communities along the Mississippi, including Davenport, have used the river and its banks as a dumping ground. It took the voice and actions of a young conservationist, Chad Pregracke, to awaken the Quad Cities communities to the environmental degradation of the river and to convince them to become preservers rather than destroyers of the "Mighty Mississippi."

In 1998, Chad founded Living Lands & Waters, a non-profit organization dedicated to cleaning up and preserving the nation's rivers and hosted the first community-based cleanup of the Mississippi in the Quad Cities called Xstream Clean-up. Since then, the Humilities have staffed the volunteer tables for the annual cleanup and joined hundreds of Quad City citizens in removing tons of garbage from the river and its shore.

At the annual cleanups, former students and other friends join the sisters. Curtis Lundy, who the Sisters of Humility taught at both St. Vincent's and Sacred Heart School in Davenport, is a committed naturalist who shares their deep concern for and care of the earth. Currently, Curtis is rehabilitating 130 acres of bluff land bordered by the Yellow River and Hickory Creek in Southeastern Iowa, including a trout stream, woods, constructed wetlands, meadows, and agricultural land. His goal is to promote a healthy habitat for the land's diverse ecosystems, which can also serve as an educational site for students to gain a greater appreciation of the delicate balance in nature.[5]

Although these care of the earth efforts by the Humilities and their friends will not by themselves solve the immense environmental problems in the world, they do represent the essential element for revolutionary societal change—the small but persistent efforts of a growing number of committed people who understand that we are all one human family who must care for and preserve the earth.

# Serving Appalachian People

In 1975, Sister Martha Mary "Marty" Conrad, an elementary teacher for thirteen years, experienced what she has called "a compelling urge to focus her efforts on ministering to poor people in Appalachia." She shared the idea with Bernadine and Ann Therese, who supported her idea. Bernadine said, "Why don't you go check out where in Appalachia you might like to minister. If your plans don't work out in Appalachia, you can look elsewhere or go back to teaching."

So, Marty and two other sisters set off to explore the possibilities in Kentucky. One of the towns they visited was Somerset, where Marty stopped at St. Mildred Church and met staff who described the needs of the community. They emphasized to Marty that St. Mildred is a church that cares about poor people and their needs. They cited as evidence the parish's monthly second collection to benefit people who need financial assistance. Marty quickly decided that this was the place for her.

When she returned to Iowa, she consulted again with Bernadine and described the work in Somerset that she would be doing. Bernadine asked what she could do to help and Marty asked for some seed money to get a car and pay her expenses until she became settled. Bernadine committed five thousand dollars over a two-year period to help her buy a car and become established in Somerset.

Somerset is a small town nestled in the foothills of the Appalachian Mountains in southern Kentucky. Located in Pulaski County, Somerset had a population of 10,500 people when Marty moved there. While the town of Somerset itself has never been the poorest place in Kentucky, over twenty-one percent of Somerset residents currently live below the poverty line. Children and older people have and continue to bear much of the brunt of poverty. Thirty-two percent of children live in poverty.[1] and many older people and families isolated in the hills outside Somerset are even poorer. Many live in shacks, have no jobs, are hungry, and live without hope.

St. Mildred Church had no formal outreach program when Marty arrived, so she began by assisting people who showed up at her home. News spread like wildfire about the sister providing help to people at her home, and the number of people who sought help made it impossible for Marty to continue to accommodate them at her home. The church, therefore, established an Outreach Center and named Marty its director.

Marty believes that her ministry to poor people in Somerset was "a radical response to the Christian gospel." However, Marty does not consider herself a revolutionary on a large scale or a political activist seeking systemic change. Instead, she believes in helping to improve the lives of individual people one by one. She lives by the philosophy expressed by a former president of the St. Mildred parish counsel, who said, "A parish that looks in on itself and only feeds itself and doesn't look out to the community to meet its needs doesn't deserve to exist."

Marty is also rooted in her deep but simple faith in God. She places her own problems and those of the people with whom she works in God's hands. According to Marty, her work in Somerset was the best job in the world because she could see the grace of God overflow in the lives of many people everyday.

During her thirty-five years as Director of the Outreach Center, Marty proved that St. Mildred Church did indeed deserve to exist. She and her volunteers served tens of thousands of poor people throughout Pulaski County. In 2008 alone, the Center served 3,263 families. Their problems were many and diverse, but their most prevalent problem was lack of adequate income to meet their basic needs and unexpected emergencies. For example, a woman came into the center distraught. Her husband had finally gotten a job after months of unemployment, but was picked up for a fine he had not paid for the prior three years. Their baby was seriously ill and had to go to the doctor every week. These demands made it literally impossible for her husband to pay the fine. If he did not pay it, he would go to jail and lose his job. Marty, through the Outreach Center, loaned him the money to pay the fine. She also found a doctor willing to treat the child for free.

A thirty-three-year old man whose wife suffers from seizures visited the center with his small son. He explained that he had attempted suicide seven times due to his lack of income and subsequent inability to feed and shelter his family or secure medicine to treat his wife's seizures. His work hours had been cut back and he was in danger of losing his job because he did not have any way to pay for the required skid-proof boots and black belt. Marty helped him get the boots and belt he needed so that he could keep his job and also secured the necessary medication for his wife.

A tall man with a small child asked for a few dollars for gas so that he could get to the hospital to see his wife and their newborn baby, who needed immediate surgery. One of the Center volunteers asked the man why he was not working. The man opened his shirt and showed the scars from a recent heart-surgery. After getting the check for gas, the man picked up the small boy. The volunteer noticed that the child had only one eye and the father explained that he was giving his son a bath when he noticed his eye was protruding. So he took his son to the doctor who diagnosed a malignant eye tumor that had to be removed.

On almost a daily basis Marty encountered homeless individuals and families. When homeless people showed up at her home in the middle of the night or appeared at the Outreach Center, Marty never turned them away. One night, a mother and five young children, four girls and a boy, showed up at her door around midnight. They had no place to stay for the night, so Marty invited them to stay with her. The youngest child, who was about five years old, kept hugging her while saying, "I'm so glad you're alive." Marty knew that meant that the little girl was grateful to have a safe place to stay, and she herself was also grateful because these children were her "special visitors in the night." When they left the next day, one of the older girls left Marty one of her treasures, a Canadian penny.

Another night, Marty took into her home a woman with two small children who had no home, no money for a motel, or no place to stay for the night. Like other homeless mothers, she was afraid that she would lose her children if she could not find them a safe place to stay. They stayed for two nights. Many other homeless people over the years slept in the church, the rectory, or at Marty's home. Some stayed only a night; others stayed several weeks. Marty and other Center staff would give them money for a motel room or gas money to get to a family member's or friend's home.

Marty, through the Outreach Center, also helped people who lived in substandard or dangerous housing. The Center sponsored a house repair program in which college and high school students, working under the supervision of local crew leaders, repaired homes, or in some instances built new ones. One of the home repairs involved closing holes in a house to prevent the constant infestation by rats that had been eating the toes of a small child in the family. In another house, the students built steps for an eighty-one-year old woman whose insurance was being cancelled because her back door was five feet off the ground with no steps.

The students also built ramps to make homes accessible for disabled people. For example, they built a ramp and a walkway for a twenty-five-year old woman with multiple sclerosis who had not walked since her father died five years before. When Marty and the student crew returned to finish the job, the woman was very excited. When the ramp was completed, she was no longer trapped in her home but was able to go out into the community with her mother.

The students also built a ramp and painted the house of a forty-one-year old paraplegic. When the man and his wife divorced, Marty found a caregiver for him. Describing the help Marty gave to him, the man said, "Without Marty in my life, I would not be here today."

The students built homes for people with special needs, including one for a man who had spent thirty years in a mental institution. His new house not only gave him the first place he ever had to call home, but a new sense of his own dignity as well. Another was for the family of a man who had completely withdrawn from life after he had been seriously hurt in a logging accident. A third house was built for the large family of a man injured when a truck rolled over his back. When he recovered from the accident, he spent the next eight years serving as a volunteer at the Outreach Center.

While the Center's housing program made a real difference in the lives of many people in Somerset, it also made a difference in the lives of the students who participated in the program. The people of Somerset shared their lives and stories with the students who came away with a new understanding and appreciation for the rich spirit and strong faith of the Appalachian people.

In parts of Pulaski County that had no fire departments, people frequently lost their homes to fire. To help remedy this problem for one community in the county, the Outreach Center gave a semi-truck full of clothes donated by people in Iron City, Michigan to the people of Tateville, who sold the clothing at a big yard sale and used the proceeds to buy equipment for a fire department just being established.

Hunger was a very real problem in Somerset and the surrounding county, so Marty helped organize a food pantry in the furnace room of the church. For many years, this pantry was the primary source of food for many poor people in Pulaski County. Over time, the church pantry expanded with the help of other community agencies to become God's Food Pantry, a countywide pantry that in 2009 provided just over five hundred thousand meals to poor families and individuals.[2] With the help of parishioners and businesses in the community, Marty put on a community Thanksgiving dinner each year for thirty-five years, serving hundreds of persons in need.

In addition, Marty organized people in the parish to solve other problems, such as a dangerous railroad crossing at which many people had been killed over the years. After investigating the crossing and the circumstances of the prior deaths, the team found that a dangerous grade in the road leading to the crossing and the lack of automatic controls to bar cars from crossing when trains approached caused the deaths. Within just a few weeks time, they solved both problems and prevented future deaths at the crossing.

Marty also focused her attention on people who were poor in spirit. She describes "sharing God's graces with those in broken relationships, in bondage to destructive drugs, those living in violent situations, those who were sick and in hopeless conditions, those in jail, and those without faith." Through the years, she learned that her best tool was listening. She understood she couldn't solve their problems for them, but she could listen to them and provide the support necessary for them to face and resolve their own problems. By doing so, she preserved their pride and dignity.

After thirty-five years in Somerset, Marty returned to Iowa—not to retire, but to join Humilities living in the River Bend neighborhood on the north side of Des Moines. This inner city neighborhood has many of the same problems she had faced in Kentucky, low-income and homeless people in need of food, shelter and clothing as well as pervasive problems of drugs and prostitution.

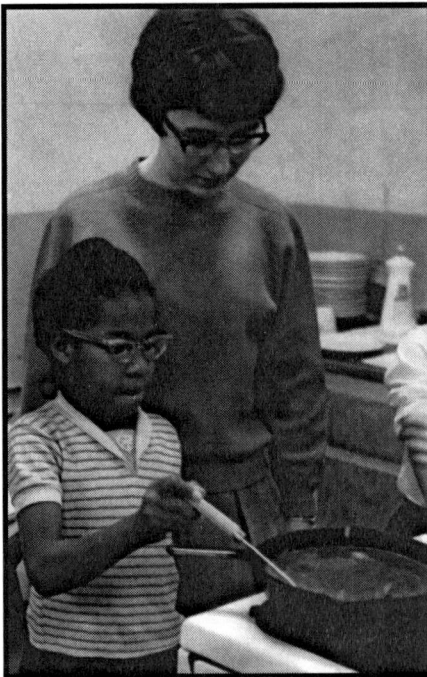
Sister Marty Conrad and friend

Since 2002, Sisters Ramona Kaalberg, Donna Schmitt, Johanna Rickl, Ursula Keough, and Lynn Mousel, along with Rose Arnoldy, a Seeds of Hope volunteer, have, at various times, been members of the River Bend community while carrying out their regular jobs. They have no set agenda, but simply respond to the needs presented by the residents of the neighborhood. Over the years, they have served meals for the homeless on the Salvation Army's breakfast truck, developed community gardens, and volunteered at the Catholic Worker House and the St. Vincent de Paul outlets. For many years, Donna Schmitt served as resident manager of a low-income apartment building. They have provided arts and crafts classes for older residents and neighborhood children, and organized summer festivals and community block parties for the neighborhood. In short, they just try to be supportive neighbors. Marty feels right at home there and is currently using her outreach skills honed over thirty-five years in Appalachia to help meet the needs of her River Bend neighbors.


Sister Mary Rehmann, like Marty, also began a journey in the mid-1970s that eventually led her to Appalachia, where for twenty years she provided legal representation to poor West Virginians. Mary's first stop on her journey, however, was Chicago, Illinois. After teaching for fourteen years, Mary moved to Chicago in 1973 to become a member of the three-person staff of the National Assembly of Religious Women (NARW).

The two years Mary worked at NARW were exciting times. Women on NARW's staff and national board were creative and courageous women who became leaders in their individual communities and national leaders of religious women. NARW sought to harness the collective power of women to build a world of peace and justice, specifically emphasizing the elimination of systemic injustices that directly impacted the lives of women and children. To achieve this goal, NARW mobilized sisters as well as lay women and men across the United States through Ministry for Justice workshops.

NARW also promoted and strengthened Sisters Councils and facilitated communication among religious congregations across the country during the period of major change following Vatican II. Through its monthly publication, *Probe*, NARW publicized new areas of ministry by sisters. While editing an issue of *Probe* in 1975 about women in law, Mary began thinking seriously about becoming a lawyer. When some of the contributors to that issue of *Probe* encouraged her, Mary entered DePaul University School of Law in Chicago, with the goal of combining her interest in both law and the environment.

After completing law school in 1978, Mary joined the enforcement section at the Illinois Environmental Protection Agency (IEPA). At that time, IEPA and other states, were translating the broad goals of the landmark Clean Air and Clean Water Acts into specific standards governing the quantity and type of pollutants that could be legally discharged into the air or public waters. At the IEPA, Mary worked with engineers, statisticians, public health specialists, and field staff to develop and organize evidence to support adoption of regulations proposed by the water and air divisions of the agency. Although Mary believed then, as she does today, that such environmental protection requires both national and global action, she used the legal tools available to her in the 1970s and 80s to try to preserve the nation's air and water not only for the current generation of citizens, but for future generations as well.

After eight years at the IEPA, Mary took a sabbatical at the Women's Theological Center in Boston. As part of her studies, Mary worked with women in prison. This work made a lasting impression on her and contributed to her decision to refocus her legal work on directly serving poor persons.

In 1987, Mary moved to Williamson, West Virginia, a small mining town and railroad hub in Mingo County with a population around 3,500 people. She served as the sole legal aid lawyer in the county. In this position, Mary was responsible for representing low-income persons in divorce, child custody, public benefits, landlord/tenant disputes, consumer collection, education, and social security cases. Her practice was intense and, at times, very difficult. When one of her clients lost custody of her child, Mary was so devastated that she considered leaving the practice of law.

In 1990, Mary's interest was sparked by the lack of portability in health insurance coverage and the exclusions of pre-existing conditions from health insurance coverage, which prevented people from securing necessary medical care. After moving to Morgantown, WV in 1991, Mary researched the "gaps" in access to health care in the area under the auspices of the local free health clinic. When she found a severe lack of services and insurance coverage for persons with mental illness, she decided to do something about it.

Mary returned to the legal aid program and began representing low-income disabled people who had been denied disability income benefits under the Supplemental Security Income (SSI) program. For those who have no Medicaid coverage at the time of their application for SSI, a denial of the SSI income benefits also results in a denial of medical care coverage under the Medicaid program. As many people who are denied SSI benefits suffer from mental illness or chronic pain, the denial of SSI and consequently of Medicaid leaves them without access to medical care necessary to treat their debilitating conditions.

When the mid-term elections of 1994 returned Republicans to the majority in Congress, they slashed funding to legal aid programs throughout the country. When the funds for legal aid were cut by a

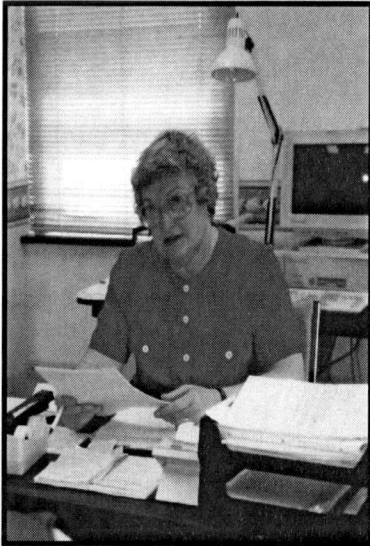

Sister Mary Rehmann

third in 1995, Mary's job was eliminated. Undaunted, Mary opened a private law office specializing in representing low-income disabled people who were denied Social Security Disability (SSDI) as well as SSI benefits. Mary advertised that she took "the tough cases"— the ones where the person's disability was rooted in illnesses with subjective symptoms such as mental illness and chronic pain. Low-income disabled people with "tough cases" flocked to her practice. Mary also took court appointments in which she represented children or parents in custody cases and served as a volunteer lawyer in domestic abuse cases.

She finally closed her practice in 2008 when she was elected president of the Sisters of Humility. In her ten years in private practice, Mary had successfully represented hundreds of poor disabled people. More often than not, she secured for them SSDI or SSI benefits, which in turn made them eligible for Medicaid or Medicare. Mary's long time commitment to poor people was one of the reasons the Humilities chose her to serve as their current president.

In 2010, Mary joined more than sixty other religious leaders representing the majority of women religious in the U.S. in signing a letter to Congress supporting enactment of the Health Care Reform

Act (HCRA). They stood with the Catholic Health Association's 2100 Catholic hospitals in expressing a view at odds with the position of the U.S. Conference of Catholic Bishops, who opposed the enactment of the Health Care Reform Act on the alleged grounds that the Act would provide federal funding for abortions. In their letter, Mary and the other leaders of religious communities pointed out that HCRA does not in fact authorize the use of federal funding for elective abortions. Instead the Act provides an additional $250 million investment in support for pregnant women, which is "the real pro-life stance."[3] Since the act also expands health care coverage to millions of citizens who currently do not have it, supporting the HCRA was for Mary a moral imperative.

# Making Miracles Happen in the Quad Cities

The Sisters of Humility have served poor people in Davenport, Iowa for over a century. Starting in 1897 and for the next eighty years, they cared for and taught orphans at St. Vincent's Home and taught immigrants at St. Alphonsus School and at Marycrest College. For the past forty years, a number of Humility sisters have focused their efforts on housing and other essential supports for Davenport's low-income and homeless families and individuals.

In the late 1960s, when the sisters were freed to choose where they would work and what they would do, Sisters Germaine Dermody, Miriam Therese Foley, and Teresa Gomez decided they would work on improving the educational levels of poor children in Davenport's Central Community Circle neighborhood. This inner-city neighborhood, at the time filled with deteriorating housing, was home to many low-income single parent families. Because of the instability of its residential base and the influx of drugs, Central Community Circle in the 1960s was a dangerous neighborhood.

When these Humilities moved into the neighborhood, they found it virtually locked down due to the high crime rate. So they went house to house knocking on doors, introducing themselves, and explaining the programs they intended to offer children.

Germaine and Miriam Therese both initially taught at Lincoln elementary school, the Central Community Circle public school. Teresa founded and served as the director of the first Head Start program in Davenport, which she located on Sixth Street in the heart of the Central Community Circle neighborhood. In addition to their day jobs, all three tutored neighborhood children at night, on weekends, and during school vacations.

As the demand for tutoring services grew, Germaine in 1968 established the Sixth Street Community Center, which became a home for hundreds of children where they could get advice, tutoring, and boxing lessons. As Germaine described the center, "It's a place where people with an idea can try it out. If it is successful, it usually keeps on going." The guiding spirit of the center, according to Germaine, was that "everyone helps one another—that's what it is all about."[1]

Volunteers staffed the Center and the tutoring program especially turned out to be a great success. Sixty or more volunteer tutors—college students, housewives, and teachers—twice a week provided the children of the neighborhood the personal attention and support necessary to help them learn and the positive relationships missing in many of their lives. As tutors worked one-on-one with the children, the program always had a waiting list of children seeking admission.

The boxing program for boys eleven and older served as an outlet for pent-up frustrations and stress from inner-city living. Alveno Pena, a professional boxer, directed the program with the help of volunteers, taught both boxing skills and sportsmanship. In 1968, three boys from the center made it to a national boxing competition.[2]

For ten years, Germaine directed the center and became a legend not only in the Central Community Circle neighborhood, but also in the broader Quad Cities area. In the 1980s, Germaine served as lead teacher in the Head Start program and then resumed teaching at Lincoln elementary school for many more years. When she retired, she continued to tutor children through the Center for Active Seniors, Inc.

**Sister Teresa Gomez**

For eighteen years, Miriam Therese taught at Lincoln School and tutored at the Sixth Street Center. She was a superior teacher, who cared deeply about her students and worked hard to help them succeed. Teresa, after directing the Head Start program for a number of years, focused on providing shelter to homeless people and seniors. She also became known as a premier scavenger for coats, shoes, food and other supplies for homeless people.

All three of the Central Community Circle pioneers lived long lives, during which they continued to serve poor and other disadvantaged persons. Tom Wolfe, one of the volunteers at the Sixth Street Center, aptly captures the significance of their work in a 2006 tribute published by the *Quad-Cities Times*:

**Sisters Germaine Dermody and Miriam Therese Foley**

> Margaret Meade once said that a small group of dedicated people could change the world. I don't think Sister Germaine Dermody . . . changed the whole world, but she did change a small part of it, and she certainly improved the lives of many impoverished Davenport citizens for many years. She also helped many others, such as me, see what practicing the social gospel was all about if one "really" practiced what one preached.
>
> Sister Germaine and other very special people such as Sister Miriam Therese and Sister Teresa Gomez served the poor in the most humble manner for years in this city, and I was privileged to have known them. There is an old Irish blessing that says, "May you ever have a kindly greeting from them you meet along the road." That is how Sister Germaine and her friends lived, and all of us can learn from their example.[3]

Beginning in the 1980s, other Sisters of Humility joined the effort to serve low-income persons and families in Davenport, especially in the Central Community Circle neighborhood. In the early 1980s, Sister Ramona Kaalberg, while teaching full time at Marycrest, joined Project Renewal, a group of religious and lay volunteers who lived communally and operated after-school and summer programs for children of Central Community Circle. Ramona's volunteer "job" was to serve as a "caring presence" for children, who stopped by the Project Renewal house after school. She found that simply listening to the children seemed to fill a void in their lives.

Two years later, Sister Mary John Byers, decided that the neighborhood was just the right place for balancing her spiritual counseling and retreat work with service to poor families. Mary John and Ramona moved into a condemned house on Sixth Street, fixed it up and opened it to the neighborhood. Their home became a site for the common prayer life of the Project Renewal community as well as a gathering place for both adults and children in the neighborhood. Ramona focused on the children and Mary John became the friendly community sounding board for women of the neighborhood. She served them coffee, listened to their troubles, and supported them in their roles as mothers of young children and the sole providers for their families.

Mary John, at various times during her thirteen years in the neighborhood, also organized volunteers to become mentors for neighborhood children, offered art classes on the weekends for them, and created what she called her "clown ministry." She dressed the children up in clown costumes, grease painted their faces, and took them with her when she went to visit elders and sick people in nursing homes. According to Mary John, the children loved the experience and she enjoyed watching them learn to give back to others in the community. When reflecting in 2001 on her years in the Central Community Circle neighborhood, she said, "I found God in that neighborhood more than in any other place or any other work I have done."

In the spring of 1987, after the Humilities moved their headquarters to Davenport, Sisters Mary Ann Vogel and Joann Kuebrich convened a group of sisters to explore the current unmet needs of the Quad Cities and determine how they might best help meet them. Calling themselves the "Dream Team," they began their work by consulting with educators, advocates for low-income people, health care providers, church leaders, representatives of the legal system, and staff of community service agencies, foundations, and city governments throughout the Quad Cities area.

They discovered that affordable housing, particularly for older persons and single parent families, quickly rose to the top of the list as the most pressing need. The Humilities decided to focus on single parent families because, by doing so, they felt they could help change lives two generations at a time. As the sisters did not want to become just landlords, they set out to create a model supportive housing program that would provide a way out of poverty and homelessness for single parent families.

The members of the Dream Team from the beginning saw this project as a joint venture between the Humilities and the broader Quad Cities community. Developing community ownership of the project, they believed, was critical not only to secure the necessary financial support to serve the expanding numbers of low-income single parent families in the community, but to ensure that the program became a permanent resource in the community. Therefore, they created Humility of Mary Housing, Inc. (HMHI) as an independent 501c(3) corporation, with a board of directors comprised of both Sisters of Humility and members of the broader community. Currently, the HMHI board of directors is made up of three Sisters of Humility and nine members from the Quad Cities region.

From 1990 to 2001, Mary Ann served as both the full time financial director of the Sisters of Humility and the financial director of HMHI. With a no-interest loan from the Sisters of Humility payable in ten years, HMHI in 1990 bought its first home for single parent families, a four-plex apartment complex on Columbia Avenue in Davenport. Over the past twenty-one years, the Sisters of Humility, both corporately and individually, have contributed additional financing and volunteer assistance necessary to expand the program and ensure its success.

To help get HMHI off to a good start, Mary Ann's mother, Gertrude, began her tradition of holding what she calls "Fresh Start" sales to support HMHI. During the past twenty-one years, Gertrude's Fresh Start sales have yielded over $169,000 for HMHI. Gertrude, at ninety-one, is unstoppable. She spends a day or more at HMHI each week sorting and cataloguing donations for the annual sale. She hopes that the Fresh Start sales will be an ongoing HMHI tradition.

In 1990, HMHI hired Sandra (Sandy) Walters as the executive director and initial social services coordinator for the organization. Germaine Dermody recommended Sandy as she had a history of successfully working with single parent families and other vulnerable

**Sister Mary Ann Vogel and friends**

people, and had the passion, courage, and determination to make the project succeed. Sandy also had solid relationships with church communities, a willingness to trust in the generosity of the Quad Cities community, and a belief that "miracles can happen." All of these qualities were core job requirements as HMHI at the time had the meager sum of thirty thousand dollars to pay Sandy's salary and all other expenses of the corporation. Undaunted by the meager amount of secure funding, Sandy and Mary Ann forged ahead.

In collaboration with board members, Sandy designed the HMHI supportive housing program, which she and Mary Ann implemented for the first time at the Columbia Avenue complex in 1990. This program provides affordable furnished apartments at below market rates based upon each family's income and a structured living environment designed to help parents become self-sufficient. Upon admission, an HMHI social worker meets with the parent and they jointly create a plan aimed at overcoming the obstacles that might prevent him/her from independently supporting and caring for his or her children. They agree upon specific goals for growth in the parent's educational levels and job skills as well parenting, housekeeping, budgeting, meal planning, and time management skills. Throughout the family's residency at HMHI, a social worker meets with the parent on a regular basis to provide encouragement and whatever assistance is necessary to help the parent succeed. HMHI also provides a food pantry, clothing, hygiene and household supplies, life skills classes, tutoring, access to computers, and counseling.

As HMHI seeks to foster a strong sense of community among residents, staff, and volunteers, celebrating birthdays, Halloween, Easter, Christmas and other important events is integral to the living experience at HMHI. Although the average length of stay in the program is eighteen months to two years with a six-month transition program, the length is flexible depending upon the individual needs of each family.

HMHI's first resident was Connie and her infant daughter. While a student at St. Ambrose College, Connie had become pregnant and didn't see that she had many options. There was no family housing on campus and Connie's parents lived too far away for her to commute. So Sister Ritamary Bradley, a teacher at St. Ambrose, referred her to HMHI.

When Connie moved into HMHI's Columbia apartment complex in 1990, her child was only a month old. As a new parent, Connie needed a lot of help and support. Sandy carefully observed Connie caring for her child and provided her the supports she needed. When her daughter first began to crawl, Connie came running down the stairs, put her daughter on the floor and said, "Look, she can crawl!" According to Sandy, Connie's joy "made me want to be part of the growth of this agency."[4]

While residing at HMHI, Connie graduated from St. Ambrose and secured a job with a local physician. After a short period of time, she went to work for Alcoa and over the years has been promoted up the ranks of the company. She has since married and has two additional children. Based upon her experience at HMHI, Connie is a firm supporter of the program. She regularly speaks on behalf of HMHI at fundraising events and as part of the United Way campaign at Alcoa. Currently, Connie also serves on the board of HMHI.

Another early resident at HMHI was a homeless mom and her son. The night before they appeared at HMHI seeking help, the mom had slept on the streets and had only a can of cold green beans to eat while her son stayed at a friend's home. Sandy, after listening to the woman's story, said, "You are not going to have to do this again." And she was right. This homeless mother and her child became residents in the HMHI program during which she finished her education, secured a job at a bank, and has subsequently successfully raised her son.

Between 1990 and 2004, HMHI leased, built, or rehabbed donated properties on seventeen separate sites to provide a total of forty-seven apartments for single parent families. A substantial number of these apartments are located in the Central Community Circle neighborhood. A strong partnership between HMHI, the Sisters of Humility, and individuals and agencies in the Quad Cities have made this development possible.

Because housing for parents in recovery from alcohol or drugs quickly emerged as a high priority need, HMHI opened three apartment complexes from 1991-93 dedicated to families with a parent in recovery. These families need a lot of support, so Mary Ann served as the site manager from 1991-2003. Her work with the families in recovery was, according to Mary Ann, "a life changing experience." She lived with them through the parents' daily struggles to maintain their sobriety and saw the courage it took for them to balance these struggles with the hard work of supporting their children and creating a better life for all of them. While Mary Ann's work with parents in recovery has been hard, it has also been life saving for both parents and their children.

In July 1992, HMHI opened its first handicapped accessible site. Two years later, HMHI opened a five-plex complex dedicated to families in which the parent has a severe mental illness or traumatic brain injury with an on-site manager to assist such families.

During its first twenty-one years, HMHI served 684 parents and 1349 children. The growth and development of HMHI's first teen-age mom, Latoya, who arrived in 1994 when she was sixteen-years old with two children and no money, illustrates the value of the HMHI program. Latoya's mother firmly believed that Latoya could succeed and referred her daughter to the program. During her two-year residency, Latoya completed high school, graduating first in her class with a four-point average while supporting her family by working a night job at Greatest Grains. HMHI provided her secure housing and other necessary supports, including the glasses she needed to study and access to a computer to do her homework. Sandy taught her how to budget her money while Mary Ann tutored her in calculus. After graduating from high school, Latoya immediately enrolled at St. Ambrose College, earned an accounting degree, and became a manager at Greatest Grains, where she has worked for the last fifteen years while successfully raising her eight children. According to Latoya,

> Humility of Mary's positive environment gave me confidence that I could succeed. The goals I set kept me focused on self-sufficiency and HMHI's support helped me stay on track. Although it was hard, I managed to succeed with a lot of support from HMHI. Even after I completed the residential program, HMHI staff continued to assist me. They helped me find an apartment and furnished it. During the first year after I left HMHI, I was struggling financially. At Christmas, I got a call from a HMHI staff person, who told me that HMHI had gotten a little extra money and would like to share it with me. What a great Christmas gift! I will never forget how HMHI helped me realize the success that I knew was within me.

In 2002, three other Humility Sisters, Marilyn Schierbrock, Bea Snyder, and Nancy Schwieters joined the effort to serve Davenport's low-income families and homeless persons in the Central Community Circle neighborhood. Marilyn became a community organizer at the John Lewis Community Service Agency. On her first day on the job, the agency director, Kate Ridge, told her to "Go out and visit with the people and see what they need." Marilyn did precisely that and quickly learned that residents did not feel safe in their neighborhood. To bring people together, Marilyn started serving coffee on Wednesday mornings at the John Lewis Café. As more and more residents came together and got to know one another, they began working together on community concerns.

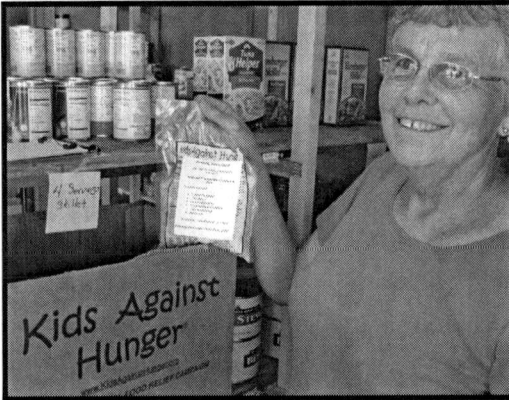

**Sister Marilyn Schierbrock**

To provide greater security for the community, Marilyn forged a personal relationship with the Davenport Police Department and then helped build a trusting relationship between the residents and police. She also developed a community watch program, which made the community safer.

The following summer Marilyn organized a community garden. The garden further fostered a cooperative relationship between the city and the residents of the neighborhood. The city tilled the soil, mapped out the garden on two empty city blocks, and built raised gardens. Marilyn got neighbors and volunteers from the Sisters of Humility to help plant the garden and the boy scouts built a patio. When the people in the neighborhood began to take pride in and own the garden, Marilyn invited them to pick whatever produce they wanted. Participating gardeners with their own plots began sharing their surplus produce with the

254

community pantry. The garden has become a showpiece in the neighborhood and is now included on city garden tours.

When Marilyn discovered that a fair number of grandmothers were raising their grandchildren and felt overwhelmed by this responsibility, she began taking them on short trips to give them some relief from their responsibilities. Through these trips, they got to know one another and began to provide each other mutual support. Marilyn has also worked with single parents in the neighborhood to help them increase their parenting skills and connect them to other services available in the neighborhood, including literacy and homemaking classes.

From 2000 to 2007, the residents became more community minded, crime went down and the Central Community Circle neighborhood became and remains a more stable, peaceful community. The services provided by Project Renewal, John Lewis, and HMHI also helped strengthen and increase the neighborhood's pride and cohesiveness. But, like a garden, a neighborhood like Central Community Circle needs constant nurturing. So Marilyn continues to walk the neighborhood, talking to the residents and assessing their needs. When new needs emerge, she does everything in her power to meet them.

In 2000, after spending fifteen years managing a soup kitchen for homeless people in Colorado, Sister Bea Snyder returned to Iowa and became a services coordinator at the John Lewis Shelter. Bea loved her work with the men at the shelter and focused her efforts on helping them resolve the myriad problems that led to their homelessness. Although many of them had had very hard lives, they were cooperative and appreciative of her work. Her bond with the men at the shelter made it difficult for Bea to leave in 2003 when she was asked to serve as the Director of the Humility Center in Davenport. At the time, Bea also had a nagging sense that John Lewis' rapid growth and lack of strong administrative structures to sustain it might destroy the network of services the homeless men with whom Bea worked depended upon.


In August 2007, John Lewis began to implode under too much debt. The first shoe to drop was the announcement that the John Lewis

Café, which had provided daily lunch to about 150 homeless or low-income people for the prior eight years, closed on August 14, 2007. This announcement caused shock waves in the community, particularly among church leaders who felt that the café was too important to let die. Leaders from the Quad Cities asked the Sisters of Humility to help them save the café. When Sister Roberta Birch, President of the Humilities, asked Bea if she would take the lead in the effort to save the café, Bea quickly agreed.

During her initial site review, Bea found that the café building required intensive cleaning and repair. She also learned that the annual operating budget for the café was approximately eighty-five thousand dollars per year. Undeterred by the problems, Bea began taking the action necessary to reopen the café.

The first issue, whether the Sisters of Humility would have to create a new legal entity to operate the café, was easily solved. Father Marvin Mottet, a member of Project Renewal in the neighborhood, and John Kelley, the social action director for the Diocese of Davenport, offered the Thomas Merton House, an existing non-profit organization, as a possible sponsor for the café. Bea accepted their offer.

Bea then publicly announced the Humilities' intention to reopen the café, but candidly stated they would need the help of the broader community to do so. Large numbers of volunteers came forward offering to repair and clean the premises, secure or donate food, help with daily services, and solicit funds to cover the costs of operating the café. United Way of the Quad Cites provided an initial grant to restore the café to operational status. Parishioners of St. Anthony's parish and

Sisters Miriam Anstey, Nancy Schwieters, Mary Ann Vogel, and Bea Snyder, with tiny resident of HMHI

other community and business groups, including King's Harvest, helped get the café ready for reopening. Individual donors and United Way, among others, provided the money necessary to operate the café on an ongoing basis.

On November 18, 2007, three months after John Lewis closed its café, Café on Vine opened for business. In its first year, the café served 43,675 meals. The community support for the café was amazing. Bea says she was "blown out of the water by how the people in the community responded." It reflected, she said, "good old mid-western values. People from the community donated all of the food served at the Café on Vine in the first year, except for salad dressings, which cost $103 for the year."

In November 2008, John Lewis Community Services, who owned the building housing the café, announced it would seek bankruptcy protection. Concerned that the café's home might be lost; Father Mottet and John Kelley negotiated a purchase of the building with grant money provided by the Scott County Regional Authority and the City of Davenport. At the same time, a Davenport couple established an endowment for the Café on Vine to be administered by the Community Foundation for the Great River Bend.

With the future of the Café on Vine secured at least for the time being, it began its second year of operation. Bea resumed her full time job at the Humility Center and turned her responsibilities at the café over to Sister Ruth E Westmoreland, a Clinton Franciscan who is both a skilled manager and passionate about the café. Bea continues to serve as a board member of the café.

The café operates with only three paid FTE staff and many volunteers. United Way grants cover some of the operating expenses and most of the food is donated. Volunteers help prepare and serve the meals, keep the café clean, do necessary repairs, and handle the café's recycling program. On Saturdays and Sundays, a family, church, or other community group makes and serves the lunch. On holidays, associate members of the Sisters of Humility provide the noon meal.

During the depths of the recession in 2008-09, the Café on Vine served approximately 55,000 meals, between 150 to 200 meals a day. No questions are asked when guests appear for lunch. The café operates on the assumption that if a person comes for lunch, he or she needs it. Although most of the café's guests are residents at the Humility of Mary Shelter or the Salvation Army Shelter, there are new people every day. According to Ruth E, who has worked at the café since September 2008 and coordinated it since June 2009, "The café is a miraculous place. I learned the meaning of 'God will provide' at the café. Whatever we need to keep the café operating and growing stronger just keeps coming through the door."

Just as the Humilities helped save the café, they also helped save the community pantry. When John Lewis shut its pantry down in early 2008, Marilyn Schierbrock "inherited it." But like other Humility of Mary projects in the Quad Cities, the Central Community Circle Food Pantry became a joint venture with members of the broader community.

Three women from United Churches—Susie Seitz, Pat Bereskin, and Karen Shapley—established the legal structure for the pantry, secured an initial operations grant, and have continued to raise the necessary funds to purchase at wholesale prices the food the pantry distributes. Marilyn buys the food, stocks the shelves, and staffs the pantry on a daily basis with the help of residents from the neighborhood. The pantry is important not only as a food distribution center, but also as a meeting place for women in the neighborhood. Although the economic status of the neighborhood has and continues to improve, hunger is still a real issue for some members of the community. The pantry and the Café on Vine are the neighborhood's collective response to this issue.

In late August 2008, John Lewis announced that it would close all its remaining programs on September 21, 2008, including its seventy-bed overnight shelter for adult men and women as well as a day shelter program which served as a refuge for anyone needing a safe place to get out of the heat or cold. It also placed in jeopardy one million dollars in annual grant funds for which John Lewis had served as the lead grantee for the housing and supportive services programs serving veterans, youth, persons with mental illness, homeless adults, single parents, and those in transitional housing struggling to acquire their own homes.

When John Lewis made its closure announcement, the HMHI board immediately faced the decision whether to assume administration of the shelter and related programs to preserve essential services for homeless people and how to do it in a manner that would not jeopardize HMHI's existing single parent family supported housing program. Both HMHI and the Quad Cities community quickly realized that HMHI was the only community-based agency capable of meeting the challenge.

But the HMHI board knew that it alone could not save the shelter and the other at-risk community-based programming in the short or long term. A significant effort from the Quad Cities community would be necessary. On September 9, 2008, Sister Mary Ann Vogel publicly announced that HMHI would form a new corporation, Humility of Mary Shelter, Inc. (HMSI) to assume responsibility for operating the shelter. But she also stated that HMSI would have to raise $250,000 to $300,000 prior to the end of the current fiscal year in order to ensure continuation of the shelter in the short term. Mary Ann also reported that additional long term funding for the shelter would be necessary as the annual cost of the shelter program is nearly one million dollars a year, and government grants cover only part of the costs.

Over the next twelve days, the City of Davenport, foundations, and other community-based organizations and businesses rallied to meet the short term funding requirements for continuation of the shelter. HMHI executive staff hired new staff to operate the shelter and community volunteers thoroughly cleaned the shelter and prepared it for occupancy. Before sundown on September 21, 2008, the Humility of Mary Shelter opened for business. HMHI board and staff, with broad support from the Quad Cities community, accomplished a seamless transition of services for homeless people residing at the shelter.

HMHI's creation of a new 501(c) (3) shelter corporation and the willingness of its executive staff to manage the Department of Housing and Urban Development (HUD) grants also preserved the additional one million dollars in funding for supportive services, transitional housing, and permanent supportive housing programs jeopardized by the closure of John Lewis. These emergency shelter and housing support services are the safety net for some of the most disabled and vulnerable citizens in Scott County.

When a *Quad City News* reporter asked Bea Snyder and Mary Rehmann why they decided to take on the challenge of these programs, Bea responded, "Why not? We're here. It's what we're about. There are people who need to have what we bring. Being women of faith, we're willing to take the risk."[5] Mary Rehmann, President of the Sisters of Humility, echoed her sentiments, saying, "This is God's work. It's our full time job. Walking with and being in the presence of those who need help . . . there is nothing like it to energize you."[6]

In the first two years of its operation, HMSI provided shelter and supportive services to over two thousand homeless persons as well as additional service coordination services to approximately two hundred persons from the Salvation Army Family Service Center and its Family Resources Domestic Violence Center. While nearly all of these people share the fear and desperation of homelessness when they arrive at HMSI, their circumstances and needs are often unique and require a custom made services plan to help them secure the permanent housing and other supportive services they need. That is the core of the HMSI program. Many of the same support services that HMHI provides to single parent families are made available to shelter participants.

As many shelter participants have long-term disabilities, they often require more than thirty days of emergency housing. For some, HMSI provides three months of transitional housing and services. For more severely disabled participants, HMSI provides permanent supportive housing. One of these permanently disabled residents is Randy, a fifty-five-year old man who came to Humility of Mary Shelter after being homeless for a year. Randy had been a long-haul truck driver who quit his job in order to care for his father. After his father died, Randy remained at his parent's home taking care of his sick mother, but he became homeless when his mother had to be transferred to a care facility and the family home was sold. By then, Randy had developed serious health problems that prevented him from working. He lived first in a shelter and later in his car. When winter arrived, Randy came to HMSI. He was thin, depressed, and had significant problems with untreated diabetes, as well as a life threatening heart condition. HMSI transferred Randy from the shelter to its "Housing First" permanent housing program for disabled persons. He had open-heart surgery and other related surgeries, his diabetes is now stabilized with both insulin and diet, and he has found a place among the caring HMSI staff. Randy has made friends in the neighborhood, volunteers at the pantry, enjoys reading, and celebrates the friendships he has made at HMSI.

HMSI also serves large numbers of veterans who seek emergency shelter through its Veterans Transitional Housing Program. This program provides service coordination and housing for twenty-four months to allow veterans to take advantage of case management, education, job training, crisis intervention, and counseling services through the VA. In 2010, HMSI received the Secretary of the Department of Veterans Affairs' Award for Outstanding Achievement in Service to Homeless Veterans. Sara Oliver, VA homeless coordinator for the Veteran's Outreach Center of Rock Island, nominated HMSI for this singular award. According to Ms. Oliver, "Life changing work is being done here."[7] In presenting the award to HMSI, Barry Sharp, director of the Iowa City VA Medical Center, stated, "You folks literally have worked miracles . . . Humility of Mary Shelter did what others would not do."[8]

Due to the success of HMSI's veterans program, the VA granted it $225,000 to expand outreach services to very low-income veterans and their families, who are homeless or at imminent risk of becoming homeless.

In reflecting back over their twenty-one years of working with HMHI and HMSI, both Sandy and Mary Ann describe a number of miracles that have happened along the way to make these programs possible, but are also quick to point out that miracles don't just happen. They are rooted in the Sisters of Humility's leadership and willingness to take risks, the generosity of the Quad Cities community, and the hard work of the HMHI and HMSI staff and volunteers.

# Doing Justice, Changing Lives in Colorado

In 1978, Mary Boland moved back to Colorado drawn by the beauty of the state and Bishop Charles Buswell's call to "come back home." They had been friends since 1965 when Mary served as a Catholic Extension Service volunteer in Pueblo. Charles was an affable, gentle man who did everything in his power to open up his diocese and allow all people to fully participate in the life of the church. Uninterested in the trappings of his office, he was a passionate leader in matters of social justice, a strong advocate for low-income and other disadvantaged people, and a persistent promoter of peace and opponent of war. In short, like Bernadine, Charles was Mary's idea of what a church leader ought to be.

Sharing community with a committed group of people was important to Mary, so when she returned to Colorado, she reconnected with the Sisters of Loretto and eventually became a co-member in their community. She also taught in the social work department at the University of Northern Colorado for a few years. But after fifteen years of teaching, Mary was eager to have a direct hand in fashioning social policy to improve the lives of people at the margins of society. In 1986, she got the chance to do precisely that when she accepted a job as the Director of Social Concerns for Catholic Charities of Denver, commonly known as "Catholic Charities" or "Charities." Mary agreed to join Catholic Charities because she firmly believed that service to low-income persons and other disadvantaged people should be at the heart of the Catholic Church's mission. She hoped that, through Charities, she would be able to carry out the social justice mission she embraced as a young college graduate when she became a friend of Bernadine and subsequently joined the Sisters of Humility in 1966.

Mary also believed that, with the resources and influence of the Denver Archdiocese, she would not only be able to meet the needs of

Charities' clients but also organize like-minded individuals and organizations to achieve substantial reforms in social policies, economic supports, and systems of care for thousands of low-income and disadvantaged people throughout the state.

Mary was a clear-headed, pragmatic woman who knew that no matter how diplomatic she was, she would have policy disagreements and problems with the church, as well as with the state and federal governments. And she wasn't wrong. During her twenty-one years at Catholic Charities, Mary had many such disagreements, but as Reverend Constance Delzell remarked in January 2009,

> Mary, a brilliant, constant, visionary woman of incomparable compassion and determination, was always on the side of the angels in these disagreements . . . Her disagreements never ended, as so many do, in moral outrage. She persistently worked for concrete change in the world by lobbying government officials, administering and reforming the social service arms of church and government, protesting exclusionary laws and policies in church and state, providing the most practical of unguents—food, housing, training, laws while engendering the most elusive—hope.[1]

During her tenure at Catholic Charities, one of Mary's responsibilities was developing the agency's public policy agenda for each Colorado legislative session and securing its approval from the Catholic Charities board. This group "was made up largely of business people, more cautious, deliberate and less able to think outside the box than Mary," said Father Martin (Marty) Lally, who served on the board at the time. When members of the board raised fiscal and other concerns, including how such policies might adversely affect the reputation of Catholic Charities, Mary politely but clearly described the factual and moral bases for her proposals. By doing so, Marty observed, Mary generally persuaded the board to adopt her proposed agenda. If board members continued to object to Mary's proposals, Mary then demonstrated how the proposed policies were fully consistent with the social policy of the Catholic Church as described in papal encyclicals and policy statements by the U.S. Conference of Catholic Bishops. According to Marty, "If Mary felt strongly about an issue, she never took 'no' for an answer."

Legislators and administrators of state and federal agencies respected Mary for her honesty and for the basic justice and fairness of the causes she championed. But Mary knew that success in legislative and administrative bodies also depends on political power. So she became a master at organizing coalitions of individuals and organizations, consolidating their power to protect and enhance the lives of low-income and other disadvantaged groups whose voices alone would not be heard.

Shortly after arriving at Catholic Charities, Mary organized a task force of churches, state, and local social service agencies, university professors, state legislators, and community-based agencies to support Charities' effort to increase benefit levels for families reliant on the Aid to Families with Dependent Children (AFDC) program. Some members of the task force thought this legislative effort was a fools' task. The legislature, they said, will never approve such an increase. Undaunted, Mary and other Charities staff moved forward to develop their proposal.

AFDC benefit levels, by law, are intended to reflect the current average costs of basic necessities, including rent, food, utilities, and clothing. As Mary believed the existing benefit levels weren't sufficient to secure such necessities, she commissioned a study of the income level needed to meet their current costs in Colorado. With the benefit of this study and strong task force support, the legislature in 1988 granted the first increase in AFDC benefit levels in over ten years. This victory, however, was short lived.

Beginning in the early 1990s, punitive bills directed at AFDC families became common in the Colorado legislature. One that really raised Mary's Irish ire was a bill to deny AFDC coverage for any child conceived after the family began receiving AFDC benefits. To defend against this and other legislative assaults on poor families, Mary turned to a new intern from the University of Denver's School of Social Work, Sister Buffy Boeson, S.L., and said, "Why don't we work on improving the AFDC program?" While Buffy was game to take on the task, she had no prior experience with either community organizing or changing social systems. But, as she recalls, "Mary had the ideas and the heart to make you want to do the project." Under Mary's tutelage, Buffy quickly gained the required skills to make the project succeed.

Together, Buffy and Mary organized AFDC recipients, connected them with members of the AFDC task force and established a new AFDC (All Families Deserve a Chance) Coalition. The AFDC recipients described in detail to other coalition members the real life disincentives of the program. Social service staff agreed with their critique of the system and worked with them to change it. Together, they and other coalition members also successfully defeated numerous punitive AFDC legislative and administrative proposals. Equally important, the AFDC recipients found their voices and became effective advocates for themselves and other families.

Core members of the AFDC coalition have continued to be strong advocates for AFDC families in the state legislature over the past twenty-three years. In fact, as recently as the spring of 2008, the Coalition secured a thirty percent increase in AFDC benefits just prior to the onset of the 2008 recession.

According to Buffy, Mary was "a genius at strategy who also had a deep reservoir of respect and support among individuals and agencies in the community, which helped her enact legislation and develop programs that were life saving for thousands of low-income individuals and families." The beauty of Mary's contact list was that the people on it actually responded whenever Mary called because they knew she was a committed and skilled advocate with a no-nonsense approach to solving the problems of poverty. They also knew they could count on Mary delivering what she promised.

One of Mary's most successful coalitions was the Coalition on Health Care Conversion. In 1997, Blue Cross Blue Shield (BCBS) announced its intention to become a for-profit corporation or, alternatively, to be sold to such a corporation. Colorado law required BCBS, as a condition of its conversion to for-profit status, to transfer the fair market value of its non-profit corporation to one or more foundations to promote and serve the health needs of Colorado citizens. BCBS's original conversion plan grossly understated its fair market value at only twenty-five million dollars. BCBS also provided no assurance that these assets would be transferred to a non-profit foundation whose sole mission was to serve the health care needs of Colorado citizens.

Catholic Charities opposed BCBS's plan during the conversion review proceedings. Ed Kahn, a private lawyer known for his commitment to public interest law, and Sister Mary Catherine Rabbitt, S.L., an attorney from the Colorado Center for Law and Social Policy, represented Charities in these proceedings. However, to ensure that they had the views and support of other groups representing the public interest, Mary organized and chaired the Coalition on Health Care Conversion, which played a significant role in formulating and supporting the positions put forth by Catholic Charities in the review proceedings before the Colorado Insurance Commissioner. In addition, Mary and Mary Catherine drafted the bylaws for the proposed Caring for Colorado Foundation to ensure that the BCBS money would actually be used to promote and serve the health care needs of Colorado citizens.

Mary Boland and
Mary Catherine Rabbitt, S.L.

After a two day hearing, the Insurance Commissioner approved BCBS's proposed sale to Anthem Insurance Companies but conditioned the sale on Anthem's transfer of $155 million to the Caring for Colorado Foundation, $130 million more than BCBS originally proposed in its application. According to Ed Kahn, "Mary, in this case as in other public interest matters, served as the conscience of the community. She was both a tireless and, more importantly, an effective advocate on behalf of the interests of Colorado citizens."

Over the past eleven years, the Caring for Colorado Foundation has creatively partnered with community-based organizations all over the state to build health care capacity, strengthen existing health care systems and link people in underserved populations to care. It has substantially expanded access to medical services in rural communities among underserved populations, increased mental and oral health services, provided training for Colorado health care providers, and expanded the health care safety net for some of Colorado's most vulnerable citizens in every Colorado county.[2]

In addition to her legislative and administrative advocacy, Mary created within Charities many programs to serve low-income people. She transformed small parish-based crisis programs into a coordinated network of storefront emergency assistance centers, where any person or family in need could secure assistance to pay rent or utilities, have access to food, clothing, medications and referrals to related community agencies. By 2006, these centers served 76,700 households on an annual basis.

Mary also established a community organizing team to work in partnership with the Metropolitan Organization for People (MOP), to empower low-income inner city citizens to identify and solve problems adversely affecting their quality of life. In order to maintain this effort, Mary served on MOP's board of directors for many years.

In 1988, Mary along with Jim Mauck, director of Catholic Charities, organized SHARE Colorado, a multi-state food distribution network that operated from 1988 until 2010. At its peak membership, SHARE Colorado served twenty-five thousand members, who, by providing two hours of service to SHARE on a monthly basis, were entitled to purchase meat, fresh fruits and vegetables, as well as staples at fifty percent of retail prices. In addition to purchasing food in bulk for its own members, SHARE also bought food at wholesale prices for community food banks, homeless missions, emergency assistance centers and other local non-profits, saving these organizations an estimated $625,000 in food expenses annually.

Services for children were always one of Mary's central concerns.

She was a consistent voice in the legislature arguing for expansion of health care for low-income children. Under her leadership, Catholic Charities became a lead agency helping low-income families enroll their children in the Colorado Child Health Plan. Mary was also the force behind Charities starting childcare centers and helped transform them into child education centers providing before and after school programs. These centers focused not only on educating children but their parents as well by offering GED and ESL classes.

Although Mary's work at Catholic Charities consumed most of her time, she also contributed her time and skills to other groups in the community. In the early 1990s, Mary renewed her friendship with Sally Brown, an ordained deacon in the Episcopal Church. Their paths had crossed earlier while both were working on increasing services to homeless people and at St. Thomas Episcopal Church where Sally served as a deacon and Mary occasionally attended services. They became close friends and eventually committed partners sharing life and home together.

In 1995, Sally was appointed to the staff of St. Andrew's Episcopal Church, an Anglo-Catholic Church located on the edge of downtown Denver near the historically black neighborhood of Five Points. Mary had desired to become a priest since she was a child, and she quickly felt at home at St. Andrews due to the church's acceptance of women as priests and deacons, its Anglo-Catholic sacramental focus, and its philosophy that the liturgy is the work of all members of the Church. She also appreciated the Church's respect for diversity and inclusion of all members. After a few years, Mary was formally received into the Episcopal Church. Although she seriously considered pursuing the priesthood at that time, she finally decided with her typical pragmatism that she was "too old" to go down that path. She did, however assume a variety of leadership roles at St. Andrew's.

After an accidental fire in October 1999 severely damaged St. Andrew's Church, the church leaders instituted a five-year plan task force. Mary served on the task force. Following exhaustive demographic, economic, and social research, Mary accurately forecasted how the area around St. Andrew's would change from an economically distressed neighborhood to a substantially redeveloped area. But she also pointed out that the low- to no-income citizens who inhabited the neighborhood around St. Andrew's would still be there in the shadows and would need the services that church members could and should provide.

Mary outlined a detailed plan of how St. Andrew's could respond to this problem. With characteristic candor, Mary told the clergy and lay leaders of St. Andrew's that she thought the fire at the church was perhaps a good thing for the members of the parish as it refocused their resources and commitment outward to the broader community beyond the church door.

One of Mary's proposals was a partnership between St. Andrew's and the Urban Land Conservancy to purchase the parking lots adjoining the Church for eventual development into affordable housing, with each partner to pay half of the costs. The partnership was forged and the land jointly purchased in 2008. The revenues from the parking lots are currently paying down the purchase loan debt, but St. Andrews and the Urban Land Conservancy remain committed to use the land to serve essential needs of the community.

John Taylor, who served as parish administrator at St. Andrew's, said of Mary, "She possessed a quiet relentlessness and an unbelievable will to achieve justice tempered by deep compassion. Tenaciousness was in her DNA." According to John, "In my sixty years of life before I met Mary, I had never met a person with her connection to others. She was able to listen to folks at the edges of society, understood their need for a decent life and worked tirelessly to help them achieve that goal." But equally important, said John, "Mary's life and action inspired others to become responsible for the needs of their brothers and sisters."

Low-income housing was one of Mary's passions. She, like Bernadine, was a financial wizard and a tough negotiator, both skills essential to becoming a successful developer of low-income housing. In 1993, when Lowry Air Force Base closed, Mary applied for and secured on behalf of Catholic Charities forty units of surplus housing for homeless persons under the federal McKinney Homeless Assistance Act. These units were used to provide transitional housing for two hundred homeless families from Samaritan House and other shelters in Denver over a four-year period. Mary also secured $745,000 in federal homeless assistance funds to create additional transitional housing and case management services to help families move from homelessness to self-support.

When the Lowry Reuse Plan called for the demolition of all transitional housing on the base, advocates accused the city of discriminating against homeless people. This controversy created a highly charged environment for negotiations. Rather than allowing negotiations to be derailed by anger and years of litigation, Mary calmly but forcefully demanded and secured on behalf of Catholic Charities two million dollars for the development of permanent affordable housing for homeless families in other locations in the metropolitan area. Mary knew that with the two million dollars, she could leverage millions more in tax credits or other public financing for new low-income housing. Other advocates for homeless people living at Lowry followed Mary's lead. Denver Mayor Wellington Webb was so impressed with Mary's handling of these negotiations that he wrote a letter to Archbishop Stafford thanking him for the "calm and responsive manner" in which Mary conducted what the Mayor acknowledged was a difficult negotiation of the Lowry Reuse Plan.

In 1995, Mary developed and secured approval for creating a new Catholic Charities Farm Worker Housing Corporation in Greeley, which now operates eighty units of housing for agricultural workers on a year round basis. In the late 1990s, Mary was also one of the founding members of the Metro Denver Homeless Initiative that administered over ten million dollars in federal housing funds to address homelessness in the metropolitan area.

When Loretto Heights College in Denver closed and most of its property was sold, Mary learned that the Sisters of Loretto had retained five and a half acres of land on the edge of the campus. After Mary Catherine Rabbitt became president of the Sisters of Loretto in 2001, Mary asked her, "What are you going to do with land you own at the Heights?" To Mary, the vacant land was already the future home of Mt. Loretto, a housing complex for low to medium-income families, with great views of the mountains and a community center where educational and social programs would be available to its residents. The Sisters of Loretto not only donated the land for Mary's project, but Mary Catherine became a full partner in its development.

Mary and Mary Catherine jointly raised the financing necessary to construct the housing and community center. That was the easy part. The harder part was getting the water rights easement necessary for construction of the project. Fred Van Leu, President of Teikyo Loretto Heights University, had a "not in my backyard" attitude towards the project and refused to grant the easement. After Mary had exhausted all reasonable negotiation efforts with him, she called in one of her chits with a Denver Planning Office official, who told Van Leu that, if he wanted to do any development at Teikyo, he'd better let Mt. Loretto proceed. That settled the easement dispute and Mt. Loretto became the first multifamily housing project built by the Denver Archdiocese in over ten years. It opened in June 2005 and six months later had become a bustling community of seventy families with over two hundred children.

According to Mary Catherine, Mary taught her a lot about housing development and finance as well as negotiating strategy. For Mary Catherine, it was the most important work she did as President of the Sisters of Loretto. In recalling the project, Mary Catherine said, "The Sisters of Loretto acquired the property in 1899 and kept it for a good purpose. Mt. Loretto was it."

While Mary was developing Mt. Loretto, Catholic Charities named her vice president for Housing and Homelessness, responsible for managing three emergency shelters, transitional housing, and case management programs for homeless families in Denver, Fort Collins, Greeley, and on the Western Slope. When the need for emergency shelter for women with children in Denver exceeded the existing resources, Mary became the project facilitator for a new shelter, the Father Ed Judy House. This shelter continues to serve as the temporary home for homeless women and children and provides services to assist the women to become self-sufficient, including GED programs, parenting techniques, counseling, employment assistance, health care, and housing assistance.

Mary also became the Executive Director of Archdiocesan Housing, Inc. (AHI) and Housing Management Services (HMS), two independent housing development and management agencies founded by Auxiliary Bishop George Evans in 1978. Under his leadership, AHI developed six large senior housing complexes and twenty-four units of family housing. After Bishop Evans died in 1985, however, AHI lost its focus. While it continued to operate its existing housing, it developed no new low-income housing between 1985 and 2005.

Mary's first task was to breathe new life into the organization that, as one staff member remarked, "needed to be shaken up." She evaluated and reorganized existing staff, tried to bring parity of salaries between men and women, and provided additional training for everyone from the maintenance staff to senior program staff. She also raised funds for and hired new staff necessary to restart the housing development mission of the agency and modernized AHI and HMS's financial and accounting systems.

Mary then refinanced the six senior housing complexes resulting in $3 million in savings, which she used to renovate and upgrade each of these complexes. She also purchased a thirty-four unit apartment complex for homeless veterans and other residents of Samaritan House from Catholic Charities, refinanced it, and used the $1.5 million savings to renovate it. Mary also assisted the Diocese of Colorado Springs to refinance two of its properties for low-income seniors and provided property management services for them, resulting in savings to the diocese in excess of one hundred thousand dollars per year. When Angela Fletcher, the Director of Housing Management Services, asked Mary how she felt about being the only woman in negotiations with the "big guns" from real estate companies or financing agencies, Mary laughed and said, "The secret is that you never let your opponents see you sweat."

Turning then to new housing development, Mary added new board members with housing development and financing experience to AHI. Together, Mary and the AHI board set a goal of developing one hundred units of low to moderate income housing each year. Mary then commenced development of low to moderate-income housing in Basalt, Colorado for low-wage workers in Aspen and low-income housing for developmentally disabled persons in Commerce City.

In 2006, Catholic Charities, with the support of Archbishop Chaput, proposed to merge AHI and HMS into Charities. Mary opposed the proposed merger in order to protect the independence and integrity of AHI and HMS as a joint housing development and management company, and to prevent diversion of its resources to other priorities of the archdiocese, including evangelization programs and increasing the archdiocese's rainy day fund. After struggling for nearly a year to prevent the merger, Mary finally lost the argument and left the agency.

The Archdiocese's loss became the Jefferson County Department of Human Services' (Jeffco's) gain. Mary became the director of Community Assistance, with responsibility for, among other things, making sure that the agency processed over 6,400 pending applications for public assistance and food stamps in a timely manner, as well as ensuring that Jefferson County low-income citizens received their welfare checks and food stamps on time each month. Mary knew that her job would be challenging because ten of the largest county human services departments in Colorado, including Jeffco, were under a court order to fix the processing delays in the system. These were due to short staffing, a culture focused more on weeding out fraud than delivering the necessary benefits, and a complicated benefits management computer system that caused more problems than it solved.

Mary faced the problems head on. She hired a new intake worker to process applications for assistance and food stamps at a satellite center more accessible to clients. She also deployed additional existing staff to complete delayed application reviews, instructing them to conduct interviews by phone rather than in person and stopping them from asking the applicants to provide more documents than legally necessary. All these measures decreased the time expended in making eligibility decisions.

Mary also took action to change Jeffco's reputation as a cold, heartless welfare agency by recruiting John Taylor to man the front reception desk. She told him that his job, similar to the Walmart greeter, was to be the open and accepting greeter of applicants, giving them the dignity and respect to which they were entitled. Mary also spent a considerable amount of time in the Jeffco waiting room. She brought apples and cookies for the children. She slowly made her way around the waiting room, talking to people, listening to their concerns and treating them as human beings. Mary, within a short time, began to change the culture of Jeffco from a bureaucratic, resistant-to-change system to a service-oriented agency that puts clients' needs first. Mary's approach to clients served as a model for staff in how to treat clients with respect and compassion.

In addition to improving the welfare system, Mary also secured authorization from the Jeffco county commissioners to develop affordable housing for veterans. Mary had many other ideas to improve services to Jeffco's low-income citizens and never stopped working on them until a rare form of cancer abruptly ended her life. Within three weeks of her last day at Jeffco, Mary died in early January 2009.

In both Denver and Jeffco, Mary is known as a brilliant social services dynamo who never saw a problem she could not fix or a social services system that could not be improved. She had a fierce commitment to systemic change, but never lost sight of the individual person in front of her. To many of those she served, Mary was "the saint," not only because of the benefits she secured for them, but for the respectful and caring manner in which she treated them.

But to those of us who knew her personally, she was also a feisty Irish woman who loved a good story, had a great laugh, and was also one of the most humble persons one is likely to meet in a lifetime. She had a low tolerance for those who "whined" as indicated by a simple sign in her office, "No Whining." She loved to argue about politics and worked for candidates she believed in. Shortly before Mary died, she insisted on going door to door for Barack Obama. When her sister Kate, a member of the opposition party, learned about Mary's canvassing, she said, "I could have saved myself a lot of angst about the outcome of the election, for clearly we did not have the power to overcome her unbelievable zeal."

Traveling with Mary, according to Sally, was always an adventure—her Good Samaritan instinct knew no bounds. When Mary saw a wounded dog on the road, she stopped, picked it up, and headed to a veterinary clinic. When she came upon an immigrant family attempting to change a flat on I-70, she stopped, gave them her own jack and spare tire, plus money for gas. When Mary saw a stranded woman and children on the side of the highway, she brought her car to a screeching halt, picked them up, and took them to their destination, or if they had no particular destination, to the next town where she would arrange emergency shelter and any other necessary services.

Mary was incredibly curious about people and the world and she was intrigued by technological innovation. She took great delight in mastering the latest in digital cameras, had a keen eye for photography, and created a splendid collection of photographs. Although she did not have time to travel to distant lands and little tolerance for being a tourist, she and Sally did enjoy spending time in the villages of northern New México and small communities on the northern California coast.

Despite her intense and packed work life, she had the ability at home or among friends to be carefree and relaxed. It may have been due in part to her daily monastic rhythm of filling her three bird feeders morning and night, caring for any injured birds, and feeding, walking, and caring for her dogs.

At Mary's funeral in January 2009, St. John's Episcopal Cathedral was packed with hundreds of people whose lives Mary had touched. Her friends, Father Marty Lally and Rev. Kent Curtis participated at the funeral mass with the Episcopal bishop and male and female Episcopal priests.

Mary's sister, Kate, described how Mary was both the prodder and the protector of the Boland family as part of her mission to quietly tend to the Boland Diaspora. She became the surrogate "mom" for nieces and nephews who, like Mary, discovered the beauty of Colorado and moved to Denver. She welcomed and watched over them through big moments and small, just as she had her mother during her declining years. With a quiet pride, Kate said:

> Most of all we remember her dedication to helping others less fortunate. She was an advocate, a fighter for others, but more than that. She was a true Good Samaritan, finding those along the way who needed a ride or a place to stay or a dresser or two. No matter the time or detour required in her schedule. This was her true calling. . . . We are all humbled by her example.

Reverend Delzell elegantly summed up Mary's life as one that fulfilled the words of the prophet of Israel, Micah, by saying, "What does the Lord require of you but to do justice, to love kindness, and walk humbly with your God." Many of us, she said,

> think justice, talk justice, hope for justice, even pray for justice, but Mary did justice . . . Many of us think and speak compassionately, promise kindness, and exhibit kindness to those in our own circle, but Mary loved kindness so profoundly and so thoroughly that her kindness extended itself in acts of mercy to the farthest range of her capacity. . . . All that Mary did, of justice, of kindness was intentional, prayerful, consistent, persistent, constant, steady, and measured until the end. A pilgrim 'til the end of her journey, she walked humbly . . . and she loved every minute of it.[3]

# Sources and Notes

One of the primary sources for this book is Sister Bernadine Pieper herself, including her speeches and letters to the community and a number of unpublished manuscripts about her life and the history of her family, the history and spirituality of the Sisters of Humility, the early history of Marycrest College, and care of the earth. Other primary sources are over fifty Sisters of Humility, as well as other persons, including Bernadine's family and persons with whom Bernadine and the other sisters depicted in this book worked. In the notes below, the names of the sisters or other persons who are sources for each chapter are listed first, followed by specific citations to written materials relied upon for each chapter. Unless otherwise noted, the sisters identified in these notes are Sisters of Humility. Bernadine Pieper's letters to the CHM community and the unpublished manuscripts cited here are in the CHM archives. Many of the events described are based on my experience as a member of the Sisters of Humility from 1960-1985 and on my discussions with Bernadine over forty years.

# BOOK I

### INTRODUCTION

Discussions with Sister Bernadine Pieper and Interview with Sister Cathy Talarico.

1  Cathy Talarico tribute in "Sister Bernadine Pieper, CHM, 1918-2000," (unpublished manuscript, February 24, 2000), 12.

2  Machado, Antonio, "Proverbs and Dreams," *Border of a Dream: Selected Poems of Antonio Machado,* trans. Willis Barnstone. Port Townsend, Wash: Cooper Canyon Press, 2004, 281.

3  Bernadine Pieper, "Footprints, The Story of the Sisters of Humility of Mary, Part I" (unpublished manuscript 1978), 5.

## FROM IOWA FARM GIRL TO SISTER OF HUMILITY

Discussions with Sister Bernadine Pieper and Interviews with Ruth Caslauka and John Holtkamp.

[1] Bernadine Pieper, "From Generation to Generation, The Nichting-Pieper Family Tree" (unpublished manuscript, December 1975) 19-21.

[2] Ibid. 20-23.

[3] Ruth Holtkamp, letter to author, October 8, 2001,1-2.

[4] While the Vatican did not publicly condemn Darwin's *On the Origin on the Species* when it was published in 1859, it did place Father John Augustine Zahm's book, *Evolution and Dogma,* Chicago: D.H. McBride & Co., 1896 on the Index of Forbidden Books. Father Zahm was also required to recant his book's thesis that Darwin's theory of evolution is consistent with Church teaching and the Bible. Pope Pius XII's 1950 encyclical, *Humani Generis is* the Church's first acknowledgment that the Church does not forbid research and discussions between experts in human science and theology with regard to the doctrine. But, according Pius XII, evolution is merely a hypothesis that is subject to the Church's right to define matters touching on revelation. Catholics, according to Pius XII, must believe that God specifically created the human soul and that all men have descended from Adam. WWW.VATICAN.VA/ . . . /HF_P-XII_ENC_12081950_HUMANI-GENERIS_EN.HTML. In 1966, Pope John Paul II, in his "Message to The Pontifical Academy of Sciences: Evolution," WWW.EWTN.COM/LIBRARY/PAPALDOC/JP961022.HTM, stated that while new findings from independent researchers contain significant arguments in favor of the theory of evolution, "any theory of evolution which regards the spirit either emerging from the forces of living matter or as a simple epiphenomenon of that matter is incompatible with the truth about man."

[5] Bernadine Pieper, "Care of the Earth: a Reflection on Creation Spirituality" (unpublished manuscript, 1998), 1.

[6] Bernadine Pieper, "E Pluribus Unum, One Among Many" (unpublished manuscript, 1978) in "Sister Bernadine Pieper, CHM, 1918-2000," 5.

## THE MARYCREST YEARS: EXPANDING MINDS AND SOLVING PROBLEMS

Discussions with Sister Bernadine Pieper and Interviews with Sisters Marie Ven Horst, Gretchen McKean, Annette Gallagher, Elizabeth Anne Schneider,

Jude Fitzpatrick, Luz María Orozco and Penelope Wink, Mary Martin Lane, Roberta Kealey, Nancy Wooldridge and John Holtkamp.

1   Bernadine Pieper, "Early History of Marycrest College 1939-1955" (unpublished manuscript, July 1999), 1.

2   Msgr. U.A. Hauber, Baccalaureate Mass Sermon preached at St. Ambrose College, 1954, WWW.WEB.SAU.EDU/125/SPIRITDAYSTORIES. HTM.

3   Pieper, "Early History of Marycrest College," 12-13.

4   Marie Ven Horst, letter to author, September 30, 2001, 2-3.

5   Luz María Orozco, "Vintage Bernadine," *The Crest*, 2000, reprinted in "Sister Bernadine Pieper, 1918-2000," 37.

6   Lisa Mullins, letter to author, 2001, 1.

7   Roberta Kealey tribute in "Sister Bernadine Pieper, CHM, 1918-2000," 19-20.

8   John Holtkamp tribute in "Sister Bernadine Pieper, CHM, 1918- 2000," 11.

## CHANGING COURSE BY RECLAIMING
## THE COMMUNITY'S ROOTS

Discussions with Sister Bernadine Pieper and interviews with Patricia McGuire Rock, Sisters Mary John Byers, Micheline Curtis, Harriet Ping, Cathy Talarico, Ann Therese Collins, Madeline Marie Schmidt and Roberta Brich.

1   Cardinal Franz König, "Vatican II: the Highlight of My Life," 1, HTTP:// WWW.VATICAN 2VOICE.ORG/5DEPTH/OFMYLIFE.HTML.

2   Vatican Archive, quoted in Peter Hebblethwaite. *John XXIII, Pope of the Council,* London: Geoffrey Chapman/Cassell, 1984.

3   *Perfectae Caritatis,* WWW.VATICAN.VA/.../VAT-II_DECREE_19651028PERFE CTAECARITATIS.HTML.

4   Ecclesiae Sanctae, HTTP://WWW.VA/HOLY_FATHER/PAULVI/MOTU_ PROPRIO/DOCUMENTS/HF_P-VI_MOTU-PRORIO_19660806_ECCLESIAE- SANCTAE_EN.HTML.

5   Pieper, Bernadine, "A Path of Humility and Truth: Historical Reminiscence," *Review For Religious* (July-August 2000), 359-367, is a primary source for this chapter.

6   Pieper, *"Footprints,"* 27-28.

7   Elizabeth T. Knut, "The Beguines," December 1992,1-7, WWW.USERS.CSBSJU.EDUC/EKNUT/XPSS/BEGUINES/HTML.

8   Pieper, *Footprints, 30-34.*

9   Ibid. 32.

10  Ibid. 31, 33.

11  Ibid. 49.

12  Ibid. 58, 64.

13  "Our Spirit," WWW.CHMIOWA.ORG/HERITAGE.CFM.

14  Pieper, *Footprints, 73-75.*

15  Ibid. 79-84.

16  Ibid. 92-137.

17  Madeline Marie Schmidt, "Sisters of Humility of Mary Come to Ottumwa: The Ottumwa Foundation, First Fifteen Years, 1877-1892" (unpublished manuscript, February 1998), 1.

18  Ibid. 2.

## HONEST BROKERING OF THE RENEWAL PROCESS

Discussions with Sister Bernadine Pieper and Interviews with Eleanor Anstey, Sisters Mary Ann Vogel, Ann Therese Collins, Teresa Gomez and Delphine Vasquez.

1   Bernadine Pieper, Christmas Day 1966 letter to the CHM community, 2.

2   Bernadine Pieper, Veteran's Day 1966 letter to the CHM community, 2.

3   Roberta Brich, October 1, 2001 letter to author, 3.

4   Bernadine Pieper, September 13, 1966 letter to the CHM community, 1.

5   Barbara Miller, "Decrees on Government and Self-Determination," *Kiosk* (February 1970), 14.

6   Bernadine Pieper, March 31, 1967 letter to the CHM community, 1.

7   Bernadine Pieper, May 6, 1968 letter to the CHM community, 2.

8   Caspary, Anita, M. *Witness to Integrity.* Collegeville: Liturgical Press, 2003, 119 -148.

9   Ibid. 157-158.

10  Ibid. 174-175.

[11] Ibid. 179.

[12] Stammer, Larry B., "Mahoney Offers Apology for His, Church's Failings," *Los Angeles Times*, March 8, 2000, Sec. B: 1.

## REACHING ACCORD ON BASIC PRINCIPLES

Discussions with Sister Bernadine Pieper and Interviews with Sisters Ann Therese Collins, Marie Ven Horst and Mary John Byers.

[1] Bernadine Pieper, April 23, 1969 letter to the CHM community. Poem: "To You, People," translated by Tupikina-Glaessner, Dutton & Mazbakoff-Koriak, from BRATSK STATION AND OTHER POEMS by Yevgeny Yevtushenko, translated by Tupikina-Glaessner, Dutton & Mazbakoff-Koriak, copyright © 1966 by Sun Books Pty. Ltd. Used by permission of Doubleday, a division of Random House, Inc.

[2] Bernadine Pieper, A Week Before Christmas 1972 letter to the CHM community, 2.

[3] Bernadine Pieper, October 8, 1968 letter to the CHM community, 1-2.

[4] Ibid. 2.

## GREASING THE WHEELS OF RENEWAL

Discussions with Sister Bernadine Pieper and interviews with Eleanor Anstey,Sisters Ann Therese Collins and Bea Snyder.

[1] Bernadine Pieper, August 2, 1976 report to the CHM community, 1-7.

[2] Ibid.

## FOUNDING THE LATIN AMERICAN MISSIONS

Discussions with Sister Bernadine Pieper and interviews with Sisters Ana María Orozco and Judith Cararra.

[1] Bernadine Pieper, June 29, 1967 letter to the CHM community, 2.

## WIDENING THE TENT/
## EXTENDING THE COMMUNITY'S REACH

Discussions with Sister Bernadine Pieper and interviews with Mary Martin Lane, Lisa Mullins and Pat Knopick, Director of the CHM Associate Program.

1   Anne Morrow Lindbergh, Excerpt from *Unicorn and Other Poems, 1935-1955*, New York: Pantheon Press, 1956, 14.

2   Lisa Mullins, 2001 letter to author, 1.


## INTEGRATING PRAYER, SIMPLICITY OF LIFE, WORK AND COMMUNITY

Discussions with Sister Bernadine Pieper, and interviews with Sister Mary John Byers, Mary Boland, and Vicky Reeves.

1   Bernadine Pieper, February 24, 1967 letter to the CHM community, 1.

2   Bernadine Pieper, August 31, 1967 letter to the CHM community, 1.

3   Bernadine Pieper, April 1973 letter to the CHM Community, 3, quoting Abraham Joseph Heschel. *Moral Grandeur and Spiritual Audacity,* ed. Susan Heschel, New York: Farrar, Straus and Giroux, 1997, 116.

4   Bernadine Pieper, April 1973 letter to the CHM Community quoting Abraham Joseph Heschel. *Man's Quest for God,* New York: Scribner Publishing Co., 1954, 5.

5   Bernadine Pieper March 5, 1969 letter to CHM community, quoting Gladys Taber's untitled poem, which is reprinted with permission of Anne E. Colby, the granddaughter and representative of Mrs. Taber's heirs, who hold all copyrights to Mrs. Taber's work.

6   Bernadine Pieper, May 1972 letter to the CHM community, 1.

7   Bernadine Pieper, August 2, 1975 report to the CHM General Assembly, 4.


## RISK TAKERS, NOT NESTERS

Discussions with Sister Bernadine Pieper and Interviews with Sisters Ann Therese Collins, Jeanie Hagedorn, and Joanne O'Brien.

1   Bernadine Pieper, May 10, 1970 letter to the CHM Community, quoting excerpt from Albert Camus' "Statement at Dominican Monastery of Latour, Maubourg, France" in 1948, reprinted in *Resistance, Rebellion, and Death,* New York: Random House, 1960, 73.

2   Bernadine Pieper, May 10, 1970 letter to the CHM Community, quoting Daniel Berrigan. *America Is Hard To Find,* New York: Doubleday & Company, 1972, 36-37, reprinted with permission of John Dear, literary administrator for Daniel Berrigan.

## CHANGING MISSION WHILE PRESERVING COMMITMENTS

Discussions with Sister Bernadine Pieper, and Interviews with Sisters Joann Kuebrich and Ann Therese Collins, Mary Boland, Jim and Mary McCue, Eleanor Anstey, Dr. Lyle Hellyer and Nancy Roberson.

[1]  Bernadine Pieper, April 19, 1975 letter to the CHM community, 3.

[2]  Jim Crane, "Sister Bernadine Leads the Way at Ottumwa Heights," *Ottumwa Courier*, 1998.

[3]  Excerpt from "Little Gidding" from *Four Quartets*, copyright 1942 by T.S.Eliot, renewed by Esme Valerie Eliot, reprinted by permission of Houghton Mifflin Harcourt Publishing Company, Faber and Faber Ltd. All rights reserved.

## FOSTERING PEACE AND JUSTICE THE QUAKER WAY

Discussions with Sister Bernadine Pieper and Interviews with Pam Solo, Judy Danielson, Mikel Johnson, Ramona Gomez, Bill Ramsey and Sister Ramona Kaalberg.

[1]  Acceptance Speech for the Award of the Nobel Prize in 1947 by Henry Cadbury on behalf of the American Friends Service Committee, HTTP://AFSC.ORG/NOBEL-PRIZE.

## BUILDING COMMUNITY IN THE IOWA HEARTLAND

Discussions with Sister Bernadine Pieper and Interviews with Fathers Dave Polich and John Zeitler, Betsy and Brian Terrell, Regina Lynch, Joan Jackson, Pastor Carman J. Lampe, Veronica Ray and Debbie Murphy.

[1]  Brian Terrell tribute in Sister Bernadine Pieper, CHM, 1918-2000, 15-17.

[2]  Dave Polich tribute in Sister Bernadine Pieper, CHM, 1918-2000, 28; Dave Polich 1992 letter in support of Bernadine Pieper's nomination for the Lumen Christi Award, 1-2.

[3]  Carmen J. Lampe 1992 letter in support of Bernadine Pieper's nomination for the Lumen Christi Award, 1.

## PROMOTING LITERACY AND BRIDGING THE RACIAL DIVIDE

Discussions with Sister Bernadine Pieper and interviews with Sister Helen Strohman, Sister Janita Curoe, BVM, Linda Johnson, Azikiwe (Azi) Kambule, and Sis Wohner.

[1] Bernadine Pieper, January 8, 1995 letter to Mary and Jim McCue, 3; Bernadine Pieper, 1996 Application to the Conrad N. Hilton Fund For Sisters seeking Funding for the Rainbow Literacy Project, 1-2.

[2] *Green v. County School Board of New Kent County*, 391 U.S. 430, 442 (1968).

[3] *Alexander v. Holmes County Board of Education et al*, 396 U.S. 19 (1969) 78.

### GOING OUT AS A SHOOTING STAR

Discussions with Sister Bernadine Pieper and interviews with John Zeitler, Sister Jude Fitzpatrick, Joann Kuebrich, Mary John Byers, Cathleen Real, and Roberta Brich.

[1] Bernadine Pieper, "E Pluribus Unum – One Among Many," in "Sister Bernadine Pieper, CHM 1918 -2000," 8.

[2] Jude Fitzpatrick, "History of Our Lady of the Prairie Retreat," 2010, 1-2.

[3] Bernadine Pieper, "Spirituality of the Sisters of Humility," (unpublished manuscript, January 1998, 16-17.

[4] Roberta Brich, October 1, 2001 letter to author, 1.

[5] Barb Arland-Fye, "God is With Us, God is With Me – Sister Bernadine Pieper, on Dealing with a Terminal Illness." *Quad-City Times*, October 4, 1997.

[6] Bernadine's Summary of Tasks She Completed Before She died in "Sister Bernadine Piper, CHM 1918-2000," 27.

# BOOK II

### THE WITCH DOCTOR OF CHIAPAS

Discussions with Sister Bernadine Pieper and interviews with Sister Ana María Orozco, Luz María Orozco, and Elizabeth Anne Schneider.

[1] Ana María Orozco, "Letters from the Cloud Forest," (unpublished letters to her donors, October 1968 through Easter 2004. These 200+ letters describe in more detail her thirty-six years of providing medical care and other services in the Highlands of Chiapas. The events described in this chapter represent only a sampling of Ana María's work among the Chiapanean people.

[2] Ana María Orozco, September 1985 letter, 1.

[3] Ana María Orozco, May 30, 1971 letter, 1-2.

[4]    Ana María Orozco, St. Phillip of Jesus 1972 letter, 1.

[5]    Ana María Orozco, February 1972 letter, 1.

[6]    Ana María Orozco, February 26, 1984 letter, 1.

[7]    Ana María Orozco, January 1977 letter, 1.

[8]    Ibid.

[9]    Ana María Orozco, September 1975 letter, 1.

[10]    Ana María Orozco, February 1979 letter, 1-2.

[11]    Ana María Orozco, September 19, 1987 letter, 1.

## PRESERVING MAYAN CULTURE & EMPOWERING ITS PEOPLE

Discussions with Sister Bernadine Pieper and interviews with Michel Andraos, Sister Ana María Orozco, Luz María Orozco, Johanna Rickl, and Penelope Wink.

1    Michel Andraos, "Praxis of Peace, The Pastoral Work and Theology of Bishop Samuel Ruiz and the Diocese of San Cristóbal de las Casas, Chiapas, Mexico," Ottawa, ON: National Library of Canada, 2000, 36-37.

2    Ibid. 38-39.

3    Thomas Benjamin, "A Time of Reconquest: History of the Mayan Revival and the Zaptista Rebellion in Chiapas," *The American History Review,*" Vol. 105, No. 2, April 2000, 8.

4    June 21, 1997 Pastoral Letter issued by the Diocese of San Cristóbal de las Casas, Chiapas, Mexico, App. I of Andraos, *Praxis of Peace, 213-218.*

5    Ibid. 215.

6    Jose Virtuoso, "The Government Turns on the Church of the Poor," *Envio Digital,* No. 155, June 1994, 3-4, http://www.envio.org.ni/articulo/1777.

7    "The Zapatistas Response to México̱n Terrorism from Above," 2, HTTP//WWW.MATTKAPKO.COM/INDEPTH/ZAPATISTAS.HTML, October 21, 2010.

## LIVING THE "PREFERENTIAL OPTION FOR THE POOR"

Interviews with Carol Anne Guckeen von Eschen, Sisters Johanna Rickl, Penelope Wink, and Nancy Wooldridge.

[1] Michel Andraos, "Indigenous Leadership in the Church: The Experience of the Diocese of San Cristóbal de las Casas, Chiapas, Mexico," *Toronto Journal of Theology*, January 21, 2005, 59.

[2] Ibid. 62.

[3] Wink, Penelope, CHM, "Weaving New Visions," *The CHM Flame*, Spring 2009, 5.

## FORGING FRIENDSHIPS AND IMPROVING LIVES IN LATIN AMERICA AND AFRICA

Interviews with Maxine Lloyd Brice, Sisters Delphine Vasquez and Irene Muñoz.

## CARING FOR THE SICK AND VISITING THE IMPRISONED

Discussions with Sister Bernadine Pieper and interviews with Katy Doyle, Sisters Suzanne Wickenkamp, Kayleen Heffron, Irene Muñoz, Hilary Veith, Cathy Talarico, JoAnne Talarico, Nancy Schweiters, Joan Sheil and Kay Holland.

[1] "Pioneers of Healing," *The CHM Flame*, Fall 2009, 2.

[2] Vittetoe, Marie, CHM, "Last Two Standing in Ottumwa Healthcare," *The CHM Flame*, Fall 2009, 4.

[3.] "Minds Meet at Mitchellville," *Phoenix, Vol. 1 No. 2*, winter 1984, 1.

## TRAINING MED TECHS TO CARE FOR THEIR OWN COMMUNITIES

Interviews with Sister Marie Vittetoe.

[1] "Three DMO Physicians share their story of their medical mission to Haiti," 1, WWW.DMOS.COM/HAITIJOURNAL.ASP; "Iowans return from work in Haiti," 1, WWW.KCCI. COM/R/22384026/DETAIL.HTML.

[2] "Large Trauma Hospital in Haiti Turns Town into Hospital Village," 1-2, *EIN Presswire*, January 27, 2010.

[3] Deb O'Hara-Ruckowski, "Haiti Post-Earthquake –Just One Perspective," *Hôpital Sacré Coeur*, Spring 2011, 4, reprinted with permission by the Crudem Foundation.

[4] Press Release from the Crudem Foundation describing the Helping

Hearts Cookie Haitian relief project initiated by Homeless clients of the St. Patrick's Center in St. Louis, Mo. September 22, 2010, 1-2, reprinted by permission of the Crudem Foundation.

## MAKING VALUES THE HEART OF EDUCATION

Interviews with Sisters Micheline Curtis, Roberta Brich, Rosalind (Rosie) Restelli, and Camille Clark.

[1] Eckerman, Marcia, CHM, "Their Cheerleader," *The Mustard Seed, A Celebration of 125 Years in America,* July 17, 1989, 49.

[2] "The Camille Clark Award for Exemplary Service," *The CHM Flame,* Summer 2007, 3.

## TAKING BACK THE CHURCH THROUGH NON-VIOLENT RESISTANCE

Interviews with Sister Caridad Inda.

[1] Gutiérrez, Gustavo. *A Theology of Liberation: History, Politics and Salvation,* trans. Caridad Inda, CHM and John Eaglson, rev.ed. Maryknoll, NY: Orbis Books, 1988.

[2] Gene Sharp, *From Dictatorship to Democracy, A Conceptual Framework for Liberation.* Boston: Albert Einstein Institution, 2003, 10.

## SHAPING CULTURE THROUGH MEDIA LITERACY

Discussions with Sister Bernadine Pieper and Interviews with Sister Elizabeth Thoman.

[1] Elizabeth Thoman, Vol.1, Issue 4, March 2006, "Media Literacy: Transforming Education in the 21st Century," *The CHM Flame,* Spring 2007, 1.

[2] Bellony, Lisa, "Photos by Cancer Surviving Nun Inspire Prayer," June 12, 2008, www.ncnwr.org/news-item.php?ID=5.

## SERVING HISPANICS AND LATINOS & ENRICHING ALL OUR LIVES

Discussions with Sister Bernadine Pieper and Interviews with Sisters Irene Muñoz, Molly Muñoz, and Maxine Lloyd.

[1] Renee Sedlacek and Shannon Regan, "Juntos Todos Aprendemos!," *Community Impact*, Vol. 1, Issue 4, March 2006, 1-4.

## STANDING UP AND PAYING UP PERSONALLY

Interviews with Elizabeth Loescher, Sisters Joanne O'Brien, Elaine Hagedorn, Jeanie Hagedorn, Roberta Brich, Patricia Miller, and Elizabeth Anne Schneider.

1. "Catholic Peace Ministry Honors Women Religious for 'Waging Peace,'" 1 EBOOKBROUSE.COM/CATHOLIC-PEACE-MINISTRY-HONORS RELIGIOUS,PDF.

2. September 9, 2008 Announcement by the Sisters of Humility of their commitment to anti-torture campaign, 3, HTTP//QCRCAST.BLOGSPOT. COM.

## CARING FOR THE EARTH

Discussions with Sister Bernadine Pieper and Interviews with Sisters Miriam Ehrhardt, Kathleen Hanley, Roberta Brich and Cathleen Real.

1. Bernadine Pieper, October 16, 1974 letter to the CHM Community, 1.

2. Bernadine Pieper, "Why Do We Need A New Creation Story" (undated, unpublished manuscript)1.

3. "A Short History of the Earth Charter Initiative, WWW. EARTHCHARTERINACTION.ORG/ABOUT_THE_INTIATIVE_HISTORY_2T. PDF.

4. "Preamble of the Earth Charter," 1-4, HTTP//WWW. EARTHCHARTERINACTION.ORG/CONTENT/ PAGES/READ-THE-CHARTER. HTML.

5. Karen Brook, "Shared Missions," *The CHM Flame,* Summer 2007, 6.

## SERVING APPALACHIAN PEOPLE

Interviews with Sisters Martha (Marty) Conrad and Mary Rehmann.

1. "Somerset, Kentucky, "*Wikipedia,* July 19, 2001.

2. "God's Food Pantry," WWW.GODSFOODPANTRYSOMERSET.ORG/.

3. "Catholic Sisters' Letter of Support of Health Care Reform Bill, March 17, 2010, WWW.NETWORKLOBBY.ORG/LEGISLATION/ CATHOLIC-SISTERS-SUPPORT-HEALTH-REFORM-BILL.

## MAKING MIRACLES HAPPEN IN THE QUAD CITIES

Discussions with Sister Bernadine Pieper and Interviews with Sisters Ramona Kaalberg, Mary John Byers, Mary Ann Vogel, Joann Kuebrich, Marilyn Schierbrock, Bea Snyder, Harriet Ping, Nancy Schweiters, Roberta Brich, and Mary Rehmann, Sister Ruth E. Westmoreland, OSF, Sandra Walters and Latoya Pegues.

1   Elizabeth Thoman, "Focus," *Kiosk*, No. 1, February 1970, 23.

2   Ibid. 24.

3   Wolfe, Tom, "Sister Set Example for Humble Living," *Quad City Times*, January 31, 2006, 1, reprinted with permission from the Quad City Times.

4   Thompson, Kelly, "Humility of Mary Housing: Twenty Years of Changing Lives – Our Agency's History, Present and Future," *Humility Housing Inc. Annual Report July 1, 2009 – June 30, 2010*, 36.

5   Ann McGlynn, "'This Is God's Work', Humility of Mary Sisters Step in to Operate Homeless Shelter, *Quad City Times*, September 20, 2008, A8, reprinted with permission by the *Quad City Times*.

6   Ibid.

7   Brian Wellner, "Humility of Mary Shelter Wins National Award," *Quad City Times*, December 24, 2011, 2, reprinted with permission by the *Quad City Times*.

8   Ibid. 2-3.

## DOING JUSTICE, CHANGING LIVES IN COLORADO

Discussions with Mary Boland and interviews with Rev. Sally Brown, Sisters Buffy Boesen, S.L. and Mary Catherine Rabbit, S.L., Kathleen O'Malley, S.L., James Mauch, John Taylor, Beth Taylor, Mark Miliotto, Angela Fletcher, Kent Kroeber, Rev. Marty Lally, Kate Boland, Patrick Filter, Nan Morehead, Ed Kahn, Rev. Constance Delzell and Sue Kenny.

1   Contance Delzell, Sermon preached at Mary Boland's Funeral, January 15, 2009, 2-3.

2   Caring for Colorado Foundation, "Building the Capacity to Care," 2011.

3   Delzell Sermon, 3. About the Author

# Acknowledgments

This book has been a collaborative effort. I am indebted to the many Sisters of Humility and their friends, whose names are recorded in the Sources and Notes section of the book, who generously shared with me their stories and described the remarkable work the sisters have done over the past fifty years. Without your contributions, I could not have written this book.

The CHM archivists, Sisters Joan Sheil and Micheline Curtis, as well the CHM communications director, Lisa Martin Bellomy, patiently tracked down documents and photos necessary for the book. Sisters Mary Rehmann and Johanna Rickl, the current president and vice president of the Sisters of Humility, provided essential institutional support for the project. I owe each of you my thanks.

I am also grateful to JoAnn Slater, Sally Brown, Kathleen Hoebel, and Sister Luz Maria Orozco, who cheerfully read and critiqued this book in its various stages of development, provided me helpful insights about the strength and weaknesses of each draft and encouraged me during the ups and downs of its writing. I am also thankful to Sisters Susan Marie Maloney, S.N.J.M. and Cecily Jones, S.L. for their clear critiques and practical recommendations for revising the book. Thanks also to Mary Watters for rescuing me at times with your computer skills during the writing phase of this project.

To my sister, Colleen Hayes, your cover design is beautiful. Thank you.

Finally, my thanks to Caleb Seeling and Sonya Unrein of Samizdat Creative Services for your design and editing work, as well as shepherding this book and me through the publishing process.

# About the Author

Kathleen Mullen is a lawyer who for thirty-five years has shone a spotlight on the unmet needs of low income, elderly, disabled and other disadvantaged people in Colorado while enforcing their legal rights. Her passion for such work grew in part out of her friendship with Sister Bernadine Pieper and other members of the Sisters of Humility of Mary of Iowa. This book, her first, is a tribute to Bernadine and provides a sampling of the important peace, justice, and care of the earth work carried out by members of the Sisters of Humility over the past fifty years. Ms. Mullen lives in Denver, Colorado.

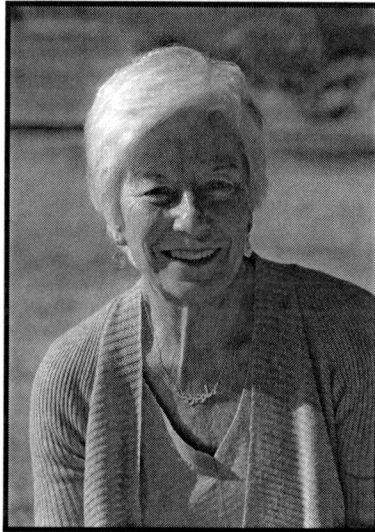

CPSIA information can be obtained at www.ICGtesting.com
Printed in the USA
LVOW130224081112

306382LV00006B/1/P